PUBLIC AND PRIVATE FINANCING OF HIGHER EDUCATION
Shaping Public Policy for the Future

Edited by
Patrick M. Callan and Joni E. Finney

With Kathy Reeves Bracco
and William R. Doyle

AMERICAN COUNCIL ON EDUCATION ★
ORYX PRESS ★
Series on Higher Education
1997

The rare Arabian oryx is believed to have inspired the myth of the unicorn. This desert antelope became virtually extinct in the early 1960s. At that time several groups of international conservationists arranged to have 9 animals sent to the Phoenix Zoo to be the nucleus of a captive breeding herd. Today the oryx population is over 1,000, and over 500 have been returned to the Middle East.

© 1997 by American Council on Education and The Oryx Press
Published by The Oryx Press
4041 North Central at Indian School Road
Phoenix, Arizona 85012-3397

Published simultaneously in Canada
Printed and bound in the United States of America

∞ The paper used in this publication meets the minimum requirements of the American National Standard for Information Sciences—Permanence of Paper for Printed Library Materials, ANSI Z39.48-1984.

Library of Congress Cataloging-in-Publication Data

Public and private financing of higher education: shaping public
policy for the future / edited by Patrick M. Callan . . . [et al.].
    p. cm.—(American Council on Education/Oryx Press series on higher education)
    Includes bibliographical references and index.
    ISBN 1-57356-116-9 (alk. paper)
    1. Education, Higher—United States—Finance. 2. Education, Higher—United States—Finance—Case studies. 3. Finance, Public--United States. 4. Finance, Public—United States—Case studies. 5. Higher education and state—United States. 6. Higher education and state—United States—Case studies. I. Callan, Patrick M. II. Series.
LB2342.P785   1997
379.1'214'0973—dc21   97-29457
                                                          CIP

Dedicated to

Dennis A. Collins
with gratitude for his friendship, counsel, and support.

P.M.C. and J.E.F.

CONTENTS

LIST OF FIGURES
AND TABLES

PREFACE

The financing and accessibility of higher education are major issues of social and educational policy. Yet it would be difficult to identify a public policy area that has undergone as much change with as little public discussion or explicit policy direction as the financing of American higher education in recent years. The respective responsibilities of students, families, colleges and universities, and government have altered significantly, but with little debate and without any public policy consensus.

Three major changes in state and federal higher education finance have included: a shift of responsibility away from public and governmental sources to students, families, and institutions; a shift from grants to loans as the predominant form of student financial assistance; and an increasing reliance on allocated tuition fees as a source of student financial assistance for students in private and public colleges and universities. These changes have occurred incrementally over the past decade and a half, but have accelerated in the 1990s. Considered individually, these changes may have been reasonable responses to particular circumstances. But their cumulative impact creates a fundamentally different public policy for financing higher education than existed even a decade ago. The consequences are twofold: whatever consensus and public policy framework may have existed in the past concerning the responsibility for paying for higher education has eroded; and increasingly of late, terms like "privatization" are used to describe (and in some cases, to prescribe) the recent past and possible future. The danger is not that the system of financing higher education has changed and will continue to do so, but rather that long-term systemic changes will result from unexamined and undebated responses to short-term considerations—state budget shortfalls, in particular. The ultimate result may be a drastically altered system of finance that is disconnected from broader national, state, and institutional purposes and directions.

There will never be a permanent or simple solution to the issues of financial responsibility for higher education, but the long-term stakes are too high to allow the issue to be settled by short-term policy drift. These issues require national debate and state-by-state resolution. This book was written to help frame and stimulate that debate by providing a deeper understanding of recent developments in higher education finance, of the policy responses to those developments in particular states, and of the increasingly volatile context of public finance in the United States. It is directed primarily to policy leaders in higher education and government, including college and university presidents and trustees, governors and legislators and their staffs, state higher education boards, and scholars and policy analysts in the field of higher education.

The book is divided into two parts, with the first analyzing national trends and the second focusing on the financing of higher education in five states. In the opening chapter, Brian M. Roherty places higher education finance in the context of public finance and budgeting at the state and federal levels, and he identifies political, economic, and demographic forces confronting policy makers. The second chapter by David W. Breneman and Joni E. Finney reviews the major changes in public finance at the state level in the 1990s, and raises important policy questions and alternatives. Chapter 3 is based on the deliberations of the National Roundtable on the Public and Private Finance of Higher Education, a two-day roundtable meeting of state governmental and higher education leaders and policy experts who reviewed drafts of the earlier chapters, and sought to clarify and frame the policy agenda facing the nation and the states. An afterword to Part One by Robert Zemsky, Gregory R. Wegner, and Maria Iannozzi helps to describe the debate over privatization, a term that has become pervasive but that carries a multitude of meanings and has enormous consequences for public policies regarding higher education.

The five chapters in Part Two narrow the focus from national and regional trends to examine more closely the financial circumstances of five states from 1990 through 1995: California, Florida, Michigan, Minnesota, and New York. These studies also provide information on the policy responses of state governments and of colleges and universities during this period.

The research for this book and the convening of the National Roundtable on the Public and Private Finance of Higher Education were supported by The Ford Foundation, The James Irvine Foundation, and The Pew Charitable Trusts. The California Higher Education Policy Center and the Pew Higher Education Roundtable cosponsored the project that led to the development of this book.

The editors would like to thank the authors of the chapters for their contributions to this book: Kathy Reeves Bracco, David W. Breneman, Joni E. Finney, Maria Iannozzi, Mario C. Martinez, Thad Nodine, Brian M. Roherty, Yolanda Sanchez-Penley, Joan E. Sundquist, Gregory R. Wegner, and Robert Zemsky. Several people reviewed the case studies and offered helpful comments and suggestions: Richard Richardson, Joseph Burke, Patrick Dallet, William Proctor, David Leslie, Phil Lewenstein, William Pickens, and Marvin Peterson. Listed in the appendix are the members of the National Roundtable on the Public and Private Finance of Higher Education. Their thoughtful discussion of these issues shaped the content of chapter 3. Our appreciation also goes to Heather Jack, who proofread several revisions of the text; William R. Doyle, who provided research support for the book; and to Thad Nodine, who edited it for the center. The editors also thank the staff from ACE and Oryx Press, who supported and encouraged us to develop this book: Jim Murray, Susan Slesinger, and Anne Thompson. Special thanks go to Christine Davis and John Wagner, who edited the final version of the text.

Patrick M. Callan
Joni E. Finney

LIST OF EDITORS
AND CONTRIBUTORS

KATHY REEVES BRACCO is senior policy analyst at the California Higher Education Policy Center. She has led national projects on student transfer and higher education governance. Prior to her current position, she was research associate for the National Center for Research in Vocational Education.

DAVID W. BRENEMAN is university professor and dean of the Curry School of Education at the University of Virginia. Prior to his current position, he was visiting professor at the Harvard Graduate School of Education and senior fellow at The Brookings Institution. He is author of *Liberal Arts Colleges: Thriving, Surviving, or Endangered* (1994), published by Brookings, and *Finance in Higher Education* (1993). He has also authored numerous national and state reports on financing higher education and community colleges.

PATRICK M. CALLAN is executive director of the California Higher Education Policy Center. Prior to his current position, he was vice president for the Education Commission of the States and executive director of the California Commission for Higher Education. He is author of numerous reports and articles on higher education policy issues related to educational opportunity, and the finance and governance of higher education.

WILLIAM R. DOYLE is a research assistant with the California Higher Education Policy Center. He has completed research on California college students and on the finance and governance of higher education.

JONI E. FINNEY is the associate director of the California Higher Education Policy Center. Prior to her current position, she was director of policy studies at the Education Commission of the States. She has directed national projects and is coauthor of *By Design or By Default* (1994) with Patrick M. Callan. She has authored policy reports on assessment, teacher education, and the finance of higher education.

MARIA IANNOZZI is a consulting writer and editor specializing in education research and policy. She is affiliated with the Institute for Research on Higher Education at the University of Pennsylvania and the National Center for Postsecondary Improvement at Stanford University.

MARIO C. MARTINEZ has worked in both the public and private sectors in finance and strategic planning. His current research areas are the governance and finance of higher education. He is currently affiliated with Educational Systems Research, where he is completing a survey of state legislatures and their views on educational technology.

THAD NODINE is a writer, editor, and independent consultant specializing in education and social services. He is the editorial consultant for the California Higher Education Policy Center. He is also a lecturer in humanities at the University of California at Santa Cruz.

BRIAN M. ROHERTY is executive director of the National Association of State Budget Officers. In this capacity, he advises state budget directors and the National Governors' Association on matters of fiscal management, federal budget policy, and other policy issues of intra- and interstate concern. He was formerly budget director of the Minnesota Department of Finance.

YOLANDA SANCHEZ-PENLEY is a faculty member in business and management for the Maricopa Community College District in Arizona. She is involved in campus policy committees related to academic advising and educational software. She coordinated the North Central Association of Colleges and Schools' self-study for Chandler-Gilbert Community College.

JOAN E. SUNDQUIST is affiliated with the University of Pennsylvania and has served as a Graduate Fellow at the Institute for Research on Higher Education. Prior to her current activities, she was fiscal analyst for the legislative committees of the Minnesota House of Representatives, charged with developing the state higher education budgets.

GREGORY R. WEGNER serves as senior liaison for colleges and universities throughout the country that have convened campus roundtables in conjunction with the Pew Higher Education Roundtable. He joined the University of Pennsylvania's Institute for Research on Higher Education in 1987, where he is now associate director. He is managing editor and coauthor of the periodical publication, *Policy Perspectives*.

ROBERT ZEMSKY is the founding director of the University of Pennsylvania's Institute for Research on Higher Education. In 1986, the Institute was invited to develop and host the Pew Higher Education Roundtable, sponsored by The Pew Charitable Trusts. He serves as director of the National Research and Development Center on the Educational Quality of the Workforce, funded by the federal government. He is author of *Unfinished Design* (1988) and *The Structure of College Choice* (1983) with Penney Oedel. He is also the author of several scholarly articles. He is currently engaged in a major study of the underlying costs of an undergraduate education.

PART
ONE

· · · · · · · · ·

National Trends

CHAPTER 1

The Price of Passive Resistance in Financing Higher Education

Brian M. Roherty

I n the natural order of things, it is not unusual for state budgeting to be characterized as a derivative activity of government. From a vantage point just beyond the decision making, planners in particular hurl the assertion that policy *ought* to drive budget rather than the other way around. But in practice, as the United States moves ever closer to the *fin de siècle*, the interface between policy and budget may now be fully transparent: they are one and the same. There is no way to interpret the landscape of state finance without a concurrent understanding of the policy choices that are implicit in the numbers.

In the fall of 1996, the fiscal condition of the states is strong, steady, and poised for change. With respect to revenues, there seems to be a broad-based consensus not to raise taxes. Economic growth continues slowly but steadily. It seems unlikely that there will be a repeat of the high spending of the 1980s since those states and regions with the highest economic growth, such as states in the West, tend to be more politically conservative. States in the Middle Atlantic and New England regions continue to lag behind the rest of the nation, although these regions too are showing signs of recovery. States have reestablished positive balances in their general funds, and combined balances are now higher than they have been in more than a decade.[1]

From an intergovernmental perspective, state finances now appear to be advantageously positioned between a federal government burdened with debt and preparing for devolution, and local governments that are struggling in many cases from a point of vulnerability at the bottom of the fiscal food chain. Large cities and counties appear to be especially vulnerable in the period ahead.

On the policy frontier, the winds of change are blowing and the terms of debate are moving away from what have been cries for minimalist government back toward a more centrist view. The origin for this new equilibrium may lie in the fact that the "Republican revolution" has now run its course. Beginning with the Budget Enforcement Act in 1990, "the revolution" defined the 1990s with its early emphases in the 1992 presidential race on the macro issues of budget discipline and health care reform. These themes united the two major political parties in the same way that "safe communities," "family values," and a "contract with America" came to define the pivotal elections in 1994.

By way of contrast, the 1996 election provided a critical juncture for both parties. In the case of the incumbent President, it offered a defining opportunity to turn back the revolution and its congressional legions; for the challengers, it was an opportunity to complete what their party sought throughout the final decade of the twentieth century. The revolution would either approach its *denouement,* or it would be dead.

In either event, the terms of debate now point toward a new horizon. The emerging fundamentals in this policy debate include renewed emphases on character and leadership,[2] the failure of elites and contemporary political institutions,[3] and in some cases calls for completely new "political models."[4] Although some have gone so far as to announce *la fin de la démocratie,*[5] others have offered more hopeful forecasts that range from new economic arguments[6] to a more traditional call for moderation and balance in overcoming the imperfections of democracy.[7]

THE FISCAL VARIABLES

Trends in State Finance

During the 1980s, state revenues more than doubled from $276 billion to $625 billion.[8] There were no significant changes in the mix of taxes, intergovernmental revenue, or other charges. But as the high-flying eighties were coming to an end, economic growth began slowing and in August 1989, 49 governors saw the handwriting on the wall and signed a letter to Congress "expressing their concern with the impact of recent Medicaid mandates on their budgets."[9]

That impact was being driven by 33 mandated and 18 optional expansions of Medicaid during the last half of the 1980s.[10] When they wrote that letter, however, the governors only suspected the recession that arrived the following summer and by the time it ended in the spring of 1991, much had changed.

From 1990 to 1992, Medicaid began crushing state budgets with annual increases of 20.6 percent, 28.0 percent, and 29.5 percent.[11] State budgets grew by 9.1 percent from 1990 to 1991, and grew another 10.1 percent from 1991 to 1992. As shown in table 1.1 and depicted graphically in figure 1.1, Medicaid's share of state spending nearly doubled from 10.2 to 19.2 percent of state budgets from 1987 to 1995.[12] In 1990, Medicaid spending first displaced higher education as the second largest state spending category, second only to elementary and secondary education.

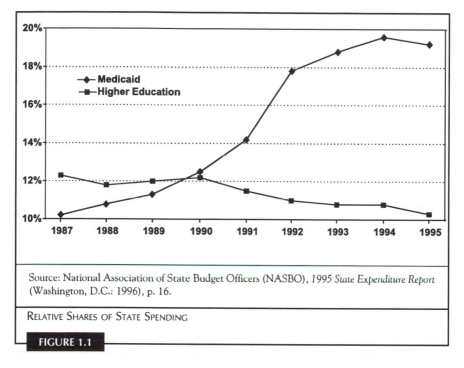

Source: National Association of State Budget Officers (NASBO), *1995 State Expenditure Report* (Washington, D.C.: 1996), p. 16.

RELATIVE SHARES OF STATE SPENDING

FIGURE 1.1

Overall, as shown in figure 1.2, annual state budget increases have shown a steady downward trend since about 1985. Current year budgets (1996) and proposed budgets for 1997 point toward the lowest increases in almost 15 years even though final numbers are likely to be slightly higher than current projections.

The fiscal discipline shown by states is largely attributable to the fact that there are balanced budget requirements of one form or another in all 50 states except Vermont.[13] In addition, in all states other than North Carolina, the governors have some form of veto authority (40 have line-item veto authority).[14] As a result, the fiscal frameworks in which state budgets are developed and approved are significantly different from those of local governments or that of the federal government.

TABLE 1.1

SHARES OF STATE SPENDING BY FUND SOURCE, 1987–1995

Fund Type & Year	Elementary & Secondary Education	Higher Education	Cash Assistance	Medicaid	Corrections	Transportation	All Other	Total
FY 1987:								
General Funds	34.2	15.5	5.3	8.1	5.0	1.4	30.4	100
Other State Funds	9.0	11.0	0.4	0.7	0.6	26.8	51.5	100
Federal Funds	11.5	6.4	10.3	26.0	0.1	13.7	31.9	100
Bond Funds	6.8	6.4	0.0	0.0	13.4	26.3	47.0	100
Total Funds	22.8	12.3	5.2	10.2	3.0	10.6	36.1	100
FY 1988:								
General Funds	34.5	15.5	5.1	8.7	5.2	1.3	29.7	100
Other State Funds	10.0	11.8	0.4	0.6	0.9	28.3	48.0	100
Federal Funds	11.4	3.4	11.1	27.0	0.1	12.4	34.6	100
Bond Funds	0.4	8.2	0.0	0.0	14.6	20.4	56.4	100
Total Funds	23.0	11.8	5.3	10.8	3.2	10.3	35.5	100
FY 1989:								
General Funds	34.6	15.2	5.0	9.0	5.3	1.3	29.7	100
Other State Funds	9.9	12.8	0.5	0.7	1.0	26.9	48.2	100
Federal Funds	11.3	3.4	10.4	28.7	0.1	12.8	33.4	100
Bond Funds	19.5	11.1	0.0	0.0	6.5	21.0	41.9	100
Total Funds	23.4	12.0	5.1	11.3	3.2	10.1	35.0	100
FY 1990:								
General Funds	33.5	14.6	4.9	9.5	5.5	1.3	30.8	100
Other State Funds	10.6	15.3	0.5	1.4	0.8	25.7	45.7	100
Federal Funds	11.5	3.2	10.4	31.8	0.1	12.8	30.2	100
Bond Funds	1.7	10.0	0.0	0.0	14.5	30.1	43.7	100
Total Funds	22.8	12.2	5.0	12.5	3.4	9.9	34.2	100
FY 1991:								
General Funds	33.4	14.1	5.3	10.5	5.7	1.1	29.9	100
Other State Funds	8.4	14.0	0.6	2.5	0.7	26.0	47.7	100
Federal Funds	10.8	3.6	10.3	34.7	0.1	10.2	30.4	100
Bond Funds	13.7	11.0	0.0	0.0	13.9	28.7	32.6	100
Total Funds	22.0	11.5	5.3	14.2	3.5	9.4	34.0	100

TABLE 1.1 (continued)

SHARES OF STATE SPENDING BY FUND SOURCE, 1987–1995

Fund Type & Year	Elementary & Secondary Education	Higher Education	Cash Assistance	Medicaid	Corrections	Transportation	All Other	Total
FY 1992:								
General Funds	34.0	13.5	5.1	12.1	5.6	0.8	28.8	100
Other State Funds	7.2	14.4	0.5	6.5	0.6	23.9	47.0	100
Federal Funds	10.3	2.6	8.9	40.9	0.1	9.5	27.7	100
Bond Funds	3.3	14.4	0.0	0.0	11.9	34.6	35.8	100
Total Funds	21.2	11.0	4.9	17.8	3.2	9.1	32.9	100
FY 1993:								
General Funds	34.8	13.1	5.1	13.3	5.7	0.9	27.2	100
Other State Funds	6.5	15.1	0.5	7.1	0.6	23.1	47.2	100
Federal Funds	10.2	2.6	7.3	40.8	0.1	9.5	29.6	100
Bond Funds	21.1	14.6	0.0	0.0	9.4	22.3	32.6	100
Total Funds	21.5	10.8	4.5	18.8	3.1	8.7	32.5	100
FY 1994:								
General Funds	33.8	13.0	4.9	14.0	6.2	0.9	27.3	100
Other State Funds	7.1	14.8	0.4	6.5	0.8	22.6	47.9	100
Federal Funds	9.8	2.4	6.8	42.2	0.1	9.5	29.3	100
Bond Funds	5.0	24.7	0.0	0.0	11.8	21.1	37.3	100
Total Funds	20.5	10.8	4.2	19.6	3.4	8.7	32.8	100
FY 1995:								
General Funds	33.8	12.7	4.6	14.3	6.5	0.8	27.3	100
Other State Funds	9.0	13.8	0.4	5.7	0.8	22.1	48.3	100
Federal Funds	9.8	2.5	6.5	41.5	0.1	9.3	30.4	100
Bond Funds	7.2	17.3	0.0	0.0	17.8	25.8	31.9	100
Total Funds	20.9	10.3	4.0	19.2	3.6	8.7	33.3	100
FY 1987-95 Combined Total:								
General Funds	34.0	14.0	5.0	11.4	5.7	1.1	28.9	100
Other State Funds	8.4	13.8	0.5	4.0	0.8	24.6	47.9	100
Federal Funds	10.6	3.1	8.7	36.4	0.1	10.7	30.5	100
Bond Funds	9.2	14.1	0.0	0.0	12.7	25.8	38.2	100
Total Funds	21.8	11.3	4.8	15.6	3.3	9.4	33.8	100

Source: National Association of State Budget Officers, 1995 State Expenditure Report, April 1996.

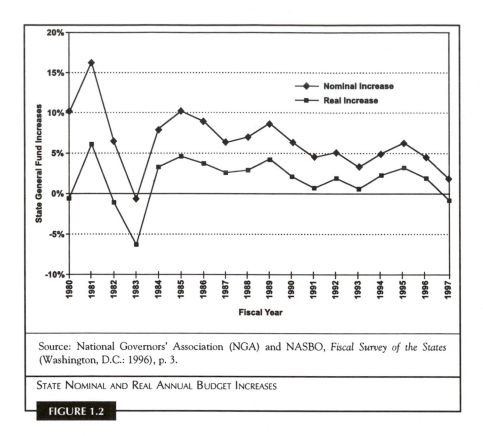

Source: National Governors' Association (NGA) and NASBO, *Fiscal Survey of the States* (Washington, D.C.: 1996), p. 3.

STATE NOMINAL AND REAL ANNUAL BUDGET INCREASES

FIGURE 1.2

As the nation moves into the last half of the 1990s, state finances appear to have stabilized but have remained sensitive to a number of factors. In the absence of structural reform, the "crowding out" phenomenon of the early nineties is likely to continue unabated. The "usual suspects," namely Medicaid, corrections, and public safety—and possibly elementary and secondary education—loom as the winners, with higher education and local government aid the probable losers.

Second, the revenue base for most states is at risk due to the inability of states to effectively tax emerging information technologies, telecommunications, and service industries;[15] potential issues of tax compliance in small businesses, where much of the job growth is occurring; and most importantly, the potential legal and other compliance problems associated with "digital cash." Together these three factors have created a somewhat fragile revenue structure that is unikely to be strengthened by tax increases in the short run.

Despite some signs of change, the mood of the country remains cautious toward government. In relation to state government, there seems to be a general lack of confidence in the four "core businesses" that make up more than three-quarters of state budgets, namely public education, health care, higher education, and public assistance. The extent to which these systems are able to regain the public's confidence may turn out to be more important than any other factor in the years ahead. Together they present an enormous challenge for our country's elected leadership, but reforms are underway.

None is perhaps more significant than the underlying *quid pro quo* in the devolution of programs from the federal government to the states and local governments. Governors throughout the United States are united in their willingness to take less money in exchange for "flexibility and simplicity."[16] Although this notion is not new, what is radical is that the governors agreed to share responsibility for balancing the federal budget and agreed to less money for the states. As a result, the movement toward a balanced budget gained significant momentum, and even the president's budget for 1997 reflected a full about-face in the view of a number of commentators inside and outside his party.[17]

With respect to higher education, the upward trend in tuition and the recent spike in student loans (see figure 1.3) portend fundamental choices ahead for higher education across the United States. With the media telling students that they can expect to earn twice as much over their lifetimes from investing in stocks as compared with investing in their degrees, the debate about the "value" of higher education seems to have moved beyond the academy.[18] This debate will take place against the backdrop of a 14 percent real decline in federal support for postsecondary education from 1980 to

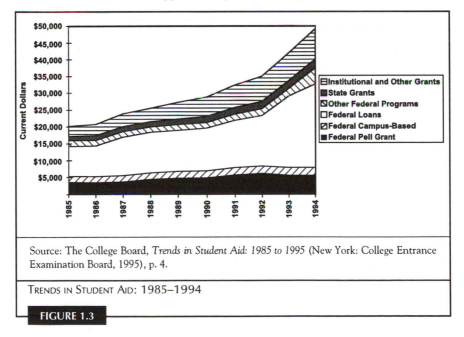

Source: The College Board, *Trends in Student Aid: 1985 to 1995* (New York: College Entrance Examination Board, 1995), p. 4.

TRENDS IN STUDENT AID: 1985–1994

FIGURE 1.3

1995,[19] slowing federal support for research and development,[20] and a clear agenda in Congress to hold the line in these areas. In particular, it is worth noting that the Department of Defense accounts for 49 percent of total federal spending on research and development, and it received a 2 percent reduction in 1995 alone.

Trends aside, there are two wild cards that could seriously alter the landscape of state finance should they occur: a recession during the devolution of the federal government or passage of the balanced budget amendment. In the case of a recession, it would simply mean that the strains would be that much greater. In the case of a balanced budget amendment, it is generally assumed that another vote on the amendment is likely in 1997. Should that pass, most observers have concluded that state approval would not be far behind. As a result, the impact of a balanced budget amendment could be felt within two years as contrasted with the six- or seven-year federal phase-down that is otherwise assumed, given the current policy debate.

State and Regional Variables

In the early 1990s, almost all the states felt the effects of the recession. The East Coast states and California were most dramatically affected while the Rocky Mountain and Plains regions were the least adversely affected. Of the 10 largest states with nonfarm employment, only Texas showed a job gain from June 1990 to June 1992. Unemployment was almost 8 percent nationally in 1991,[21] but declined steadily to about 5.5 percent in 1995.

According to the Conference Board and other sources, there has been a weakening in the influence of national economic policies since about 1985, which is being replaced by regional patterns that are determining national economic performance. For example, the North American Free Trade Agreement (NAFTA) has impacted Texas and the Southwest, whereas consolidation in the health care industry has tended to affect states such as California, Illinois, Massachusetts, and Pennsylvania. Defense cutbacks and military base closings have affected employment levels during the early 1990s, with Charleston, South Carolina, and the San Francisco Bay area being most affected.[22]

By 1995, nearly all areas of the United States had seen some positive economic growth and the gap between regions was narrowing. The federal government was forecasting steady but slow growth trending down to a range of about 2.0 to 2.5 percent throughout the forecast period. The Southwest was expected to outperform the rest of the nation because of its lead in high technology and export trade. The Rocky Mountain states and the Far West were expected to grow at a rate above the national average, particularly if California was excluded from the projections. Unemployment remained low throughout those regions, except in California where it remained at nearly 8 percent.

During this period, manufacturing was expanding on the Plains while it remained weak in the Middle Atlantic states. The Great Lakes, Southeast, and New England regions all remained steady with their underlying fundamentals essentially unchanged.

Throughout the early 1990s state budgets grew less and less as the federal reserve took a firm hand in managing the economy. During this period, revenue per full-time-equivalent (FTE) student in 1994 constant dollars increased at all types of higher education institutions between 1977 and 1992. According to the National Center for Education Statistics, "while revenues per FTE student increased, government appropriations per FTE student fell at all types of institutions."[23] During this period, tuition and fees took up the slack and maintained a steady upward slope throughout the 50 states.

Throughout the United States there was increasing interest in state revenue and expenditure limitations. Of the 27 states with limitations, 10 were in place in the 1970s, 8 more were added in the 1980s, and 11 more in the 1990s to date; 17 are constitutional and 10 remain statutory. More than half are indexed to the growth in personal income and all but five are tied to spending growth rather than revenues.[24]

In one sense, on the reverse side of revenue and expenditure limitations are public referenda. Although data on referenda are scarce, there is little doubt that they act as cost drivers in many cases. One of the most frequently cited examples is in California, where, as a result of Proposition 98, there is a minimum state-funded guarantee for K–12 schools and community colleges.

These developments—combined with slow growth, a fragile revenue structure, federal devolution, and state balanced budget requirements—point toward an almost unmanageable compression in state budgets for the last half of the 1990s. Nevertheless, since "things that are unsustainable tend to end,"[25] some states have already begun the process of fundamental reform. Most states, however, chose a "wait and see" attitude throughout 1995, hoping for a federal budget deal that would offer a framework for their own reforms.

In addition, states took some solace in passage of the Unfunded Mandates Reform Act of 1995 (P.L. 104-4), which was aimed at assessing the effects of federal regulatory actions on state, local, and tribal governments. The act requires procedural protections if the fiscal effect of proposed actions exceeds $50 million. Although this legislation was appropriate from the point of view of states, it remains to be seen whether it has any practical effect. This is in part due to the fact that most mandated costs on state governments have come from state and federal courts rather than legislative bodies. For example, nearly half the states (24) are currently in litigation over their systems of school finance.[26]

Ironically, higher education is the only core function of state government that has been essentially untouched by litigation over its finances. The other core functions have become cost drivers in state finance in part because of the judiciary, rather than due to the budgetary or appropriations processes. Without a right for residents to attain higher education, and without an equal protection argument, higher education faces tough competition for funding in the years ahead.

Demographic Variables

From 1983 to 1993, enrollment growth was strong in higher education throughout the United States, with 14 states experiencing growth above 25 percent. The high-growth states were primarily in the West—New Mexico (53 percent), Colorado (39 percent), and Arizona (28 percent)—and the Southeast—Georgia (50 percent), Florida (41 percent), Alabama (36 percent), and South Carolina (30 percent).[27] For 1996, however, states with the highest number of high school graduates include California, Texas, New York, Pennsylvania, and Illinois.

In the period from 1995–96 to 2005–06, the U.S. Department of Education is projecting overall enrollment growth of about 6 percent, and an increase of 7 percent in bachelor's degrees awarded. As table 1.2 reveals, however, the demographics that underlie these aggregates are wide-ranging. In Arizona and California, the number of high school graduates is projected to increase by 47 percent, and in Nevada by 77 percent. Throughout the West and Pacific Northwest—along with Texas, Florida, and Illinois—the number of high school graduates is expected to increase substantially, while in other areas of the United States there will be negative or slow growth.

Among the top 10 states for projected enrollment growth, seven have expenditure limitations (and five of these seven have constitutional expenditure limitations). Nevada is perhaps an anomaly in these rankings due to its small base and the fact it has encouraged out-of-state students from adjacent counties to attend its schools by taking advantage of a low out-of-state tuition policy. In Florida and California, however, the projected increases come on top of large current populations, which include many who are below the national median family income. Although state support in both of these cases has been negotiated upward in the near future, the prospects beyond that are less clear. In Arizona, the governor has proposed paying students to go to out-of-state colleges rather than build new ones in-state.

The remaining six states in the top ten for projected enrollment growth are all projected to grow by about 30 percent. In the smaller states of Delaware and New Hampshire, state support has been double-digit in 1995–96 compared with the prior year. In Maryland, the state provides a funding formula for private colleges such as Johns Hopkins, a policy that will set up increased pressure as it confronts its 34 percent projected growth.

TABLE 1.2

Projected Change in the Number of High School Graduates, 1995–96 to 2005–06 (in Percent)

Alabama	0	Louisiana	(14)	Ohio	5
Alaska	19	Maine	9	Oklahoma	(1)
Arizona	47	Maryland	34	Oregon	19
Arkansas	6	Massachusetts	27	Pennsylvania	15
California	47	Michigan	5	Rhode Island	22
Colorado	32	Minnesota	19	South Carolina	12
Connecticut	20	Mississippi	(8)	South Dakota	1
Delaware	38	Missouri	8	Tennessee	12
Florida	56	Montana	7	Texas	17
Georgia	29	Nebraska	4	Utah	5
Hawaii	13	Nevada	77	Vermont	16
Idaho	(2)	New Hampshire	38	Virginia	34
Illinois	18	New Jersey	16	Washington	30
Indiana	3	New Mexico	15	West Virginia	(23)
Iowa	(3)	New York	12	Wisconsin	10
Kansas	13	North Carolina	23	Wyoming	(15)
Kentucky	(5)	North Dakota	(13)		

Source: *The Chronicle of Higher Education Almanac* 42, no. 1 (September 1995), p. 6.

In the remaining states of Virginia, Colorado, and Washington, growth in state support has been modest. In Virginia, Governor Allen's proposed reductions were never fully accepted by the state legislature, as contrasted with Colorado where the legislature increased the higher education budget $32 million over what was requested. In Washington State, allocations for higher education are down by more than 8 percent since 1991, even though institutions of higher education received a modest increase in the 1995 session.

There seems to be no real pattern in how states finance higher education. Instead, other policy drivers seem to lie beneath the surface of these data, and it is those currents that lead away from the numbers and into the policy environment in which they are established.

THE POLICY ENVIRONMENT

In a clinical sense, an exogenous variable may be thought of as an agent introduced from, or produced, outside the organism. Higher education has a long history of ignoring exogenous agents, preferring instead to define the academy from within. This tendency, traditionally defended under the rubric of academic freedom and faculty governance, served it well over many centuries and well into the twentieth century. Now, however, these outside agents appear eminent, and their clamor may well shape the future of higher education.

The Core Businesses Analogy

Each level of government has its own identity. It has what it perceives to be its own revenues and responsibilities, even though these change on the margin over time. These functions do not occur by accident, but are established constitutionally, in statute, and by past practice.

In the case of the federal government, most citizens do not understand that more than half the $1.6 trillion spent each year goes to citizens over 65 years without consideration of their ability to pay.[28] The remainder of the budget goes to defense (15 percent), domestic priorities (10 to 15 percent), entitlements for non-seniors, and debt service on the national debt. Most of the entitlement spending is for health care rather than income support and nearly two-thirds of the health care goes to seniors and the disabled rather than "the poor." These priorities were no more "planned" than they are generally understood.

The federal government receives its revenue from individual income taxes (39 percent), social insurance (33 percent), corporate income taxes (11 percent), borrowing (9 percent), and excise taxes (4 percent).[29]

Local governments were traditionally in the business of providing public education and "services to property." This meant trash pickup and other aesthetics, public safety, water, sewers, and other local infrastructure. But those days are gone; local government today is made up of more than 86,000 units[30] that are now coconspirators along with the states and the federal government in housing, health care provided through hospitals and public health programs, social services, and direct services ranging from populations that have been deinstitutionalized to students who are seeking admission to two- and four-year institutions in their local communities.

The revenue base for local governments has traditionally been the property tax and fees. In recent years, some metropolitan areas in particular have been successful in obtaining dedicated sales and income taxes. Nevertheless, by most accounts, local government has a stable but inadequate revenue base to handle the many functions headed its way in the twenty-first century.

When viewed from the perspective of the general fund, state government has four "core businesses." These are the functions that are supported by tax dollars rather than fees. In most states they rank in the same order of funding and together account for more than three-fourths of state general fund spending: K–12 education, health care, higher education, and public assistance. (Outside the general fund, there are two other major systems: transportation and environmental protection.) Together these systems constitute the purpose, or mission, of state government.

The problem confronting most governors, however, is that the public believes that the states' four core businesses are broken. In this context, "broken" means that the public generally lacks confidence in these systems. Elected officials generally prefer not to acknowledge this problem in elective politics. In many large metropolitan areas, parents view public education as a hopeless last resort; health care remains expensive, tenuous, and lacking the comprehensive reform the American people unanimously endorsed in the 1992 elections; higher education is viewed as a malaise in which tuition is rising to the point of disenfranchising what is left of the middle class; and public assistance policies of the last 30 years are thought to be unworkable even among those who designed them.

New governors elected in the fall of 1996 face this upward slope. One of their tasks, as with any new administration, is to assess promises made during the campaign. Although governors tend to bring into office their own philosophies about each of their core businesses (examples being to reform welfare or the public schools), these individual philosophies tend to be refined and prioritized in the months that follow. In each case, the aspirations and challenges are not unlike a business plan where winning and losing are clear. Goals are then established for the term of office, and from that point the broad outlines of an administration are less likely to change. This is because politics is so heavily influenced by the media and their methods of reporting the news,[31] along with the fact that governance ultimately requires consensus, and consensus does not coalesce in a world of surprises.

As a result, higher education within any state is in competition for the governor's and legislators' attention. Understanding that perspective is important, if only for tactical purposes. It is probably fair to say that most governors view higher education with more than a little skepticism. Yet many who work in higher education profess not to understand why.

First, most university administrators seem to skim over the fact that they are *in competition* with the other businesses of state government, or alternatively, they don't understand the nature of that playing field. Whereas other systems tend to serve children and other vulnerable populations who cannot pay for their services, colleges and universities have a wide range of fundraising mechanisms. As a result, higher education is perceived by elected officials to be better situated than the competition *no matter how current issues are cast.* If the governor supports higher education in a zero-sum game, the trade-off is clear. This competition with other state services is an exogenous problem that can be managed, but since it is often misunderstood, it can result in the unintended patina of arrogance.

Second, higher education has often argued that it should be able to bargain from outside the set of rules otherwise applicable to state government. For example, in some states the statutes say that no public employee salary may exceed that of the governor. But as everyone knows, this has never included selected faculty—in the old days in the medical school, but today in the business school, law school, and any other department where outside "compensation" is available. University administrators have accounts available to them from private gifts and other sources that mock the rules others must abide by. The matter of compensation does nothing to diminish the patina.

Campaign finance is a somewhat related issue that is seldom discussed. Elected officials, particularly those seeking statewide office, are reluctant to "take on" higher education since it is such an important source of organization and financing for their campaigns. As a result, they tend to communicate their "concerns" in a guarded manner and, unlike other contexts where gubernatorial or legislative staff can be used to deliver a more direct message, *no direct message is provided* since it would produce the same unwanted outcome.

Third, governance is too often raised as an excuse for why something cannot happen, rather than as an affirmative responsibility. Again one has to consider the competition. The competitors have no governance argument to make, and the 1990s have been unkind to their budgets. They too are tired of the endless demands for more accountability, measured outcomes, privatization, and reengineering; yet they have no alternative but to comply.

Fourth, it has become very hard outside the academy to understand its "mission." In a competitive environment, a clear sense of purpose is a prerequisite to funding. Accepting multiple missions, creating a hierarchy of institutions ranging from flagship universities to two-year community colleges, and diversifying in many directions may lead higher education to necessary destinations; but it may also lead to malaise.

Allan Bloom described the *real motive* of education to be the search for a good life,[32] and his defense of liberal education was a direct attack on the relativism he so strongly opposed in higher education. More recently, this theme arose among the self-proclaimed *digerati*, who have now concluded that information alone is hollow, and that the pursuit of truth may be of some importance.[33] In a related attack on relativism and its prominence in the university, one commentator recently deplored what he described as "the transparent bias in higher education for things that are true over things that are false."[34]

This is the milieu surrounding higher education as it pleads its case in the public square. It is incumbent on those in higher education to discern and communicate its *real motive* and the multiple businesses that necessarily underlie it. If teaching is no longer a core business in a flagship university, then it must be explained to the citizens, because they are restless and more sophisticated, and the debate about funding in state capitols has consequences.

The Impact of Devolution on the States

Most Americans have never heard of the Budget Enforcement Act. As legislation goes, it was fairly simple; but it slammed the door on the 1980s and singularly defined the terms of debate for the 1990s. It introduced an ideology that came to be known as "the Republican revolution" and contained the first effective framework for federal budgetary discipline in many years. The act categorized all spending into two areas: entitlements and discretionary spending, and established "pay as you go" rules for entitlements and hard targets for discretionary spending. The ultimate objective was to produce a balanced federal budget, and it appears that this framework is nearing completion.

The revolution has run its course. As always, it remains to be seen whether the revolution provided the end point, or the starting point, for change. The broad outlines of the "budget agreement" are unlikely to be adopted until the spring of 1997, but the brush strokes are clearly discernible. Overall spending will slow down over the next six to seven years until the budget is closer to being balanced. On the discretionary side of the budget, the domestic program (all programs other than defense and entitlements) will experience the only real reductions in the budget (20 percent) in nominal terms over the next five to seven years, and defense will remain stable or grow slightly in real terms.[36]

With respect to entitlements, the debate always turns to the healthcare twins, Medicaid and Medicare, and "welfare reform." It seems clear that there will not be "comprehensive" health-care reform, but rather a policy resolution of Medicaid similar to what the governors recommended in 1996,[37] complete with an allocational fight over the actual dollars during 1997. Medicare is likely to be addressed once all other aspects of "the deal" are complete. This could easily be part of a broader multiyear "commission-style" look at Social Security and Medicare together. Welfare reform is apparently complete for the moment, essentially along the lines the governors recommended early in 1996.[38]

As a result, the federal budget over the next five to seven years is likely to grow slower—by about $1 trillion—than current law projections. States will be given the responsibility to decide how this change is absorbed, which means that there will be multiple approaches rather than "one size fits all." In theory, states will be given the "simplicity" (read: block grants) and "flexibility" (read: deregulation) to make their tasks manageable. In addition, a recent U.S. Supreme Court decision[39] seems to have further strengthened state sovereignty in ways that could prove to be substantial.

But this is far from the whole story. To appreciate the magnitude of this "agreement," one has to recall how it was crafted. First, it was a comprehensive package that had four tracks: (1) the normal appropriation process (13 bills); (2) the budget resolution (covering reductions in the entitlements); (3) the tax cut package (originally $245 billion and now about $100 billion); and (4) the debt ceiling (originally $5 trillion, but now raised to $5.5 trillion). These were the negotiating levers that the parties relied on. Sometimes the levers brought results, sometimes they did not.

More importantly, more than enough money seemed available to "fix the problem," and most informed observers knew the deal was "doable" from the onset. The targets set in the spring of 1995 required reductions of about $1.5 trillion over seven years. Everyone knew that "all roads lead through the entitlements," which make up half the federal budget. The entitlements were the driving force behind the deficit, and $600 billion *a year* in entitlements is non-means-tested.[40] Second, health care reform was sure to offer significant multiyear savings once an agreement was reached. Third, everyone—including the chairman of the Federal Reserve—was saying that some adjustment could be made in the automatic cost of living escalators (COLAs) throughout the federal budget. These adjustments could yield hundreds of billions of dollars depending upon the figure chosen. And finally, there were always tax expenditures available—along with shifts in the economy or in economic projections—to help with the details. The Congressional Budget Office had the cookbook[41] and everybody from the Kerry Commission to the greenest freshman knew how to use it.

One issue remains on the table. The way things work in Washington, there can only be one "insanely great issue" at a time. The issue selected tends to coincide with each session of Congress—as did health care reform in 1992, deficit reduction in 1994, and the budget deal in 1996. Next comes intergenerational equity. With the glide path for the budget now in sight, the spotlight is likely to turn next to Social Security and Medicare, since neither is means-tested, yet nearly every major expenditure for future generations is need-based.

The Income Gap

Now that a budget agreement appears to be in sight, the pendulum seems ready to swing back toward social policy and how the services of government are *distributed*. Not only is there a significant intergenerational inequity, but there is an equally important distributional problem with income in the United States. This is particularly important for the delivery of services by American colleges and universities because in the case of higher education, which is highly leveraged with student loans, the demand function is going to be mapped by income dynamics during the next decade.

According to the most recent estimates,[42] the top 1 percent of federal tax filers pay almost a third (29 percent) of the federal personal income tax; the top 5 percent pay almost half (47 percent); and the top half pay *virtually all* of the more than $600 billion collected (95.2 percent) (see figure 1.4). Most people are not aware of this; most would not believe it if they were told. On the surface the estimates appear strongly progressive, but in fact they are not since the top half of households may pay 95 percent of the tax while possessing 85 percent of the income.

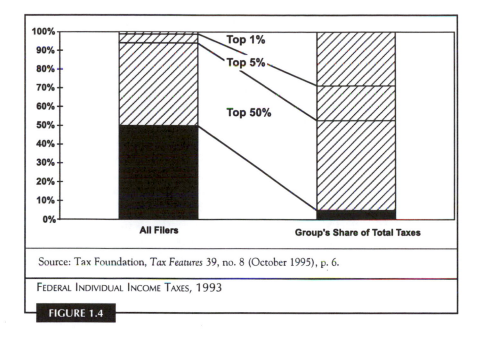

Source: Tax Foundation, *Tax Features* 39, no. 8 (October 1995), p. 6.

FEDERAL INDIVIDUAL INCOME TAXES, 1993

FIGURE 1.4

In short, the income gap is simple to describe. As figure 1.5 reveals, half the households retain 85 percent of America's income, and the other half retain 15 percent.

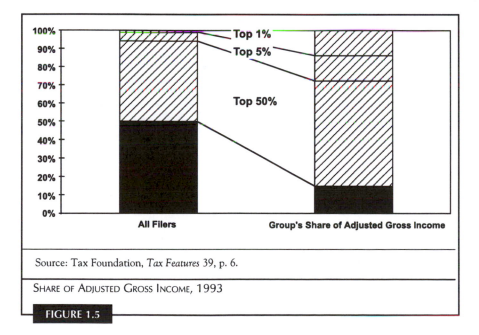

Source: Tax Foundation, *Tax Features* 39, p. 6.

SHARE OF ADJUSTED GROSS INCOME, 1993

FIGURE 1.5

These income figures raise profound questions about the future of the United States, especially regarding the role of higher education. In 1994, nearly 75 percent of the freshmen enrolled in colleges and universities came from families above the median income,[43] and it seems reasonable to conclude that an even higher percentage actually completed a degree program.

Conversely, information about current live births suggests that increasing numbers of children are being born into poverty, let alone below the median household income. In 1994, 37 percent of the population from 0 to 5 years was on Medicaid and that number is rising each year.[44] In some states it is now estimated that half of live births occur under Medicaid.[45]

Current projections of higher education enrollment are categorized by sex, attendance status, control of institution, type of institution, level, full-time-equivalency, and age, *but not by ability-to-pay*.[46] As a result, the projections are more reflective of data availability than common sense. Ability-to-pay may be the most important issue if one examines the trends in median income—whether measured by median family income (which includes two-parent households) or median household income (which includes single-parent households as well). Using the most recent statistics for the population as a whole, median household income began to *decline* in 1990, and by 1993 it declined to a level below that of 1985.[47] As figure 1.6 reveals, this pattern is shown in median family income, which is used by The College Board in their analyses. Conversely, it appears that median household and median family income for those enrolled in higher education—as opposed to the population as a whole—

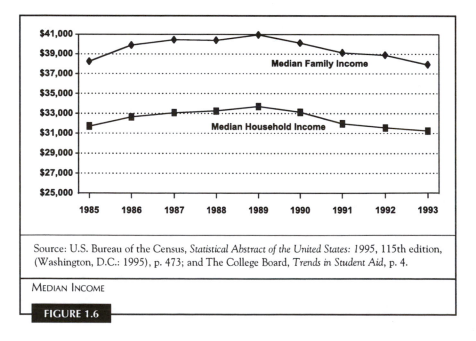

Source: U.S. Bureau of the Census, *Statistical Abstract of the United States: 1995*, 115th edition, (Washington, D.C.: 1995), p. 473; and The College Board, *Trends in Student Aid*, p. 4.

MEDIAN INCOME

FIGURE 1.6

may actually be rising, although the data to verify this are apparently not yet available. As the median income of those enrolled in higher education stretches further from the median income of the population as a whole, the projected high demand for higher education dissolves.

The Higher Education Act is scheduled for amendment in 1997. Currently, the federal government provides 75 percent of the available student aid, which is actually down 5 percent from 10 years ago.[48] Continuing the trend of the past 15 years, the largest single source of aid in 1994–95 was federal loans, nearly three-quarters of which are subsidized.[49] The number of students borrowing unsubsidized loans increased 178 percent in 1995 over the prior year—from 751,000 to over two million borrowers. Federal grant aid was steady for the same period, although the purchasing power of the Pell Grant has declined steadily over the past decade, down 50 percent in private schools and down about 40 percent in public institutions.

The income gap is about more than numbers. Although its impact stretches widely across the social horizon, it may be most important to higher education. In the period from 1980 to 1994, the cost of higher education outpaced the cost of automobiles by 500 percent, overall inflation by 400 percent, and even medical care by 70 percent.[50] This trend cannot be made up by student aid, and certainly not by loans. Something else must change.

The Policy of Passive Resistance

For a variety of reasons, state government has in many cases adopted a policy of passive resistance in financing higher education. Governors and legislators—unable to gain the understanding and support of institutional leaders, concerned about their own political futures, jealous of the "tenured radicals," and envious of the perceived stability and safety inside the academy—have *allowed natural forces to take their course.* The policy of passive resistance poses definite consequences for society in general and the academy in particular.

CONCLUSION

Tuition will continue to rise since decisions are being made incrementally from one year to the next and because there is no assurance that further support will remedy the internal structural problems now facing higher education. Forces much larger than higher education are creating an environment in which all public institutions will have to compete with one another for marginal funding, but with far fewer resources to share.

Institutions of higher education must move quickly beyond some of their old fundamentals, such as tenure, teaching loads, and the like, to answer directly whom they intend to serve in the years ahead, and how they will serve them. Colleges and universities must implicitly answer whether they will play a role in righting the wrongs of our society, as called for by Secretary of Education Riley,[51] or whether they plan to sit out the next "insanely great issue" of our time.

Technology, "new political models," and a renewed sense of public service will be some of America's next reference points. The future will not be singular for higher education, any more than it will be for states as they tackle the challenges of federal budget devolution. In diversity there is strength, and in pluralism there is great hope. Society rightly looks to the academy for wisdom; the academy must now complement that strength with compassion in charting our way into the twenty-first century.

NOTES

1. National Governors' Association (NGA) and the National Association of State Budget Officers (NASBO), *Fiscal Survey of the States* (Washington, D.C.: 1996), p. 12.
2. For a discussion of these topics see Stephen Carter, *Integrity* (New York: Basic Books, 1996), and the essays on presidential leadership edited by Robert A. Wilson, *Character Above All* (New York: Simon and Schuster, 1995).
3. For a discussion of these topics see Christopher Lasch, *The Revolt of the Elites and the Betrayal of Democracy* (New York: Norton, 1995), and Jean-Marie Guéhenno, *The End of the Nation-State*, translated by Victoria Elliott (Minneapolis: UM Press, 1995).
4. See Guéhenno, *The End of the Nation-State*, and Henry Mintzberg, "Managing Government, Governing Management," in *Harvard Business Review* (May–June 1996), pp. 75–83.
5. Guéhenno, *The End of the Nation-State*, p. 138.
6. For new economic arguments see: Kevin Kelly, "The Economics of Ideas," in *Wired* (June 1996), p. 148; Bill Gates, *The Road Ahead* (New York: Viking, 1995); and Robert Eisner, "No Need to Sacrifice Seniors or Children," in *Wall Street Journal* (2 February 1996), p. A10.
7. See Mintzberg, "Managing Government, Governing Management."
8. U.S. Bureau of the Census, *State Government Finances: 1980*, Series GF/80-3 (Washington, D.C.: U.S. GPO, 1981); and U.S. Bureau of the Census, *State Government Finances: 1989–90*, Series GF/90-5 (Washington, D.C.: U.S. GPO, 1991).
9. U.S. General Accounting Office, *Medicaid Expansions: Coverage Improves but State Fiscal Problems Jeopardize Continued Progress*, GAO/HRD-91-78 (Gaithersberg, MD: 1991), p. 13.
10. Ibid., p. 40.
11. NGA, "Medicaid and the States: History and Current Issues," press release (8-93), Washington D.C., 31 January 1993, p. 1.
12. NASBO, *1995 State Expenditure Report* (Washington, D.C.: 1996), p. 16.

13. Ron Snell, "State Balanced Budget Requirements: Provisions and Practice," National Conference of State Legislatures, Denver, p. 4 (forthcoming on the World Wide Web at http://www.ncsl.org/).

14. NASBO, *Budget Processes in the States* (Washington, D.C.: 1995), p. 11.

15. See National Conference of State Legislatures and NGA, *Financing State Government in the 1990s*, edited by Ron Snell (Denver: 1993).

16. Honorable Howard Dean, et. al., unpublished letter to Honorable Bill Archer, 23 February 1995.

17. Jackie Calmes, "Clinton's Fiscal 97 Budget Reflects Major Shift Toward Ending Deficits and Big Government," *Wall Street Journal* (6 February 1996), p. A16.

18. "College Quiz: Put Dollars in Stocks or in Scholars," *Washington Post* (28 April 1996), pp. H1+.

19. National Center for Education Statistics, *Federal Support for Education: Fiscal Years 1980 to 1995*, NCES 95-215 (Washington, D.C.: U.S. GPO, 1995), p. 6.

20. National Science Foundation, *Federal Funds for Research and Development: Fiscal Years 1993, 1994, 1995* (Arlington, VA: 1995), p. 1x.

21. NGA and NASBO, *Fiscal Survey of the States* (Washington, D.C.: 1992), p. 27.

22. NGA and NASBO, *Fiscal Survey of the States* (Washington, D.C.: 1994), p. 15.

23. National Center for Education Statistics, *The Condition of Education 1995*, NCES 95-273 (Washington, D.C.: 1995), p. 156.

24. National Conference of State Legislatures, "Survey of Legislative Fiscal Officers, State Revenue and Expenditure Limitations," unpublished paper, April 1996.

25. Herb Stein as cited in Peter G. Peterson, "Will America Grow Up Before It Grows Old?" in *The Atlantic Monthly* 277, no. 5 (May 1996), p. 55.

26. NASBO, *1995 State Expenditure Report*, p. 27.

27. *The Chronicle of Higher Education Almanac* 42, no. 1 (September 1995), p. 10.

28. Although this number remains open to debate, it is primarily the result of four programs (Social Security, Medicare, Medicaid, and federal retirements). Added to this would be a prorated share of all other services where there are shared benefits.

29. *Budget of the United States Government: Fiscal Year 1997*, Supplement (Washington, D.C.: U.S. GPO, 1996), p. 2.

30. U. S. Bureau of the Census, *Statistical Abstract of the United States: 1995*, 115th edition (Washington, D.C.: U.S. GPO, 1995), p. 297.

31. See James Fallows, *Breaking the News: How the Media Undermine American Democracy* (New York: Pantheon Books, 1996).

32. Allan Bloom, *The Closing of the American Mind: How Higher Education Has Failed Democracy and Impoverished the Souls of Today's Students* (New York, Simon and Schuster, 1987), p. 34.

33. See Guéhenno, *The End of the Nation-State*.

34. Alan Sokal, "A Physicist Experiments with Cultural Studies," in *Lingua Franca* (May–June 1996), p. 62.

35. See Congressional Budget Office, *The Economic and Budget Outlook: Fiscal Years 1997–2007* (Washington, D.C.: U.S. GPO, May 1996).

36. See Congressional Budget Office, *The Economic and Budget Outlook: An Update* (Washington, D.C.: U.S. GPO, August 1995).

37. NGA, "Restructuring Medicaid," policy position adopted winter meeting, Washington, D.C., 1996.

38. NGA, "Welfare Reform," policy position adopted winter meeting, Washington, D.C., 1996, revised March 1996.

39. *Seminole Tribe of Florida v. Florida*, Supreme Court of the United States, No. 94-12, 27 March 1996.

40. Congressional Budget Office, *Economic and Budget Outlook: 1997–2007*, p. 46.

41. Congressional Budget Office, *Reducing the Deficit: Spending and Revenue Options* (Washington, D.C.: 1995).

42. Tax Foundation, *Tax Features* 39, no. 8 (October 1995), p. 6.

43. *The Chronicle of Higher Education*, p. 17.

44. U.S. Department of Health and Human Services, Health Care Financing Administration, *Medicaid Statistics: Program and Financial Statistics, Fiscal Year 1994*, HCFA Pub. No. 10129 (Baltimore: 1996), p. 36.

45. For further information on counting the poor, see: Sass, "Passing the Buck"; Jane Katz, "Who's On Welfare?" in *Regional Review* (Federal Reserve Bank of Boston, summer 1995), p. 18; and Steven Pearlstein, "For Richer, For Poorer: An Election-Year Primer; Americans' Economic Status: Who's Got the Right Numbers?" in *The Washington Post* (5 May 1996), pp. H1+. For a more extended explanation of how the poor are measured, see Sharon Parrott, *The CATO Institute Report on Welfare Benefits: Do CATO's Numbers Add Up?* (Washington, D.C.: Center on Budget and Policy Priorities, 1996).

46. National Center for Education Statistics, *Projections of Education Statistics to 2005*, NCES 95-169 (Washington, D.C.: U.S. GPO, 1994), p. 11.

47. U.S. Bureau of the Census, *Statistical Abstract: 1995*, p. 473.

48. The College Board, *Trends in Student Aid: 1985 to 1995* (New York: College Entrance Examination Board, 1995), p. 3.

49. Ibid.

50. Karen Heller and Lily Eng, "Why College Costs So Much, Pushing Many out of the Market," in *Philadelphia Inquirer* (31 March 1996), pp. A1+.

51. Karen Heller and Lily Eng, "For Many, College is Slipping Out of Reach," in *Philadelphia Inquirer* (1 April 1996), pp. A1+.

BIBLIOGRAPHY

Advisory Commission on Intergovernmental Relations, *Significant Features of Fiscal Federalism: Revenues and Expenditures*, M-190-II, Washington, D.C., 1994.

Advisory Commission on Intergovernmental Relations, *Significant Features of Fiscal Federalism: Budget Processes and Tax Systems*, M-197, Washington, D.C., 1995.

American Association of Retired People, *The State Economic, Demographic and Fiscal Handbook 1993*, Washington, D.C., Public Policy Institute of the American Association of Retired Persons, 1993.

Bane, Mary Jo, and David T. Ellwood, "Is American Business Working for the Poor?" in *Harvard Business Review* 69, no. 5, September–October 1991, pp. 58–66.

Bloom, Allan, *The Closing of the American Mind: How Higher Education Has Failed Democracy and Impoverished the Souls of Today's Students*, New York, Simon and Schuster, 1987.

Budget of the United States Government: Fiscal Year 1997, Washington, D.C., U.S. GPO, 1996.

Callan, Patrick M., "Public Purposes and Public Responsibilities," San Jose, CA, California Higher Education Policy Center, November 1994.

Calmes, Jackie, "Clinton's Fiscal 97 Budget Reflects Major Shift Toward Ending Deficits and Big Government," in *Wall Street Journal*, 6 February 1996, p. A16.

Carter, Stephen L., *The Culture of Disbelief: How American Law and Politics Trivialize Religious Devotion*, New York, Basic Books, 1995.

———. *Integrity*, New York, Basic Books, 1996.

Chronicle of Higher Education Almanac 42, no. 1 (September 1995).

The College Board, *Trends in Student Aid: 1985 to 1995*, New York, College Entrance Examination Board, September 1995.

"College Quiz: Put Dollars in Stocks or in Scholars?" in *The Washington Post*, 28 April 1996, pp. H1+.

Collender, Stanley E., *The Guide to the Federal Budget, Fiscal 1996*, Washington, D.C., Urban Institute Press, 1995.

The Common Fund, *A Chartbook of Trends Affecting Higher Education Finance 1960–1990*, Westport, CT, 1992.

Congressional Budget Office, *The Economic and Budget Outlook: An Update*, Washington, D.C., U.S. GPO, August 1995.

———. *The Economic and Budget Outlook: Fiscal Years 1996–2000*, Washington, D.C., U.S. GPO, January 1995.

———. *The Economic and Budget Outlook: Fiscal Years 1997–2007*, Washington, D.C., U.S. GPO, May 1996.

———. *Reducing the Deficit: Spending and Revenue Options*, Washington, D.C., U.S. GPO, February 1995.

Davis, Bob, and Lucinda Harper, "Reason for Hope: Middle Class's Fears About Coming Markets Bode Well for U.S. Firms and for Living Standards," in *Wall Street Journal*, 29 March 1995, pp. A1+.

Dean, the Honorable Howard, unpublished letter to the Honorable Bill Archer, 23 February 1995.

Dyson, Esther, "Friend and Foe," in *Wired*, August 1995, pp. 106+.

Eisner, Robert, "No Need to Sacrifice Seniors or Children," in *Wall Street Journal*, 2 February 1996, p. A10.

Fallows, James, *Breaking the News: How the Media Undermine American Democracy*, New York, Pantheon Books, 1996.

Gates, Bill, *The Road Ahead*, New York, Viking, 1995.

Guéhenno, Jean-Marie, *The End of the Nation-State*, translated by Victoria Elliott, Minneapolis, UM Press, 1995.

Hancock, LynNell and John McCormick, "What to Chop," in *Newsweek* 127, no. 18, 29 April 1996, pp. 59–67.

Hauptman, Arthur M., Federal and State 'Macro' Policies for Financing Higher Education in the United States, unpublished speech, April 1996.

Heller, Karen, and Lily Eng, "And Now, College Applicants, the Envelope Please," in *Philadelphia Inquirer*, 3 April 1996, pp. B1+.

———. "Financial Aid is Eating Away at Colleges' Fiscal Health," in *Philadelphia Inquirer*, 2 April 1996, p. A9.

———. "For Many, College is Slipping Out of Reach," in *Philadelphia Inquirer*, 1 April 1996, pp. A1+.

———. "Spending Millions to Raise Millions," in *Philadelphia Inquirer*, 2 April 1996, pp. A1+.

———. "State Schools Grow Less Affordable," in *Philadelphia Inquirer*, 3 April 1996, pp. A1+.

———. "Why College Costs So Much, Pushing Many out of the Market," in *Philadelphia Inquirer*, 31 March 1996, pp. A1+.

Howard, Philip K, *The Death of Common Sense: How Law is Suffocating America*, New York, Random House, 1994.

Katz, Jane, "Who's on Welfare?" in *Regional Review*, Federal Reserve Bank of Boston, summer 1995, p. 18.

Kelly, Kevin, "The Economics of Ideas," in *Wired*, June 1996, p. 148.

Kliesen, Kevin L., "A Fiscal Devolution," in *The Regional Economist*, Federal Reserve Bank of St. Louis, October 1995, p. 5.

Lasch, Christopher, *The Revolt of the Elites and the Betrayal of Democracy*, New York, Norton, 1995.

Lubman, Sarah, "Campuses Mull Admissions Without Affirmative Action," in *Wall Street Journal*, 16 May 1995, pp. B1+.

Mathews, David, "The Public's Disenchantment with Professionalism: Reasons for Rethinking Academe's Service to the Country," in *Journal of Public Service and Outreach* 1, no. 1, spring 1996, p. 21.

Millbank, Dana, "Old Flaws Undermine New Poverty-Level Data," in *Wall Street Journal*, 5 October 1995, pp. B1+.

Mintzberg, Henry, "Managing Government, Governing Management," in *Harvard Business Review*, May–June 1996, pp. 75–83.

National Association of State Budget Officers, *1992 State Expenditure Report*, Washington D.C., 1993.

———. *1995 State Expenditure Report*, Washington D.C., 1996.

———. *Budget Processes in the States*, Washington D.C., 1995.

————. *Restructuring and Innovations in State Management*, Washington D.C., 1996.

National Conference of State Legislatures and the National Governors' Association, *Financing State Government in the 1990s*, edited by Ron Snell, Denver, 1993.

National Conference of State Legislatures, "Survey of Legislative Fiscal Officers, State Revenue and Expenditure Limitations," unpublished paper, April 1996.

National Education Association, *1994–95 Estimates of School Statistics*, West Haven, CT, 1995.

National Governors' Association, "Medicaid and the States: History and Current Issues," press release dated 31 January 1993 (8-93), Washington, D.C.

————. "Restructuring Medicaid," policy position adopted winter meeting, Washington, D.C., 1996.

————. "Welfare Reform," policy position adopted winter meeting, Washington, D.C., 1996, revised March 1996.

National Governors' Association and the National Association of State Budget Officers, *The Fiscal Survey of the States*, Washington, D.C., April 1996.

National Public Radio, *All Things Considered*, "The Income Gap Series," 5–8 February 1996, Washington, D.C. (transcript inquiries 202-414-3232).

National Science Foundation, *Federal Funds for Research and Development: Fiscal Years 1993, 1994, 1995*, NSF 95-334, Arlington, VA, 1995.

Parrott, Sharon, *The CATO Institute Report on Welfare Benefits: Do CATO's Numbers Add Up?* Washington, D.C., Center on Budget and Policy Priorities, 22 April 1996.

Pearlstein, Steven, "For Richer, For Poorer: An Election-Year Primer; Americans' Economic Status: Who's Got the Right Numbers," in *The Washington Post*, 5 May 1996, pp. H1+.

Peterson, Peter G., "No More Free Lunch for the Middle Class," in *New York Times Magazine*, 17 January 1982, pp. 40+.

————. "Will America Grow Up Before It Grows Old?" in *The Atlantic Monthly* 277, no. 5, May 1996, pp. 55–86.

Sandel, Michael J., *Democracy's Discontent: America in Search of a Public Philosophy*, Cambridge, MA, Harvard University Press, 1996.

Sass, Steven, "Passing the Buck: The Intergenerational Transmission of Wealth," in *Regional Review*, Federal Reserve Bank of Boston, summer 1995, p. 12.

Seminole Tribe of Florida v. Florida, Supreme Court of the United States, No. 94-12, 27 March 1996.

Sharpe, Rochelle, "Students May Pay Much More for Student Loans," in *Wall Street Journal*, 20 July 1995, pp. B2+.

Snell, Ron, "State Balanced Budget Requirements: Provisions and Practice," Denver, CO, National Conference of State Legislatures (forthcoming on the World Wide Web at http://www.ncsl.org/).

Sokal, Alan, "A Physicist Experiments with Cultural Studies," in *Lingua Franca* 6, no. 4, May–June 1996, pp. 62–64.

Sowell, Thomas, *The Vision of the Anointed: Self Congratulation as a Basis for Social Policy*, New York, Basic Books, 1995.

Tanner, Michael and Stephen Moore, "Why Welfare Pays," in *Wall Street Journal*, 28 September 1995, pp. A20.

Tax Foundation, *Tax Features* 39, no. 8, October 1995.

U.S. Bureau of the Census, Current Population Reports, Series P60-184, *Money Income of Households, Families, and Persons in the United States: 1992*, Washington, D.C., U.S. GPO, 1993.

———. *65+ in the United States*, Washington, D.C., U.S. GPO, Special Studies, P23-190, 1996.

U.S. Bureau of the Census, *Government Finances: 1989–90*, Series GF/90-5., including unpublished updates, Washington, D.C., U.S. GPO, 1991.

U.S. Bureau of the Census, *State Government Finances: 1980*, Series GF/80-3, Washington, D.C., U.S. GPO, 1981.

U.S. Bureau of the Census, *State Government Finances: 1992*, Series GF/92-3, including unpublished updates, Washington, D.C., U.S. GPO, 1993.

U.S. Bureau of the Census, *Statistical Abstract of the United States: 1995* (115th edition), Washington, D.C., U.S. GPO, 1995.

U.S. Department of Education, National Center for Education Statistics, *The Condition of Education 1995*, NCES 95-273, Washington, D.C., 1995.

———. *Digest of Education Statistics 1995*, NCES 95-029, Washington, D.C., 1995.

———. *Federal Support for Education: Fiscal Years 1980 to 1995*, NCES 95-215, Washington, D.C., U.S. GPO, 1995.

———. *Basic Student Charges at Postsecondary Institutions: Academic Year 1993–94*, NCES 94-223, Washington, D.C., U.S. GPO, 1994.

———. *Projections of Education Statistics to 2005*, NCES 95-169, Washington, D.C., U.S. GPO, 1994.

U.S. Department of Health and Human Services, Health Care Financing Administration, *Medicaid: An Overview*, HCFA Pub. No. 10965, Baltimore, MD, 1995.

———. *Medicaid Statistics: Program and Financial Statistics Fiscal Year 1994*, HCFA Pub. No. 10129, Baltimore, MD, 1996.

U.S. General Accounting Office, *Medicaid Expansions: Coverage Improves but State Fiscal Problems Jeopardize Continued Progress*, GAO/HRD-91-78, Gaithersburg, MD, June 1991.

Votruba, James C., "Strengthening the University's Alignment with Society: Challenges and Strategies," in *Journal of Public Service and Outreach* 1, no. 1, spring 1996, p. 29.

Wall Street Journal, "No Guardrails," editorial, 18 March 1993, p. A12.

Walshok, Mary Lindenstein, "New Approaches to Funding University Public Service and Outreach," in *Journal of Public Service and Outreach* 1, no. 1, spring 1996, p. 37.

Wilson, Robert A., editor, *Character Above All*, New York, Simon and Schuster, 1995.

Wingspread Group on Higher Education, *An American Imperative: Higher Expectations for Higher Education*, Racine, WI, Johnson Foundation, 1993.

Wolf, Gary, "Steve Jobs: The Next Insanely Great Thing," in *Wired*, February 1996, p. 102.

CHAPTER 2

The Changing Landscape
Higher Education Finance in the 1990s

David W. Breneman and Joni E. Finney

In the early 1970s, the Carnegie Commission on Higher Education completed a landmark study that evaluated individual and societal benefits—and responsibilities—regarding higher education. In June 1973, the commission concluded that in relation to higher education, "the proportion of total economic costs borne privately (about two-thirds) as against the proportion of total economic costs now borne publicly (about one-third) is generally reasonable."[1] The commission reached this conclusion based on, among other things, the rationale that about two-thirds of the additional earned income of college graduates is kept by those individuals, and about one-third is taken publicly in the form of taxes. Also influencing its decision was the commission's judgment about the social benefits of higher education at that time.

Current economic circumstances are pressuring public officials and educational leaders to revisit important public policy questions about who pays for, who benefits from, and who *should* pay for higher education. As of yet, however, few of these leaders fully understand or are willing to evaluate the consequences of the fiscal transformations of the 1990s. One of the most significant changes concerns reduced state support for higher education as other spending commitments—especially Medicaid and corrections—have increased dramatically. This reduced state support, coupled with steep increases in tuition and student loan burdens, has resulted in a significant shift from public to private support of higher education. Should these trends continue—and many have argued that they will—governors, legislators, and college and university officials will face even tougher decisions concerning: opportunity (how affordable and available are colleges and universities to the population at large?); costs (to what extent will institutions of higher education need to restructure their services to significantly cut costs?); and quality (what are the core services that specific colleges and universities bring to their states, and how can those services be maintained or improved?).

To more fully understand the challenges and priorities that states will face during the rest of the 1990s and into the next century, this chapter analyzes the most significant shifts in revenue sources for higher education during the recent past, with an emphasis on the economic recession of the early 1990s. In doing so, this chapter draws upon the five case studies that can be found in part II, for they explain in detail how five states financed their systems of higher education during the first half of this decade. The last section of this chapter raises issues that state and institutional leaders should address as they think about the future of higher education in their states.

MAJOR REVENUE SOURCES SUPPORTING HIGHER EDUCATION: EARLY 1990s

Overview

The financial support for higher education in the United States can be described as vast by any measure. Overall, higher education's share of the Gross Domestic Product (GDP) was nearly 3 percent in 1995.[2] Even during the recession of the early 1990s, when overall economic growth slowed from earlier decades, the proportion of the GDP spent on higher education increased. Total revenue from all sources supporting public and private higher education also increased. In 1990, total revenue from all sources supporting colleges and universities was approximately $150 billion (63 percent for public and 37 percent for private institutions). By 1994, total revenue reached approximately $179 billion, with the same percentage distribution between public and private institutions.[3]

As total revenue was increasing, however, a shift occurred in revenue sources: For the first time since the mass expansion of public colleges and universities, tuition overtook state government appropriations to institutions in providing the largest share of revenues for higher education. In 1990–91, tuition and fees for all higher education institutions nationally accounted for $37.4 billion in revenues, whereas revenues from state government appropriations to colleges and universities accounted for $39.5 billion. By 1993–94, tuition and fees had jumped to $48.6 billion while revenues from state governments rose only to $41.9 billion. In terms of share, the switch in funding sources is also apparent: The share of revenues funded by tuition increased from 25 to 27 percent from 1990–91 to 1993–94, while the share of revenues funded by state governments decreased from 27 to 23 percent during the same period.[4]

In relation to public institutions only, the shift from state funding to revenues from tuition is equally dramatic, though the portion of revenues funded by the states is still higher than the portion funded by tuition and fees. As table 2.1 reveals, however, the gap is narrowing.

TABLE 2.1

PERCENTAGE OF CURRENT REVENUE FUND FOR HIGHER EDUCATION INSTITUTIONS

	Public Institutions			Private Institutions		
	1990–91	1993–94	Change	1990–91	1993–94	Change
Tuition and Fees	16.3	18.4	12.9	40.4	42.0	4.0
Federal Government*	10.3	11.0	6.8	15.4	14.5	(5.8)
State Government	40.3	35.9	(10.9)	2.3	2.1	(8.7)
Local Government	3.7	4.0	8.1	0.7	0.7	0.0
Private Gifts, Grants, Contracts	3.8	4.0	11.1	8.6	8.6	0.0
Endowment Income	0.5	0.6	20.0	5.2	4.6	(11.5)
Sales and Services	22.7	23.4	3.1	22.9	23.2	1.3
Other Sources	2.6	2.7	3.8	4.5	4.3	(4.4)

* This category includes appropriations, unrestricted grants and contracts, restricted grants and contracts, and revenues associated with major federally funded research and development centers. This same category excludes Pell Grants; federally supported student aid that is provided to students is included under tuition and sales and services.

Source: U.S. Department of Education, National Center for Education Statistics, *Digest of Education Statistics 1996* (Washington, D.C.: 1996), pp. 333–35. Due to the difficulties in compiling data across states, 1993–94 is the most recent year that data on all institutions of higher education are available.

If one looks back to 1980–81, specifically focusing on public higher education, the changes in revenue sources are even more dramatic. Figure 2.1 demonstrates a long-term shift from public to private support for education. Although the category "private gifts and contracts" shows the highest percentage change in share and is itself an important indicator of revenue-raising priorities at public institutions, it represented only 4 percent of revenues in 1993–94. The 43 percent increase in share for tuition and fees is far more dramatic in terms of actual dollar amounts, for this category jumped from 13 to 18 percent of total revenues during the period shown. The largest drop, meanwhile, was in state government funding, both in percentage terms and dollar amounts. State government funding as a share of total revenues at public institutions fell from 46 to 36 percent, which represents a decline of 21 percent. Also, the 13 percent drop in share in federal funding is particularly important for research institutions.

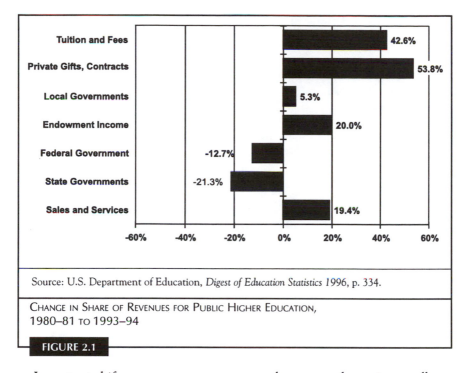

Source: U.S. Department of Education, *Digest of Education Statistics 1996*, p. 334.

CHANGE IN SHARE OF REVENUES FOR PUBLIC HIGHER EDUCATION,
1980–81 TO 1993–94

FIGURE 2.1

Important shifts among revenue sources also occurred at private colleges and universities during the same period, as shown in figure 2.2. As with public institutions, tuition revenues as a share of total funding increased significantly at the private institutions, from 37 to 42 percent of total revenues. Meanwhile, funding from the federal government as a share of overall revenues fell from 19 to 15 percent, which represents a 23 percent decline in share during this period. Federal funding is particularly important for private institutions due to their extensive involvement in research. The increase in the share represented by state governments in figure 2.2 is largely an anomaly, for state governments make up a very small portion of revenues at private institutions. The state government share during the period shown increased only from 1.9 to 2.1 percent of total revenues—an increase that looks significant in terms of percentage change, but is small in terms of overall funding.

If one excludes sales and services (e.g., hospitals, dormitories, restaurants), the shift in revenues from public to private sources is even clearer—and more pronounced (see figure 2.3). Some finance experts view this perspective of change as the most important, arguing that higher education's involvement in hospital services and other auxiliary enterprises masks the most important trends in higher education finance. The share of these revenues funded by tuition and fees increased from 27 to 37 percent (a 35 percent increase), while the share funded by state governments dropped from 40 to 31 percent (a 21 percent decrease). As a result of this shift, the share of these revenues funded by tuition and fees is now larger than the share funded by state governments.

State Revenues

In the early 1990s, a number of observers (for instance, Atwell, Breneman, Hauptman, Johnstone, Schapiro, and Zemsky[5]) began arguing that recent

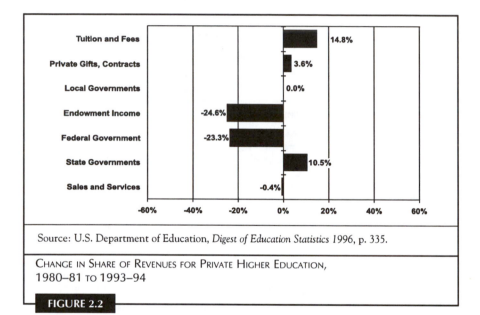

Source: U.S. Department of Education, *Digest of Education Statistics 1996*, p. 335.

CHANGE IN SHARE OF REVENUES FOR PRIVATE HIGHER EDUCATION, 1980–81 TO 1993–94

FIGURE 2.2

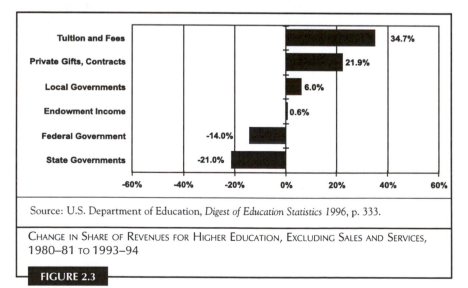

Source: U.S. Department of Education, *Digest of Education Statistics 1996*, p. 333.

CHANGE IN SHARE OF REVENUES FOR HIGHER EDUCATION, EXCLUDING SALES AND SERVICES, 1980–81 TO 1993–94

FIGURE 2.3

trends in the financing of higher education are not simply another cyclical downturn in state support for higher education, but rather a new era of reduced support likely to be long-lasting. The arguments have been based on the view that most state governments have been experiencing structural deficits brought on by obligations passed down from Washington for social services; growth in medical spending; demographic changes increasing the need for K–12 funding increases, prison spending, and aid to the elderly; and the pressure not just to refrain from tax increases, but to reduce taxes.

From this perspective, higher education has been portrayed as one of a small number of state-supported activities that is discretionary in nature, setting up the potential for legislatures to cut spending there. Additional arguments have focused on states passing up higher education in favor of other state priorities, a result, perhaps, of the years of criticism begun by William Bennett when he was secretary of education. A third view has focused on the ability of colleges and universities—unlike most state activities—to raise funds from nonstate sources, including tuition increases, private fund raising, and federal grants.

Whatever the mix of reasons present in each state, we now know from Steven Gold's work that higher education spending did indeed fall as a share of state outlays from 14.0 percent in 1990 to 12.5 percent in 1994—the only area to take such a large decline.[6]

Federal Revenues

A similar pattern is present in federal support for higher education. Grants for students comprise a declining share of total federal student aid. From 1990 to 1996, grant dollars declined from 49 to 42 percent of all federal aid allocated. Loans jumped during the same period from 48 to 57 percent. Campus work-study fell from 3.0 to 1.2 percent.[7] As college costs outpaced inflation during the late 1980s and 1990s, the purchasing power of the Pell Grant, the largest federal grant program, fell sharply. According to The College Board, the maximum Pell Grant now buys less than 30 percent of the average tuition, room and board, and fees at public colleges.

Growth in student borrowing was the most visible change in federal funding during the first half of the 1990s. Stafford Loans—the oldest and largest of the federal education loan programs—jumped by about 43 percent from 1990 to 1994.[8] In 1992, the federal government established the Unsubsidized Stafford Loan Program, for which all students are eligible—and students have flocked to it. In two years it has grown to provide $7.5 billion to more than two million students, so that it now represents about one-third of federal loan volume and accounts for half the increase in student loan volume since the 1992 reauthorization.[9]

Federal support for research grew from $9 billion in 1990 to $11.8 billion in 1994.[10] Continued growth in federally sponsored research may be problematic as the federal government works to reduce the deficit, balance the budget, and devolve responsibilities to the states. Behind these numbers, a conflict in funding research has been brewing. Due to increased pressure on limited research dollars, federal agencies tend to spread their funds over more proposals, causing gaps in funding that institutions have been trying to close with their own funds.[11] During the 1980s, for instance, institutional support for research was the second fastest growing source of research expenditures, accounting for about 8.5 percent in private universities and 23 percent at public ones by the end of the 1980s.[12] The pressure to reduce federal spending has had an impact on all forms of federal support to colleges and universities.

Tuition Revenues

While sharp tuition increases marked the early years of the 1990s (as shown in table 2.2), political resistance to additional tuition increases has increased as low- and middle-income families express fears about college being priced out of reach. As a consequence, the past two years have witnessed only modest increases in public tuition levels in most states. It no longer appears politically

---

TABLE 2.2

NATIONAL AVERAGES IN RESIDENT UNDERGRADUATE TUITION (IN DOLLARS)

	Universities		State Colleges and Univ.		Community Colleges		Private 4-Year	U.S. CPI*
	Nat'l Ave.	% Change	Nat'l Ave.	% Change	Nat'l Ave.	% Change	Nat'l Ave.	% Change
1991	2,156		1,735		947		9,391	4.2
1992	2,410	12	1,940	12	1,052	11	10,017	7 3.0
1993	2,627	9	2,123	9	1,148	9	10,498	5 3.0
1994	2,837	8	2,277	7	1,231	7	11,025	5 2.6
1995	3,032	7	2,402	6	1,314	7	11,709	6 2.8
% Change, 1991–95		41		39		39		25 11.9

* CPI figures are based on calendar rather than fiscal years.

Sources: Washington State Higher Education Coordinating Board, *Tuition and Fee Rates, 1994–95: A National Comparison* (Olympia: 1995), tables 1, 5, 9. Data for the private institutions are from *Chronicle of Higher Education Almanac* 38–42, no. 1 (September 1991 to September 1995 editions). Data for the U.S. Consumer Price Index (CPI) are from the U.S. Department of Labor, Bureau of Labor Statistics, "Consumer Price Index for All Urban Consumers, U.S. City Average," October 1996.

feasible to continue double-digit tuition increases, at least for in-state under-graduate students.

The heavy reliance on tuition revenues during the early part of the 1990s and the corresponding high rate of student borrowing represent a generational shift in the responsibilities of paying for higher education from parents to their children. Experts offer a number of opinions about why tuition has increased so rapidly. A recent study completed by the General Accounting Office cites two factors most responsible for the increase in tuition in public institutions: the rise in institutional expenditures and higher education's greater dependency on tuition as a source of revenue.[13] In fact, according to this report, if the shares of funding, by source, had remained constant at 1980 levels, tuition could have been 30 percent lower than it was at the end of 1995.

Sources of Voluntary Support

Colleges and universities have increasingly turned to philanthropy to make up some of the revenue losses, with mixed results. The big change has been the growth of private fund raising by public institutions, but only the most prestigious universities have realized much from this source. Of the total $12.7 billion given to public and private colleges and universities in 1995, 20 top universities in the country accounted for approximately 23 percent of all giving.[14] Fewer than 1,000 institutions receive 84 percent of all private contributions.[15] Overall, private fund raising by colleges and universities experienced a 30 percent gain from 1990 to 1995. The increases in giving are displayed by source in table 2.3.

TABLE 2.3	
CHANGE IN VOLUNTARY SUPPORT FOR HIGHER EDUCATION, 1990–1995 (IN PERCENT)	
Alumni	42
Other Individuals	32
Corporations	18
Foundations	28
Religious Organizations	4
Other Organizations	34

Source: *Chronicle of Higher Education Almanac* 43, no. 1 (September 1996), pp. 17–18.

Private Colleges and Universities

Private colleges and universities, faced with an excess supply of spaces at posted prices, have increased their tuition discounts dramatically. In a recent study of 147 private colleges and universities, tuition discounts increased by more than 28 percent from 1990 to 1995.[16] The study showed a wide range of tuition discounts among various types of private institutions. Tuition discounting became so commonplace in small private colleges with relatively low tuition—representing one end of the continuum—that at a third of these institutions, 10 percent (or fewer) of the freshmen paid the published tuition price. Of all the institutions surveyed, fewer than half of the students paid the published tuition price. The practice of tuition discounting raises questions about the role of financial aid in these institutions. Aid dollars are being used more frequently, it appears, to attract the right "mix" of students, rather than to offset the price of college for needy students.

In response to this climate, some colleges have decided to cut tuition since they had so few full-paying students left (for instance, Muskingum College, Bennington College, and North Carolina Wesleyan College). Haggling over the net price of college became the norm, as more and more families learned that they could bargain with most colleges over the actual price to be paid by the family. Many nonselective private colleges have squeezed about all of the net tuition revenue gains out of their markets, and will find themselves in increasingly difficult financial straits if some form of public policy response is not forthcoming.

STATE POLICY RESPONSES: 1990–1995

Overview

The case studies found in part II provide in-depth examinations of fiscal trends and changes in five states: California, Florida, Michigan, Minnesota, and New York, from 1990 to 1995—as well as state and institutional policy responses to these changes. Case study researchers found a varied range of responses to the changing fiscal climate of the 1990s. No single state can be considered "average" or "normal." It is useful for this reason to look at how these particular states fared and determine to what extent, if any, we can learn more about the common problems states face, as well as learn more about the range of policy responses to these problems.

To better understand the fiscal context of each state, case study researchers collected data from the state and drew upon national comparative data sources as well. The following section summarizes case study findings, and places these findings within a larger national context.[17]

The Context of Change, 1990–1995: Undergraduate Enrollment, Participation, and Growth in Higher Education

In 1994–95, overall undergraduate enrollment in higher education was about 12 million students nationwide.[18] The case studies show that during the first half of the 1990s, enrollment increased slowly in Michigan and more rapidly in Florida. During the same period, enrollment at New York's and Minnesota's colleges and universities declined in fairly small numbers. California's enrollment declined more substantially, by about 200,000 students—mostly at the community college and state university systems.

Enrollment levels alone, however, provide an incomplete picture of change in the states. Enrollment may increase due to increases in the population or because of improved recruiting efforts. A more complete picture of how the changes of the 1990s affected educational opportunity for young people can be seen by also examining the trends in the number of high school graduates from 1990 to 1995, as shown in table 2.4. This table also shows the full-time-equivalent (FTE) student enrollment in higher education per new high school graduate.[19]

TABLE 2.4

HIGH SCHOOL GRADUATES AND COLLEGE ENROLLMENT, CASE STUDY STATES

	% Change in High School Graduates (1990–95)*	FTE Public Higher Education Students per New High School Graduate[†]	
		1990	1995
California	11.0	4.92	4.51
Florida	8.2	2.92	3.64
Michigan	0.0	3.27	3.71
Minnesota	5.7	3.42	3.32
New York	2.8	2.59	2.81

* The figures in this column are based on projections beginning in 1993.

[†] A caution is in order here. Because these statistical data are based on students enrolling in public colleges and universities, those states with robust private sectors of education, like New York, look as though fewer of their students attend college compared to the national average.

Sources: Figures in the first column are from Western Interstate Commission for Higher Education (WICHE), Teachers Insurance and Annuity Association, and The College Board, *High School Graduates: Projections by State, 1992 to 2009* (Denver: 1993), pp. 22–27. Data in the second and third columns are from Kent Halstead, *State Profiles: Financing Public Higher Education, 1978–1996 Trend Data* (Washington, D.C.: Research Associates of Washington, 1996), pp. 9, 17, 45, 65.

Table 2.4 shows that the number of high school graduates, the primary pool for colleges and universities, increased in every state except Michigan, where it remained constant. The table also shows that the number of public FTE students in higher education (per new high school graduate) dropped in two states: California and Minnesota. This statistic provides the best national comparative measure on college enrollment relative to the size of the high school graduating class. States such as Michigan that experienced no growth in the number of high school graduates, but an increase in the number of public FTE students in higher education (per new high school graduate) either increased the number of high school graduates going to college or increased the enrollment of other full-time students to make up for the decline in high school graduates.

In Florida and New York, the number of high school graduates increased, as did the number of public FTE students in higher education (per new high school graduate). Florida's efforts to increase the number of high school students entering college seems to be working, given steady improvements in enrollment over the past 10 years or so.

In California and Minnesota, on the other hand, the number of FTE students in higher education (per new high school graduate) decreased while the overall pool of high school graduates increased. Of the case study states, California experienced the largest percentage increase in the number of high school graduates, *and* the largest percentage decrease in FTE students per new high school graduate.

Another important contextual factor to consider in trying to assess a state's record in college participation is the contribution of private colleges and universities. The case study states vary in the size of their private higher education sectors. New York depends most heavily on private colleges and universities to deliver education to its citizens. Minnesota is next in relying on its private colleges and universities. Even in states such as California and Florida, where the total number of students attending private colleges and universities is fairly small, state policies to support private higher education— mostly through financial aid—are important, long-standing commitments made by the state. Figure 2.4 shows the share of students educated in private colleges and universities in each of the case study states.

A final contextual factor that will affect many states over the next decade is the projected growth in the number of high school graduates, with a corresponding projected increase in college enrollments. In the next decade, half the states will see substantial increases in the number of students seeking postsecondary education. Figure 2.5 shows the wide range of growth projected

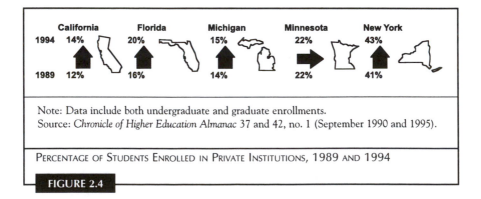

Note: Data include both undergraduate and graduate enrollments.
Source: *Chronicle of Higher Education Almanac* 37 and 42, no. 1 (September 1990 and 1995).

PERCENTAGE OF STUDENTS ENROLLED IN PRIVATE INSTITUTIONS, 1989 AND 1994

FIGURE 2.4

in high school graduates in the case study states. Nationally, high school graduates are projected to increase about 32 percent from 1992 to 2009. In the West, high school graduates are projected to increase 65 percent and in the South and South-Central United States, by 73 percent.[20]

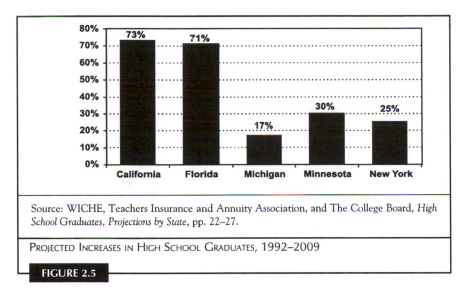

Source: WICHE, Teachers Insurance and Annuity Association, and The College Board, *High School Graduates, Projections by State*, pp. 22–27.

PROJECTED INCREASES IN HIGH SCHOOL GRADUATES, 1992–2009

FIGURE 2.5

Fiscal Changes in the States from 1990 to 1995

Although some of the changes in how states finance higher education were visible before the 1990s, many of these trends accelerated during the first half of this decade because a large part of the country was in a recession, and because higher education support declined in absolute state dollars during this period. The rapid increase in tuition, combined with growing student indebtedness, became more visible during the 1990s, even though tuition rates had been moving upward for some time. Changes in state financing of public higher education also affected private colleges and universities.

Case Study Findings

Finding One

For the first time since the mass expansion of higher education, dollars paid by students and their families (tuition) surpassed state appropriations to colleges and universities, which was previously the largest revenue source. Tuition revenue has surpassed state government appropriations to colleges and universities as the largest revenue source for higher education. In terms of actual dollars, tuition and fees for all higher education institutions nationally accounted for $37.4 billion in revenues for 1990–91, whereas appropriations to institutions from state governments accounted for $39.5 billion. In 1993–94, however, tuition and fees jumped to $48.6 billion while revenues from state governments rose only to $41.9 billion.

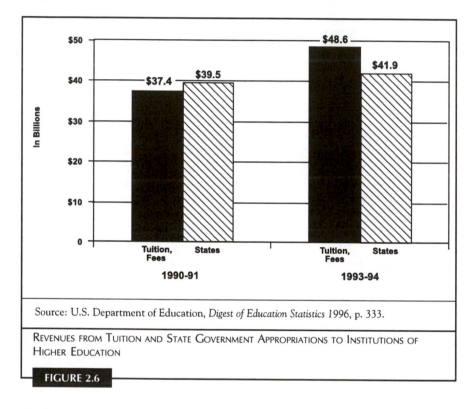

Source: U.S. Department of Education, *Digest of Education Statistics 1996*, p. 333.

REVENUES FROM TUITION AND STATE GOVERNMENT APPROPRIATIONS TO INSTITUTIONS OF HIGHER EDUCATION

FIGURE 2.6

Finding Two

Higher education's share of state budgets declined nationally and in the case study states. Higher education lost ground in the competition for state resources in the 1990s. As noted by Brian Roherty in chapter 1, beginning in 1990 Medicaid displaced higher education as the second largest state spending category (the first is elementary and secondary education); Medicaid's share of state appropriations rose from 10.2 percent in 1987 to 19.2 percent in 1995. Table 2.5 documents the declining share of state appropriations for higher education in the case study states and nationally.

TABLE 2.5

HIGHER EDUCATION SHARE OF STATE BUDGET (IN PERCENT)

	1990	1994	Change
California	13.8	11.3	(18.1)
Florida	13.2	11.4	(13.6)
Michigan	14.7	13.7	(6.8)
Minnesota	19.9	17.2	(13.6)
New York	9.8	8.5	(13.3)
U.S.	14.0	12.5	(10.7)

Source: Steven Gold, *State Spending Patterns in the 1990s* (Albany: Center for the Study of the States, SUNY, 1995), pp. 23–30.

Finding Three

For the first time in 40 years there was an absolute annual decline in state dollars for higher education. In 1992, states reached a record highof $40 billion in investment in higher education. In 1993, for the first time in 40 years, states provided fewer resources for higher education than they did the previous year—slipping to $39.8 billion. Recovery since 1993 has been steady; states invested $44.4 billion for higher education in 1996.[21]

Table 2.6 shows what happened in the five case study states in terms of appropriations per public FTE student.[22] Only Michigan and Minnesota increased state dollars per public FTE student during the period studied. California, Florida, and New York decreased state appropriations per public student, with the largest decrease—both in absolute and percentage terms—in California. Only Michigan was below the national average in state dollars per student in 1990; by 1995 Michigan moved up to the national average, while California slipped below it.

TABLE 2.6

STATE DOLLARS PER PUBLIC STUDENT

	State Dollars Per Public FTE Student		Indexed Value*	
	1990	1995	1990	1995
California	4,708	4,416	108	95
Florida	5,583	5,526	128	119
Michigan	4,194	4,648	96	100
Minnesota	4,444	4,939	102	106
New York	5,120	4,918	117	105

* National Index Average = 100.

Source: Halstead, *State Profiles, Trend Data* (1996), pp. 10, 18, 46, 66.

Finding Four

*The student share of the cost of higher education increased in all the case study states
and tuition as a share of personal disposable income increased in most states.*
Tuition as a portion of all higher education revenues (defined as state appropriations plus tuition revenues) grew at a fairly rapid pace in most states across
the country, and in *all* case study states, even those with higher state appropriations per student (see table 2.7). In 1995, tuition still ranged from a low of
20 percent of all higher education revenues in California, to a high of 45
percent in Michigan. In 1990, California, Florida, and New York were well
below the national average in this measure, while Michigan was significantly
above it. In 1995, California, Florida, and New York were still well below the
national average.

TABLE 2.7

TUITION REVENUE RELATIVE TO REVENUE SUPPORTING HIGHER EDUCATION

	Tuition Revenue Relative to Total Revenue		Indexed Value*	
	1990	1995	1990	1995
California	10.6%	20.0%	41	64
Florida	18.0%	21.4%	69	68
Michigan	39.8%	44.5%	152	142
Minnesota	26.2%	30.1%	100	96
New York	20.3%	25.7%	78	82

* National Index Average = 100.
Note: Total revenue is defined as state appropriations plus tuition revenue.

Source: Halstead, *State Profiles, Trend Data* (1996), p. 26.

From 1980 to 1995, tuition at four-year public colleges and universities rose
nearly three times as much as median household income, making it much
more difficult for low- and middle-income families to afford college.[23] With the
exception of Florida, tuition followed this same trend in the case study states,
as shown in table 2.8, which portrays tuition relative to personal disposable
income.

Data from tables 2.6, 2.7, and 2.8 reveal the broad range of public policies
across the states regarding who pays and who benefits from higher education.
Taken together, these tables show that state dollars for higher education are
declining, students and their families are paying a greater share of the cost of
higher education, and, with the exception of one state, tuition is taking a
larger bite out of personal income.

TABLE 2.8		
TUITION RELATIVE TO PERSONAL DISPOSABLE INCOME (IN PERCENT)		
	1990	1995
California	3.2	5.6
Florida	7.5	7.1
Michigan	17.4	19.3
Minnesota	9.9	11.4
New York	7.1	9.0

Source: Halstead, *State Profiles: Financing Public Higher Education, 1978 to 1995* (Washington, D.C.: Research Associates of Washington, 1995), p. 32.

Finding Five

During the first half of the 1990s, tuition increased at every type of higher education institution at a rate faster than the Consumer Price Index. In relation to this finding, see table 2.2 as well as figure 2.7.

Finding Six

Many states that increased tuition the fastest during the 1990s have frozen or dramatically slowed the growth of tuition. Of the five states (California, Massa-

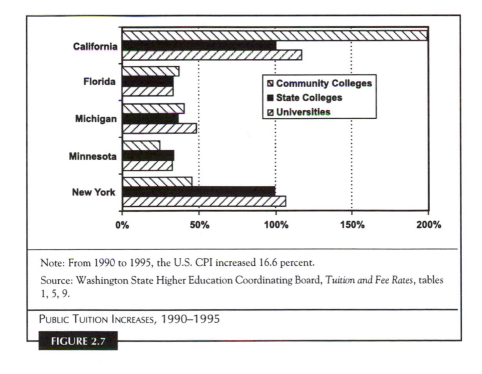

Note: From 1990 to 1995, the U.S. CPI increased 16.6 percent.

Source: Washington State Higher Education Coordinating Board, *Tuition and Fee Rates*, tables 1, 5, 9.

PUBLIC TUITION INCREASES, 1990–1995

FIGURE 2.7

chusetts, New York, Oregon, and Virginia) that raised tuition by the highest percentage from 1990 to 1995 (and also had large enrollments), four have either frozen or slowed the growth of tuition dollars in the last two years—some as the result of public backlash. Only New York continued the high rate of tuition increases into 1994 and 1995.[24] Even New York, however, froze tuition for the 1996–97 school year.

Finding Seven

State student aid programs grew, but increases did not keep pace with the need caused by rising tuition. As table 2.9 reveals, states made substantial contributions to their student aid programs during the time period studied. Total state dollars for student financial aid increased 41 percent from 1990 to 1995.[25] Of the states studied, however, none claimed that student aid dollars kept up with the double- and triple-digit increases in tuition during this period. New York, where state student aid is structured as an entitlement, was more successful in increasing aid as tuition increased, because those increases are mandated by law.

TABLE 2.9

INCREASE IN STATE GRANT AID TO STUDENTS, 1990–1995 (IN PERCENT)

California	33.0
Florida	37.5
Michigan	5.3
Minnesota	20.4
New York	25.4

Note: This table includes aid for both undergraduate and graduate students.

Source: National Association of State Student Grant and Aid Programs, *NASSGAP 26th Annual Survey Report: 1994–95 Academic Year* (Albany: New York State Higher Education Services Corporation, 1996), p. 2.

Although California's overall grant dollars increased during the five-year period, need-based state aid for undergraduates dropped by $23 million from 1991 to 1992. Similarly, while grant aid in Florida over the five-year period rose for Florida's students, state need-based aid declined by about $3 million from 1991 to 1993.

Also, as the five case studies in part II illustrate, states have widely varying priorities for state student aid dollars. For example, in 1994 Florida provided its residents with more dollars for non-need-based aid than did all the other states combined. Georgia is now moving along a similar path.

Finding Eight

Students at public institutions in many states are paying for an increasing portion of student aid through tuition increases. More public colleges and universities have, for the first time, used tuition dollars to increase their financial aid programs for students in their institutions. "Tuition discounting," a term used to describe the practice of providing institutional aid to students who cannot pay the full cost of tuition in private colleges and universities, is a practice now found in public institutions. For example, in California from 1990 to 1994, student aid dollars in the public colleges and universities dwarfed total dollars in the state aid program. Minnesota found it necessary for the first time to discount tuition at its flagship institution. In Florida, public policy requires that a percentage of tuition increases is allocated for student aid support at public institutions. Michigan colleges and universities have discretion over tuition dollars and have used these funds to support student aid. Public institutions in New York are seeking the authority to set tuition differentially across institutions, along with more freedom to use these dollars to support financial aid.

This shift in the source of financial aid raises issues of equity. California, Minnesota, and Florida have completed extensive studies about the income distribution of students in the various types of institutions in the state.[26] All three states found that, on the average, higher income students were attending the large flagship institutions with middle- and low-income students concentrated at the state colleges and universities and community colleges. The private colleges in these states drew, for the most part, students from family backgrounds with incomes higher than those students attending state colleges and universities, but lower than the flagship institutions.

The growth of institutional aid dollars from student tuition revenue raises the policy question of whether institutions or the states are best suited to distribute financial aid dollars. If the current trend of increasing institutional aid from tuition dollars continues, middle-income families will find attending public colleges and universities more expensive.

Finding Nine

Tuition discounting in private colleges and universities increased. While data are not available by state, a national study documented the findings in table 2.10, which shows that tuition discounting grew at private colleges and universities in the United States.

TABLE 2.10

INCREASE IN TUITION DISCOUNT RATE, 1990–1995 (IN PERCENT)

Small College, Low Tuition	37.5
Small College, High Tuition	28.7
Large College/University	28.0

Source: Lucie Lapovsky, "Tuition Discounting Continues to Climb: NACUBO Study Analyzes Six Years of Data," in *Portfolio* (NACUBO Business Officers, February 1996), p. 21. Data are based on a sample of 147 private colleges and universities.

Finding Ten

Students borrowed more money and more students borrowed to pay for higher education. Even though dollars for need-based grant programs increased during the 1990s, student borrowing across the five states skyrocketed from 1990 to 1995. Changes in eligibility for federal loan programs, as well as rising college prices, account for this growth. From 1990 to 1996, total loan volume in the United States grew from $15.8 billion to $28.5 billion.[27] More detailed information about trends in student borrowing is found in the case studies.

Finding Eleven

Support for state mechanisms to promote student choice to attend private colleges and universities has eroded in some states due to changes in the structure of higher education finance. Significant changes in the support of public policies relative to private colleges and universities have occurred since 1990 in California and in New York, and are also apparent in other states to a lesser degree. Although enrollment increased or held stable in private colleges and universities in the case study states during this period, tuition discounting increased and state support to private colleges decreased. The discounting of tuition and the decreased state support may undermine the investment these institutions will be able to make in their own futures.

Private colleges and universities in California and New York have historically been supported by public policies that have helped make them an integral part of the state system of higher education. Both states provide financial aid to students attending private colleges and universities. The rapid increases in tuition at public institutions have made more students eligible for state aid scholarships, including many students attending public colleges and universities. For the first time since the inception of large state programs for financial aid in both California and New York, students from public institutions are now using a greater share of state financial aid grants than are students from private colleges and universities. These programs were created to provide choice to students who wanted to attend a private college or university.

Other Policy Responses

Other policy responses to changes in the finance of higher education during the 1990s are described in the case studies. However, with the exception of Florida and Michigan, case study researchers found little evidence that the states, in responding to the changes in the 1990s, were guided by either historic or new state policies created for higher education.

Even though Florida was under significant fiscal stress during the 1990s, attempts were made to increase student participation, reduce student time in college, and begin planning to accommodate the projected increases in enroll-ment expected during the first decade of the next century. While these issues were approached largely in isolation—and none were fully resolved to the satisfaction of educational and political leaders—the state's adjustments to the fiscal pressures of the 1990s appear to have remained consistent with historic public policies in the state, particularly in maintaining access for qualified high school graduates.

Michigan, on the other hand, maintained its commitment to past public policies largely by maintaining the status quo. The state could afford this for two primary reasons. First, although state revenues dipped slightly during fiscal year 1991, revenue growth remained positive during the rest of the recession and higher education stayed a high priority for legislators. As a result, Michigan's system of higher education did not face the cuts that public colleges and universities faced in many other states. Since enrollments were not increasing in Michigan during this period, state funding per student increased significantly. Second, even though tuition increased dramatically in the state as well, students and families paid the higher rates without clamoring for change. With yearly increases in state appropriations to higher education and with a high level of public satisfaction, Michigan's colleges and universi-ties navigated the first half of the 1990s in a fairly stable environment without significant long-term changes.

Neither New York nor California could afford such a strategy. The cuts in state dollars for higher education in New York and California were much more severe than those in Florida. (Michigan's system of higher education enjoyed actual increases each year.) Moreover, the responses to New York's and California's fiscal crises were not only piecemeal and fragmentary, but they also diverged significantly from those states' historic policies. For California, the most drastic result of the early 1990s was that access to higher education decreased during this period, based on several measures described in the case study. As California began to recover from the recession, it has increased state appropriations for public higher education. The state has also begun restoring dollars to the state student aid program to support students attending private colleges and universities. Little planning has been done, however, to address how the state should accommodate the huge increases in enrollment demand expected over the coming decade.

While New York's system of higher education did not see funding cuts as deep as California's public colleges and universities, the fiscal stress on higher education in New York continued well into 1994 and 1995. During these years, tuition increases in the public institutions continued unabated—which marked a significant change in past public policy, for until the 1990s New York had very low or no tuition in its public sector. Although budgets in New York became more stable in 1996, the long-term prospects for increased higher education funding are still dim, as demands for public services increase and the governor continues to pursue his tax-cutting agenda. Unlike California, however, the state of New York has required its institutions of higher education to begin reporting regularly to the legislature on long-term strategies to improve cost effectiveness. Although policy makers and educational leaders are now asking difficult questions regarding accountability, efficiency, and productivity, it remains to be seen whether this discussion will help New York develop new long-term public policies regarding higher education.

During the 1990s in Minnesota, the state's high level of commitment to both public and private higher education eroded somewhat, causing the state's historic policies that generously supported both public and private higher education to come into question. While the state faces a moderate increase in enrollment growth over the next decade, competition for state resources is intensifying. Also increasing is the level of conflict between the public and private institutions of higher education. A proposal to move a significant portion of state funding for public colleges and universities into the state student aid program, available to students at public or private institutions, is under consideration by the governor. With a governor and many legislators also expressing interest in approaches that shift public higher education subsidies away from institutions and toward the "consumer," Minnesota may be moving toward a more "market-oriented" approach to funding higher education.

ISSUES AND OPTIONS FOR STATE POLICY

As this chapter has described, the state financing of higher education in the 1990s has brought about important structural changes in the financing of higher education in the United States, the most important of these being a dramatic increase in tuition and student borrowing, and a significant decrease in state funding. These changes have resulted in a gradual shift from the state to the individual in paying for higher education. This shift has important consequences, as Brian Roherty has described in chapter 1, concerning the composition of and the demand for higher education in the coming decades. As a result, the fiscal changes of the 1990s bring with them a wide array of public concerns that call into question, as the case studies in part II reveal in greater detail, established state priorities regarding higher education.

Priorities for Higher Education

Unfortunately, many generations find that they have backed into new priorities without having evaluated them—through isolated fiscal or institutional decisions made on an ad hoc basis in response to real and pressing short-term needs. In light of the recent shift in the burden of paying for higher education—at a time when competition for state revenues is expected to intensify and the number of high school graduates is projected to rise in many states—it is especially important that each state revisit its priorities that guide higher education policies. It is toward this aim that the following priorities for higher education, which are not meant to be exhaustive, are listed. These priorities often are in conflict, not only with one another, but also with other state priorities. Several of those listed will no doubt be prominent across many states, while others may be missing entirely from some states. It could be that states facing significant enrollment growth will find themselves adopting similar priorities—or that other factors besides projected enrollment growth are more significant determinants of state priorities.

1. Maintain or improve access to undergraduate programs, including affordability
   a. Maintain low public tuition
   b. Establish or maintain high tuition/high aid policies
2. Enhance the quality of undergraduate education
3. Enhance higher education's role in economic development
4. Ensure accountability for public funds
5. Increase specialization of function among institutions or maintain the system as is by spreading the budgetary pain evenly
6. Help private institutions survive by enhancing their ability to meet state objectives
7. Use financial pressure to force productivity increases within the institutions
   a. Force a reduction in unit costs of education
   b. Force institutions to set priorities among activities (e.g., undergraduate versus graduate programs)
8. Fund technology to enhance productivity
9. Reduce state contributions to higher education to fund other state priorities

Of course it is one thing to establish priorities publicly and another to put them into effect (through annual appropriations, governance policies, institutional decisions, and the like) and it is always the latter that proves to be the acid test. Ironically, however, those states that need to revisit their priorities most are the very ones in which publicly established policies have begun to erode without widespread public debate.

Some have argued that the underlying message of the structural changes in higher education finance during the 1990s is that access has slipped as a priority for many states. In every case study state, for instance, tuition rates and loan volume increased significantly, and in four out of five of the states, tuition was taking a larger portion of disposable income. Yet of the case study states, only in California did enrollments and other factors change so that access was reduced significantly during the first half of the 1990s. During 1994 and 1995, however, the legislature and governor in California agreed to freeze student tuition for a second year, and enrollments have increased again.

Some policy makers appear to be willing to let access slip from their grasp, perhaps on the assumption that we have done all that we can or should do in this area, or perhaps out of a sense that the system simply cannot handle the growth that will occur in some states. (In California, this growth has been referred to as "Tidal Wave II.") Not seeing any way to accommodate this potential growth, these policy makers may prefer simply not to talk about it. Others may believe that we have gone too far in our emphasis on access, and that too many young people are in college who do not deserve to be there. For whatever reason, access as a public priority has not received significant public debate, yet in relation to higher education, it is the issue that arguably affects more families more significantly than any other single issue.

Whereas access appears to have slipped from the lexicon of public debate over higher education, "privatization" has become a buzzword of late, with its meanings not entirely clear. Outsourcing seems to be one meaning, but the more profound one refers to a shift by formerly public universities into a stance of "state-assisted," and ultimately into predominantly private financial status. One dimension of this shift is the growing tendency of public institutions to recycle tuition revenue into student aid, precisely as the private institutions have been doing. Some public university presidents argue that their best policy is, to the extent possible, to behave as if they were leading private institutions. But it is not yet clear what the full impact of this strategy will be on public priorities for higher education.

Issues for Policy Makers

As states go about the task of determining their priorities (either through deliberate or ad hoc means) and as public institutions begin to adopt the revenue-raising strategies of private institutions, it is crucial that policy makers consider the effects of a general shift from state to private support of public higher education. The following issues are presented on the basis of that assumption.

1. We must better understand the effects of the increased reliance of public colleges and universities on tuition and other private revenue, and decreased reliance on state general funds. The increased reliance of tuition dollars in public colleges and universities has also influenced the financing of private institutions. Is more—or less—governmental attention being given to public institutional expenditures of state appropriations? To the amount and distribution of state appropriations for student financial aid?

2. If the changes of recent years toward "privatization" of revenue sources are structural and permanent, we need to better understand the likely effects on public and private higher education institutions and on state and federal public policies for higher education. For example, as the "equity" of state government in the enterprise decreases, how will the traditional relationships of government to the colleges and universities change with respect to accountability and regulation? Is growing deregulation likely, and if so, what form would that take?

3. It is also important to understand how the changing patterns of finance influence expectations that colleges and universities will pursue public policy goals such as access and economic development. What are the implications for public support of particular functions, such as student financial aid and capital expenditures? What are the implications for educational opportunity, affordability, access, and choice?

4. A related issue concerns how states invest their resources. Are there specific changes in state budgetary practices and policies that would encourage institutions to evolve in desired directions (for instance, by placing more emphasis on undergraduate rather than graduate programs)? Can we identify "best practices" in this area?

5. Some assert that evidence is mounting that colleges and universities have become, are becoming, or will become more responsive to market forces than in the past. If colleges and universities are becoming more responsive to markets, should government seek to achieve public purposes through the market, relying more on incentives than on general institutional support through state appropriations? In general, should public support be more focused and targeted than in the past, with less governmental responsibility for the overall well-being of institutions?

6. If colleges and universities are becoming more responsive to markets, then state and federal governments need to determine if there are

some functions of higher education that public policies should seek to insulate from market forces. If so, what are these functions? For example, is there a public policy interest in preserving and transmitting knowledge of the classical languages and cultures or in an "academic core" deemed essential for an informed citizenry or in "basic" as opposed to "applied" research?

7. Suppose it were possible for a handful of the most prestigious public universities to be privatized by replacing state institutional support with some mix of tuition, private philanthropy, and contract support. Would this be a desirable public policy? Would there be serious social costs if the most prestigious public institutions were no longer public? (This discussion assumes that privatization is not a realistic possibility for the vast majority of public four-year and two-year colleges and universities.)

8. If public tuition continues to increase, states might debate whether institutions should allocate some percentage of the increased tuition to student aid. Alternatively, states could allocate increased public funds to state-run financial aid programs rather than having each college or university mimic the selective discounting that one finds in the private sector. What is the best way to distribute student aid in public institutions?

9. Many who believe that the changes in state support for higher education of the last five years will not be reversed have argued that colleges and universities must reduce costs rather than attempt to solve their financial problems solely through increasing revenues. Although many businesses and other institutions in the United States have been following that approach recently, the degree of change has been minimal in higher education. Economist William Baumol has argued, on the other hand, that higher education fundamentally cannot achieve productivity increases, and that we must accept the fact that a steadily growing share of national income will be devoted to higher education (and also to medical care).[28] Which argument is acceptable to the public and state policy makers? Can institutions of higher education improve productivity significantly?

10. There has also been extensive discussion of the potential of the new information technologies to reduce higher education costs (or expand outreach to unserved populations), but the jury is still out on whether new technologies will produce significant reductions in the unit costs of education. Are we likely to see dramatic breakthroughs in costs from this source in the next five to ten years? If so, can public policy help to encourage this trend, or can we assume that incentives are already in place to bring these changes into existence?

11. It is difficult to address new mechanisms of finance when so many of the old ways of funding institutions are tied to how we organize our public colleges and universities. What do new forms and purposes of finance imply for governance systems? Can we identify specific governance patterns that seem best adapted to the circumstances of the next five to ten years? Are system offices (such as the University of California's Office of the President) cost-effective in a time of limited resources? And what of the regulatory powers of certain state governance structures (for instance, Illinois and Virginia)?

CONCLUSION

Clark Kerr, president emeritus of the University of California and former director of the Carnegie Commission on Higher Education, has described the mix of public and private control and financing of colleges and universities in this country as a "halfway house."[29] Changes in the financing of higher education in the 1990s have gradually shifted the burden of paying from the state to the individual. Rapidly increasing costs of operating the "house"—combined with continued intense competition for state resources in most states and projected enrollment jumps in some—threaten to exacerbate those changes. Meanwhile, many public institutions are adopting strategies similar to those of private institutions in raising revenues, yet few are seriously addressing long-term issues concerning productivity. Until state and institutional leaders begin to fully grapple with the effects of the changes in financing during the recession of the 1990s, they are unlikely to fully understand or take responsibility for the changes that are on the horizon.

NOTES

1. Carnegie Commission on Higher Education, *Higher Education: Who Pays? Who Benefits? Who Should Pay?* (New York: McGraw-Hill, 1973), p. 3.
2. U.S. Office of the President, *The Economic Report of the President* (Washington, D.C.: 1995), p. 274.
3. Appropriations, revenue, and other budgetary data are presented in fiscal years, unless otherwise noted.
4. U.S. Department of Education, National Center for Education Statistics, *Digest of Education Statistics 1996* (Washington, D.C.: 1996), p. 333.
5. Robert Atwell, "Higher Education Governance in Despair," in *Journal for Higher Education Management* 11, no. 2 (winter/spring 1996), pp. 13–19; David Breneman, *Higher Education: On A Collision Course with New Realities* (Boston: American Student Assistance, 1993); Arthur Hauptman and Anthony Carnevale, "The Economic, Financial, and Demographic Context of Ameri-

can Higher Education," unpublished paper prepared for the Seminar on Change and the Public Comprehensive University, Aspen Institute Program on Education in a Changing Society, 1996; Bruce Johnstone, "Learning Productivity: A New Imperative for American Higher Education," in *Higher Education in Crisis: New York in National Perspective*, edited by William Barba (New York: Garland, 1995); Morton Owen Schapiro, Michael McPherson, and Gordon Winston, *Paying the Piper: Productivity, Incentives, and Financing in U.S. Higher Education* (Ann Arbor: UM Press, 1993); and William Massy and Robert Zemsky, "Cost Containment: Committing to a New Economic Reality," in *Change* 22, no. 6 (November/December 1990), pp. 16–22.

6. Steven Gold, *The Fiscal Crisis of the States: Lessons for the Future* (Washington, D.C.: Georgetown University Press, 1995), p. 68.

7. The College Board, *Trends in Student Aid: 1984 to 1994* (Washington, D.C.: 1994), p. 3; and *Trends in Student Aid: 1986 to 1996* (Washington, D.C.: 1996), p. 3. Numbers for 1995–96 listed as preliminary.

8. The average Stafford Loan per student jumped from $2,712 in 1990 to $3,061 in 1994, according to The College Board, *Trends in Student Aid: 1984 to 1994*, p. 3.

9. Jacqueline E. King, "Student Aid: Who Benefits Now?" in *Educational Record* 77, no. 1 (winter 1996), pp. 21–27.

10. These data are based on federal academic research and development obligations according to a survey of 15 federal agencies by the National Science Foundation (1994 numbers are preliminary). Figures cover federal obligations, which are funds set aside for payments. Figures include spending for science and engineering projects only, and exclude spending in such disciplines as the arts, education, and the humanities.

11. Roger Geiger, "Research Universities in a New Era," in *Higher Learning in America: 1980–2000*, edited by Arthur Levine (Baltimore: John Hopkins UP, 1993), pp. 210–42.

12. Ibid.

13. U.S. General Accounting Office, *Tuition Increasing Faster Than Household Income and Public Colleges' Costs* (Washington, D.C.: 1996), p. 20.

14. *Chronicle of Higher Education Almanac* 42, no. 1 (September 1995), p. 25.

15. Ibid., pp. 17–18. Figures are based on a survey of 992 institutions, compiled by the Council for Aid to Education for 1993–94.

16. Lucie Lapovsky, "Tuition Discounting Continues to Climb: NACUBO Study Analyzes Six Years of Data," in *Portfolio* (NACUBO Business Officers, February 1996), p. 21.

17. This section draws upon data from national sources in order to compare the five states studied and to put the case study findings in a national context. Numbers in the case studies may be slightly different, since the case studies relied on a combination of national and state data. Important differences between the sets of data will be noted.

18. *Chronicle of Higher Education Almanac* 39–43, no. 1 (1992–1996 editions).

19. It is possible for a state to show an overall increase in students (head count), while experiencing a decline in the public FTE students per new high school graduate. This can happen due to an increase in the number of part-time students or due to increases in the number of high school graduates.

20. Western Interstate Commission for Higher Education (WICHE), Teachers Insurance and Annuity Association, and The College Board, *High School Graduates, Projections by State 1992 to 2009* (Denver: 1993), pp. 14–15.

21. Edward Hines, *State Higher Education Appropriations 1995–96* (Denver: State Higher Education Executive Officers, 1996). This figure does not include local property taxes appropriated for higher education.

22. It is important to note that the statistics in tables 2.6 and 2.7 are based on students attending public colleges and universities and, therefore, do not account for support to students attending private colleges and universities in the states. Also, states with large community college systems, such as California, tend to appear low on appropriations per student presented in table 2.6, due to the lower costs associated with that sector of higher education. Nevertheless, the data provide a picture of changes over time that are useful to note.

23. U.S. General Accounting Office, *Tuition Increasing Faster*, p. 19.

24. Washington State Higher Education Coordinating Board, *Tuition and Fee Rates, 1994–95: A National Comparison* (Olympia: 1995), tables 1, 5, 9.

25. National Association of State Student Grant and Aid Programs, *NASSGAP 26th Annual Survey Report: 1994–95 Academic Year* (Albany: New York State Higher Education Services Corporation, 1996), p. 2.

26. California Student Aid Commission, *Family Financial Resources of Dependent Undergraduates at California Four Year Institutions* (Sacramento: 1996); Florida Postsecondary Education Planning Commission, *How Floridians Pay for College* (Tallahassee: 1994); and Minnesota Private College Research Foundation, *Ways and Means: How Minnesota Families Pay for College* (St. Paul: 1992).

27. The College Board, *Trends in Student Aid: 1986 to 1996*, p. 4.

28. William J. Baumol and Sue Anne Batey Blackman, "How to Think About Rising College Costs," in *Planning for Higher Education* 23, no. 4 (1995), pp. 1–7.

29. Clark Kerr, *The Great Transformation in Higher Education: 1960–1980* (Albany: SUNY Press, 1991), p. 27.

BIBLIOGRAPHY

Atwell, Robert, "Higher Education Governance in Despair," *Journal for Higher Education Management* 11, no. 2, winter/spring 1996, pp. 13–19.

Baumol, William and S. A. B. Blackman, "How to Think About Rising College Costs," in *Planning for Higher Education* 23, summer 1995, pp. 1–7.

Breneman, David, *Higher Education: On A Collision Course with New Realities*, Boston, American Student Assistance, 1993.

California Student Aid Commission, *Family Financial Resources of Dependent Undergraduates at California Four Year Institutions*, Sacramento, 1996.

Carnegie Commission on Higher Education, *Higher Education: Who Pays? Who Benefits? Who Should Pay?* New York, McGraw-Hill, 1973.

Chronicle of Higher Education Almanac 37–43, no. 1, September 1990–September 1996.

The College Board, *Trends in Student Aid: 1986 to 1996*, Washington, D.C., 1996.

———. *Trends in Student Aid: 1985 to 1995*, Washington, D.C., 1995.

———. *Trends in Student Aid: 1984 to 1994*, Washington, D.C., 1994.

Florida Postsecondary Education Planning Commission, *How Floridians Pay for College*, Tallahassee, 1994.

Gold, Steven, *The Fiscal Crisis of the States: Lessons for the Future*, Washington, D.C., Georgetown University Press, 1995.

———. *Spending Patterns in the 1990s*, Albany, Center for the Study of the States, SUNY, 1995.

———. "State Support of Higher Education: A National Perspective," in *Planning for Higher Education* 18, no. 3, pp. 1989–90.

Halstead, Kent, "Quantitative Analysis of the Environment, Performance, and Operation Actions of Eight State Public Higher Education Systems," unpublished paper, San Jose, The California Higher Education Policy Center, 1996.

———. *State Profiles: Financing Public Higher Education, 1978 to 1996 Trend Data*, Washington, D.C., Research Associates of Washington, 1996.

———. *State Profiles: Financing Public Higher Education, 1978 to 1995*, Washington, D.C., Research Associates of Washington, 1995.

Hauptman, Arthur, and Anthony Carnevale, "The Economic, Financial, and Demographic Context of American Higher Education," unpublished paper prepared for the Seminar on Change and the Public Comprehensive University, Aspen Institute Program on Education in a Changing Society, 1996.

Hines, Edward R., *State Higher Education Appropriations 1995–96*, Denver, State Higher Education Executive Officers, 1996.

Johnstone, Bruce, "Learning Productivity: A New Imperative for American Higher Education," in *Higher Education in Crisis: New York in National Perspective*, edited by William Barba, New York, Garland, 1995, pp. 31–60.

Kerr, Clark, *The Great Transformation in Higher Education, 1960–1990*, Albany, SUNY Press, 1991.

King, Jacqueline, "Student Aid: Who Benefits Now?" in *Educational Record*, winter 1996, pp. 21–29.

Lapovsky, Lucie, "Tuition Discounting Continues to Climb: NACUBO Study Analyzes Six Years of Data," in *Portfolio*, NACUBO Business Officers, February 1996, pp. 20–25.

Levine, Arthur, editor, *Higher Learning in America, 1980 to 2000*, Baltimore, Johns Hopkins UP, 1993.

Massy, William, and Robert Zemsky, "Cost Containment: Committing to a New Economic Reality," in *Change* 22, no. 6, November/December 1990, pp. 16–22.

Minnesota Private College Research Foundation, *Ways and Means: How Minnesota Families Pay for College*, St. Paul, 1992.

Mortenson Research Letter on Public Policy Analysis of Opportunity for Postsecondary Education, *Postsecondary Education Opportunity*, no. 37, July 1995, Iowa City, Iowa.

National Association of State Student Grant and Aid Programs, *NASSGAP 26th Annual Survey Report, 1994–95 Academic Year*, Albany, New York State Higher Education Services Corporation, 1996.

Schapiro, Morton Owen, Michael McPherson, and Gordon Winston, *Paying the Piper: Productivity, Incentives, and Financing in U.S. Higher Education*, Ann Arbor, UM Press, 1993.

U.S. Department of Education, National Center for Education Statistics, Office of Educational Research and Improvement, *Digest of Education Statistics, 1996*, Washington, D.C., 1996.

U.S. General Accounting Office, *Tuition Increasing Faster Than Household Income and Public Colleges' Costs*, Report B-271081, Washington, D.C., 1996.

U.S. Office of the President, *Economic Report of the President*, Washington, D.C. 1996.

Washington State Higher Education Coordinating Board, *Tuition and Fee Rates, 1995–96: A National Comparison*, Olympia, 1996.

———. *Tuition and Fee Rates, 1994–95: A National Comparison*, Olympia, 1995.

Western Interstate Commission for Higher Education (WICHE), Teachers Insurance and Annuity Association, The College Board, *High School Graduates, Projections by State 1992–2009*, Denver, WICHE, 1993.

CHAPTER 3

Shaping the Future

Robert Zemsky and Gregory R. Wegner

They are images of rent landscapes and changed futures: a punctured San Francisco Bay Bridge; California State University at Northridge amid collapsed buildings and fractured walkways; and perhaps the most dramatic of these images, the Meishin Expressway in Kobe, Japan, with its sculptured pylons still intact, toppled as if by a wayward child.

Increasingly, these are also the metaphors being invoked to describe the forced, often abrupt changes now facing American higher education. What is becoming clear is that many—some would say most, a few would claim all—of the basic presumptions that underlie both the operation and financing of the enterprise are in flux. Hence a recent issue of *Policy Perspectives* was about living in an earthquake zone—about learning to build the kind of flexible institutions, public policies, and approaches to funding that will allow higher education to flourish in the face of uncertainty.[1] Metaphorically, it was about new building codes designed to preserve and enhance the academy's long-standing commitment to access and quality.

This chapter derives from the National Roundtable on the Public and Private Finance of Higher Education, jointly convened by the California Higher Education Policy Center and the Pew Higher Education Roundtable, with support from The Ford Foundation and The James Irvine Foundation (see appendix for a list of national roundtable participants). Our conversations at the roundtable meetings were intense, more than a little frightening, and in the end, remarkably optimistic. We came to understand that higher education was only at risk if it became brittle, made rigid by its own fixed costs and practices. Our discussions were informed by earlier versions of the chapters that now comprise this book.

Perhaps it was only coincidence, but California provided historical as well as geological context for our discussions. Like many other discussions of the public financing of higher education, ours began by taking account of two California-based initiatives. The first was the California Master Plan for Higher Education, that remarkably coherent vision of higher education enacted in 1960 to provide for both access and quality. As originally conceived, there were to be three distinct layers of public institutions—community colleges, state colleges, and university campuses—each stratum with a unique mission, each serving a different academic segment of the college-going population. An integral part of the Master Plan was its generous scholarship program to assist residents choosing to enroll in a private institution within the state. To ensure full access, the cost to the student was kept purposefully low.

The second California legacy was the work of the Carnegie Commission on Higher Education during the late 1960s and early 1970s, under the leadership of Clark Kerr, former president of the University of California. It was the Carnegie Commission that provided the classic formulation of the question that came to shape public policy toward higher education: "Who pays? Who benefits? Who should pay?"[2] The commission's own answer, echoing the success of the California Master Plan, was that higher education benefits not just the individual but society as a whole; the return on the societal investment is not just an educated citizenry but a more vital and productive national work force.

AN ALTERED LANDSCAPE

Today the ground has shifted from under this consensus, giving rise to a heightened sense of risk and an inordinate number of metaphors of cataclysmic change—of sea changes and tidal waves and shifting tectonic plates. The forces that underlie these changes—and their impact on the nation's colleges and universities as well as on individuals seeking to attain a higher education—are the concerns of this book.

Conflicting Demands on Public Revenue

Over the last decade, governments at every level have come to contribute less to the cost of providing postsecondary education to their citizens. Between 1980 and 1993, for example, federal support for public higher education diminished by 2 percent, while state funds over the same period diminished by a whopping 8.8 percent. Private institutions actually gained slightly in terms of nominal state dollars, but saw their federal support decline by nearly 4 percent.[3]

Behind the more dramatic declines were fundamental shifts in state budgetary priorities—the product of a political push to balance the federal budget and the resulting devolution of federal programs to state and local govern-

ments. Many states now find themselves facing structural deficits—the recur-
rent financial shortfall brought about by Washington's mandate for medical
services spending, compounded with local decisions to increase spending for
K–12 education, prisons, and aid to the elderly. All of these pressures for
funding are heightened by a political commitment to reduce taxes, which is
accompanied in some settings by voter-imposed limitations on state revenues
and expenditures. Beginning in 1990, Medicaid displaced higher education as
the second largest state spending category (eclipsed only by elementary and
secondary education); Medicaid's share of state appropriations rose from 10.2
percent in 1987 to 19.2 percent in 1995.[4] During the same period, higher
education's share of total state appropriations dropped from 12.3 percent to
10.3 percent. It was during this period that public institutions imposed rapid
tuition increases to compensate for the decline in state appropriations.

The decline in state appropriations to higher education as a proportion of
the total state budget has had a dramatic impact on the distribution of student
aid within both private and public institutions. Given their price disparity with
public institutions, private colleges and universities have found themselves
subsidizing their students by offering tuition discounts in the form of financial
aid. These discounts are financed to some degree by the "recycling" of tuition
revenues, a practice that redistributes the tuition burden by supporting students of fewer means with the dollars of those who pay the full price. More
recently, public institutions have come to adopt similar practices; yet at the
same time, some of the programs of financial assistance that states created to
help students afford private institutions are being used predominantly by
students attending public colleges or universities. This structural shift in the
distribution of publicly appropriated student financial aid has hastened private
institutions along an already expensive path of maintaining student enrollments by offering ever deeper discounts funded by all other revenues. In these
institutions, it is not at all uncommon to have one-third of gross tuition
revenues recycled into financial aid, a practice that ultimately reduces an
institution's capacity to sustain, let alone renew itself.

Rising Market Forces

As the force of public funding and initiative has diminished, the market has
come increasingly to take its place as the dominant shaper of postsecondary
education in the United States. A whole new genre of for-profit educational
providers has emerged in competition with traditional colleges and universities. Unfettered by the traditions of the academy, these specialized providers
have understood the growing demand for higher education to address interests
and needs that evolve throughout life; and they are proving that they can
provide educational programs to satisfy a consumer movement increasingly

concerned with attaining the credentials that programs of postsecondary education are expected to provide.

Just beyond the horizon is a second wave of entrepreneurs ready to combine the educational and entertainment potential of electronic technologies, creating products and services to attract both young and older learners who are accustomed to "shopping" for the services they seek. What is at risk is the near-monopoly that traditional institutions of higher education have enjoyed in the provision of postsecondary education and its credentials. Emerging instead is a commodity market in which an increasing proportion of students are buying their educations "one course at a time" from a variety of vendors, which these students consider principally as "outlets" for educational services. As this commodity market takes shape and expands, traditional colleges and universities will have to demonstrate anew that they are best qualified to define the substance, standards, and processes of higher education. Failing that demonstration, traditionally cast colleges and universities will lose much of their power to define the public good in their own terms, and hence their virtual monopoly over the credentialing function that higher education now fulfills.

In response to these emerging market forces, nearly every institution finds itself rethinking its priorities and the means by which it delivers educational services. A few of the most prestigious and selective private institutions will not feel substantial pressure to change, and some highly regarded public institutions may seek to "privatize" in order to preserve what is most important to themselves. Some of the nation's most successful public research universities, feeling a disconnection between their internal values and the priorities of their state patrons, now ponder their futures as independent or quasi-independent institutions that rely primarily on their own competitive ability and the generosity of their alumni. By far the majority of colleges and universities, however, will be forced to adapt to an environment of heightened competition from different types of higher education providers. Some institutions that prove incapable of meeting the challenge of new competition may fail; others will adapt successfully, becoming in the process more entrepreneurial and market-driven, despite the pressure of tradition exerted by accreditation agencies.

A Diminished Sense of the Public Good

In combination, these forces have undermined a consensus that for 40 years has guided public policy: that those who benefit and those who pay for higher education are part of the same collective "we" of public purposes. Whether this change is deliberate or simply an accommodation to constrained resources, the new messages are: The primary return on the investment in education is individual, rather than collective; the public good is synonymous with the choices and well-being of those individuals; and those who benefit directly should assume the greatest share of the cost. Some still search for a spirit of collective commitment to the public well-being that looks beyond "getting one's own" to a concern for the ability of all members of a population to find opportunity through education. Others reply that in an age of federal devolution, multiple claims on public funds, and universal tax resistance, cost considerations and market forces necessarily shape the opportunity agenda.

FAULT LINES

Added to these largely external forces has been a set of institutional attitudes and practices that have placed higher education even further back in the queue for public funding. While colleges and universities still claim societal purpose, legislative critics in particular sense that, if left to its own devices, the academy would address change largely by remaining the same. The sluggishness with which colleges and universities recast curricula or pedagogy, their inability to take significant advantage of the new technologies to improve their students' capacities to learn, the veil of tenure that protects faculty from the kind of accountability that is common in other professions—all become part of an argument that sees a "disconnection" between higher education and the world without, a perception that higher education as an enterprise is neither willing nor able to become efficient and responsive. Even higher education's staunchest supporters and benefactors have taken to wondering why colleges and universities are so reluctant to define and hold themselves accountable for student learning outcomes. For colleges and universities, seat time remains the common proxy for learning; students are presumed to be educated in proportion to the number and sequence of courses they pass en route to graduation. Would not, these friends ask, a more direct and useful accounting result from focusing on learning outcomes and assessing the progress students make in fulfilling those goals? Can measures of learning be devised that are readily understood and accepted both within the academy and in society generally? Those who pose these questions are particularly troubled by the academy's insistence that measurement is next to impossible, when other service professions, notably health care, have come to define publicly the outcomes they seek and to hold themselves accountable for their achievement.

Perhaps the cruelest blow to higher education is a new devaluing of research due to its overshadowing of undergraduate education. Higher education's critics have taken to asking, "Why do faculty want to teach only the best students? Why is student success so often defined as becoming 'faculty-like'? Aren't faculty paid to teach undergraduates—all undergraduates? Isn't undergraduate education the basis for most appropriations to public institutions? Why should the public pay for the faculty's preoccupation with research and publication of specialized studies? Why are there so many more newly minted Ph.D.s than there are jobs that demand their specialized training? Why should the urge of individual faculty to discover and apply knowledge transform so many four-year institutions into self-declared 'research universities' at public expense, regardless of their original mission?"

Questions of this sort are proving more than enough to blur the distinction between frivolous and important discovery, in some quarters making the term "research" synonymous with self-indulgence. What is at risk is a national consensus, three decades in the making, that once saw universities and their faculty as fundamental investments in the scientific, technological, and scholarly preeminence of the United States. If this consensus gave rise to some of the most important human advances in history, it also helped create a value system within institutions that rewards research and publication over all other forms of scholarly achievement. Viewed from without, the pervasiveness of the research ethos and its cost to taxpayers are coming to be seen as a prerogative—almost an entitlement—that faculty claim for themselves, regardless of the particular mission of the appointing institution or the importance of the research undertaken. For their part, faculty are perplexed, even offended by what they see as the mean-spirited nature of this scrutiny. "What has changed?" they ask. "Haven't we always been paid to be scholars, to be both researchers and teachers?"

The answer lies in the changing scale and homogeneity of higher education. Put simply, there are now a lot more institutions that claim a research mission, that call themselves either universities or research colleges, and that make research success a criterion for tenure. What was once the province of the few has become the domain of the many, leaving state legislators and trustees to ask: "When did we agree to pay for all this extra research? Why are state dollars expended on faculty who avoid our undergraduates?" Finding it politically difficult to distinguish between necessary and unnecessary investigation, state legislators in particular have taken to asking why any of the funds they appropriate should go to research.

The immediate result is a further eroding of the willingness to regard universities and colleges as repositories of ideas. The ultimate result, many now fear, will be a fundamental reorganization of how the nation funds research. While a dozen or so of the nation's most prestigious and best-endowed universities would continue to attract external funding for research, the majority of four-year institutions would see such funding dramatically curtailed. The concept of faculty as teacher-scholars whose teaching is informed and renewed by their own intellectual exploration would be replaced by a conception that regards most faculty as simply teachers. Few indeed would be the number of universities or, more likely, independent research institutes with sufficient resources to conduct major research projects. In the competition for a much smaller "research pie," the humanities and social sciences would find themselves largely displaced by the natural sciences, and basic research would take a back seat to that which is applied and technological.

SUSTAINING VALUES

It is this combination of public perceptions, altered state-funding priorities, and market forces that now compels colleges and universities to be more efficient and more entrepreneurial in their search for new revenues. Because the causes of reduced public funding are multiple, most people close to higher education understand that they cannot hope for a cyclical upturn that restores funding to previous levels and that obviates the need for greater accountability to both markets and public agencies. Only those with a naive idealism could hope for a full-scale return to the era of broad public finance of higher education that the Master Plan and the Carnegie Commission helped to create.

Every age embodies its own fears about change in the language and images it creates. It is a penchant of the current age to define itself through a series of "post-" constructions: post-modern, post-literate, post-rational. The frame of mind that gives rise to these constructions can make it seem that all potential for initiative is past, and the future determined wholly by forces that exceed the power of individuals or organizations to shape it. We believe the future can be shaped; the changes in funding patterns for colleges and universities do not constitute an inevitable decline of higher education. The challenge to the nation's colleges and universities, and to those who share responsibility for their continued vitality, is to posit a future that engages the commitment of all stakeholders—legislators, business leaders, institutions and their faculty, parents, students, and the general public—to sustain a system of higher education that is characterized both by quality and broad accessibility.

In the end, it will prove a question not just of vision but of values—those principles that ought to define the requirements for an educated citizenry and the purposes of a knowledgeable society. Here we see a sharp distinction between means and ends, between the current funding patterns of higher education and its public purposes. To confuse the two would be to conclude either that because higher education receives less funding today it has become less important, or that its value consists mainly in the conferring of status and distinction on those willing and able to meet the price of entry. In fact, higher education has never been more important to society—as an enabler of individuals, an engine of economic transformation, and a source of community cohesion and national awareness. The principles that have shaped the American academy and made it important to society at large ought to remain unchanged: that education is a means to personal improvement and social mobility; that inclusive rather than exclusive systems of education offer the greatest return on societal investment; and that choice—of institution as well as course of study—is itself an important guarantor of educational quality and instructional innovation. What has and will continue to change is how higher education achieves these ends. Higher education's changing circumstances must inevitably result in changed practices, in different means for realizing enduring ends.

Altered Questions

Necessarily, then, the basic questions concerning the financing of higher education—"Who pays? Who benefits? Who should pay?"—will need to be re-asked, in some cases as a means of distinguishing between the different missions that higher education fulfills: "What should be subsidized? From what sources? For what purpose?" Indeed, what is now required most is a renewed discussion of the role that public agencies and public funds need to play in ensuring a broad-based, necessarily mixed system of higher education. The questions that need to be asked in state capitals, in state higher education commissions, within the federal government, and within colleges and universities are as diverse as the constituencies that have a stake in the public's investment in higher education. From our roundtable discussion we have distilled a set of initial queries that can help promote the larger discussions we seek. The answers are likely to differ according to location, demographics, and economic circumstance. The important thing is that the questions be asked and suitable answers found among all those who control the levers of access, quality, and performance accountability in higher education.

The Roles of State and Federal Government

In what ways should the relationship of government to higher education change in response to changing public needs? Does any attempt to establish a model vision or policy amount to a waste of time in light of the considerable differences among states as well as among institutions? What should be the relationship between federal and state funding of higher education? To what extent should states be directly involved in the operation of institutions? Would the public interest be better served if a state's role were to focus primarily on evaluating, assessing, and certifying the education provided by its colleges and universities?

Access to Opportunity

The concept of access to higher education was first proposed and aggressively pursued in the 1950s and 1960s, when the college-going population was still overwhelmingly white and largely middle class. In what ways have the circumstances that brought higher education within reach of most young Americans changed in the current age? Is there a more cost-effective way to provide access and quality in an era of greater competition for public funds? In order to provide continued opportunity, what combination of providers and what funding mechanisms would optimize public and private investments in higher education?

Tuition and Student Aid Policy

What objectives—within state legislatures as well as individual institutions—should guide the setting of tuition? What mixture of tuition and financial aid will ensure the most equitable system of access to higher education? Should publicly provided student financial aid be more conditional on a recipient's demonstrated capacity to learn or on that student's ability to apply the lessons of the classroom in the world outside the academy? Where do the benefits of higher education lie on a sliding scale between purely public and purely private? If general education yields more of a public benefit and professional training more of a private benefit, should tuition levels reflect such distributions of societal and individual return on investment?

Privatization and the Public Good

To what degree do public institutions of higher education require a guaranteed funding base to succeed? Once the state is no longer the principal patron of a public college or university, to what extent should that state set institutional policy or regulate institutional practice? Would public research universities, in particular, have more robust futures as independent or quasi-independent entities? Should the public divorce its interest and support from institutions that do not have a broader public interest? Under what circumstances might the public be well served if institutions built with tax dollars were free to charge the market price for the education and services they deliver? What would the transition to quasi-independence entail, economically and politically?

Technology and Market Forces

In what ways will technology impact the nature of teaching and learning in the future? How can public policy or public investment work most effectively in conjunction with market forces to ensure that the technological transformation of higher education produces real enhancements to learning? Under what circumstances are public agencies likely to be more equitable than the market in distributing access to or funds for technology?

Better Performance Outcomes

How can the public in general and public agencies in particular ensure that they are getting fair value for public investments in higher education? In what specific ways must higher education do a better job of preparing graduates for the future? To what extent must such judgments await the development of effective measures for gauging the performance of colleges and universities? Whose responsibility is it to develop such measures? To what extent can public policy either encourage or mandate institutions to use the feedback gained from assessing student learning to improve their own performance as designers of learning experiences?

Linking Funding to Performance

To what degree should the funding of higher education be tied to the performance of either institutions or students? In what set of operations can the linking of dollars to outcomes provide a way to help colleges and universities overcome their seeming inability to realize productivity gains? What safeguards can ensure that a state government actually rewards institutions for successfully attaining performance objectives? What steps can guard against having short-term political agendas overshadow long-range objectives for improving quality?

Access and Institutional Capacity to Change

The one innovation that most clearly broadened access to higher education in the 1960s was the community college. While these largely new institutions put a higher education within reach of almost every American, they did so for the most part without requiring four-year institutions to change. How can public policy enlist the energies of all types of institutions in meeting the twin challenges of access and innovation in the current age?

The Quality and Quantity of Publicly Funded Research

What obligation do states have to fund research in public institutions? To what extent should the federal government be a major investor in the research infrastructure of principal American universities? To what extent should the public role be limited to purchasing the specific research that public representatives determine is in the interest of the nation or a particular state? Do public agencies have sufficient leverage or mandate to strike a better balance between the demand for graduate education and its supply?

PRINCIPLES FIRST

The answers to these questions are neither simple nor preordained. What the nation has lost is the consensus that once made the answering of such questions a largely derivative exercise. In the past, the answers involved not so much the "what" as the "how": How could public policy and public funds best achieve previously agreed-upon outcomes? Now, however, basic questions of ends as well as means need to be asked anew. To begin that conversation, we offer five recommendations, starting points really, that we believe provide a framework for public initiative as well as public responsibility.

1. *The nation cannot afford to have a higher education system stratified by socio-economic status and class.* A public disposition that allows demographic attributes to supplant individual promise in determining educational opportunity will lead to a society divided increasingly into haves and have-nots. Here the proof will be in the pudding. If public policy, by allowing tuitions to rise without a concomitant increase in funds for financial aid, yields a set of colleges and universities that are homogeneous by either race or economic class, then that policy is fundamentally flawed. It is simply unacceptable to suppose that lower income students should confine themselves to lower priced institutions, while those of greater means enjoy the privilege of attending more costly institutions that too easily claim the mantle of quality.

2. *The nation's colleges and universities need to see themselves and to be perceived by others as integral to a broader system of postsecondary education.* For half a century or more, access to higher education has been synonymous with access to socio-economic mobility. It is that prospect that principally accounts for higher education's expansion since World War II. It is also a promise that is proving increasingly difficult to fulfill as more and more families have sought a college education in hopes of economic advancement. Not even in the United States are "all the women strong, all the men good looking, and all the children above average." Attending college no longer ensures an "above average" future, and a four-year degree may not be the most appropriate goal for every American seeking a postsecondary education. What higher education needs now is a set of effective partnerships with other providers of postsecondary education, including the military, vocational-technical schools, corporations, and proprietary institutions, each of which has learned lessons that could contribute to a collective rethinking and improvement of teaching and learning, and to a better alignment of individual aspirations with educational settings.

3.   *The nation will be best served by a mixed economy of public and private institutions.* It is in the public interest to have a strong sector of independent colleges and universities—to ensure access, provide choice, to spur innovation, and to respond to changing markets and expectations. The current trend, however, is in the opposite direction, placing many private institutions in a vicious cycle of tuition discounting that creates structural deficits and too often makes these institutions unable to invest in their own futures or offer their students what an increasingly competitive world demands. The result will likely be a diminished private sector and hence a shrinking horizon of choice for those who would attain a college education.

4.   *Higher education's research mission belongs primarily to the nation's research universities.* The desire of institutions to enhance their reputations through expanded research functions must not be allowed to undermine the quality of undergraduate teaching and learning—within an institution, within state systems, and within the nation at large. Faculty naturally seek the intellectual renewal that accompanies the pursuit of new discovery, but it is important that this pursuit not come to eclipse the primary emphasis on undergraduate education that exists at all but a few institutions in this country. How many research universities are needed—within the nation, or within individual states— and what those institutions ought to cost the public at large is an open question. We believe, however, that what the nation needs now is less of a good thing: fewer faculty and departments that define their futures primarily in terms of the quantity of the research they produce and the size of their graduate Ph.D. programs.

5.   *Outcomes in general, and learning outcomes in particular, provide the best gauge for matching the promises of colleges and universities with the revenues they receive.* Like every other American enterprise, colleges and universities are learning the value of efficiency in pursuit of well-defined outcomes. Whether the spur that makes that lesson both important and painful is market discipline or public mandate, the academy is also learning that defining outcomes publicly is not easy, and that the corresponding sense of accountability is often elusive. For colleges and universities, a first step to greater accountability is to identify a set of outcomes that has meaning both to themselves and to the constituencies they serve. What is required now is a clearer demonstration that success in this arena has tangible rewards—greater opportunities and more public support, including more financial support.

CONCLUSION

Once, it was possible for colleges and universities to look inward and define the challenges confronting them in their own terms; they could presume that the answers to problems in society could be found in the curriculum as they defined it. Much of the academy still wishes it enjoyed that sense of autonomy and deference once accorded institutions of learning. Indeed, the question most often asked within the academy is still, "How can society be made to recognize and support the value of what we do?" In contrast, the question now regularly asked by legislators, employers, parents, and students is, "How can higher education serve us better?"

How the tension suggested by these two questions is resolved will largely determine how the nation chooses to finance its system of higher education. It is not so much a matter of specific enrollment formulae or financial aid programs as it is a search for both common and secure ground. What our own conversation taught us is that there cannot be a prescribed answer—no eleventh commandment proclaiming that "this is the way it must be done." No one knows enough to anticipate how external changes will transform the academy or its reactions to the challenges it faces. The system of higher education that emerges in the first decades of the new century will be as different from today's as the system that evolved after World War II was different from that which prevailed at the beginning of this century. Higher education will either transform itself or be transformed as new markets, new technologies, and new competitors recast the business of the business— changing, in the process, how colleges and universities organize and deliver instruction as well as how they structure and manage their enterprises. What will work least of all are policies that micro-manage the enterprise, yielding institutions that are more brittle and hence subject to convulsive change. Higher education needs public policies that facilitate this transformation, not regulations that make colleges' and universities' current modes of operation even more fixed.

Some will argue that only the discipline of the market can make colleges and universities more efficient and effective—more capable of operating with reduced revenues, more likely to respond to the needs of their stakeholders. We believe that something more than the market is required. Because there is public purpose to higher education, there is public obligation as well. The market will come to play an increasingly important, perhaps even dominant, role in determining the nature and range of learning experiences that colleges and universities provide, and the kinds and quantity of research they supply. But markets can also be shaped, by creating more knowledgeable consumers, by regulating practices and customs, and by providing subsidies that guarantee equal access to the goods and services a public market supplies. To what extent the nation wants the market for higher education to be shaped by public initiative is the question public agencies in partnership with both public and private institutions need to answer—now!

NOTES

1. This essay first appeared under the title, "Rumbling," in *Policy Perspectives* 7, no. 1 (Philadelphia: Institute for Research on Higher Education). It also appeared in *CrossTalk* 4, no. 3 (San Jose: California Higher Education Policy Center, October 1996), pp. 1a–8a.
2. Carnegie Commission on Higher Education, *Who Pays? Who Benefits? Who Should Pay?* (New York: McGraw-Hill, 1973).
3. U.S. Department of Education, National Center for Education Statistics, *Digest of Education Statistics, 1995* (Washington, D.C.: 1995), pp. 330–332.
4. National Association of State Budget Officers, 1995 *State Expenditure Report* (Washington, D.C.: 1996), p. 2.

AFTERWORD TO PART I

A Perspective on Privatization

Robert Zemsky, Gregory R. Wegner, and Maria Iannozzi

T he vice president for development at an expanding, multicampus state system of higher education needed a keynote speaker for his first annual conference of more than 100 development professionals from across the system's nearly 20 campuses. To intrigue his would-be guest, he needed to cajole and flatter, to stress the importance of obligation as well as the opportunity of addressing a rapt audience; but to have the session work, he also needed to impart a warning! Public higher education had changed; even publicly funded institutions were in the business of raising money, lots of money, and largely out of necessity. "Just five years ago," he wrote to his prospective speaker, "the state provided more than 75 percent of our funding. Today, the state supplies less than half, and by the end of the decade we expect the state to supply less than 35 percent of the funds we need. We are being privatized!"

"Privatization" has become a buzzword in higher education, carrying a multitude of meanings, covering multiple sins, and offering more than a few opportunities. Like other recent arrivals to the higher education lexicon, the term derives from the vernacular of another domain. For government agencies, privatization means assigning to a private contractor tasks that were once routinely undertaken by public employees: collecting garbage, running municipal hospitals, manning prisons, and in a few cases even taking over the management of public schools. More broadly, privatization is part and parcel of the devolution of authority from Washington to states and localities, the remaking or unmaking of public welfare, and—not so coincidentally—often the rationale given for using public funds to create school vouchers so that families can choose their children's schools from among an expanding set of both private and public providers. A primer on privatization would include a range of definitions to the following effect:

- the conscious decision on the part of government to transfer to private management and responsibility certain functions that had formerly been organized and carried out by public agencies;
- the phenomenon that results from a government's inability to fund its agencies at previous levels, often implicitly transferring a greater degree of authority and initiative to individual agencies or institutions, while continuing to vest nominal control in government;
- the initiatives taken by public agencies and by institutions to reduce costs by outsourcing functions and/or to increase revenues by raising the prices they charge for the services they deliver; and
- the actions that proceed from a public perception that government itself has become cumbersome and inefficient, that taxation is excessive and tax dollars are not well spent, and that government should exert a smaller influence in public and private life.

In politics, privatization has become a term of art, a way of talking about the rise of markets and the demise of public policies and initiatives. "Being privatized" may, at first, sound like something that is done to an institution—a deprivation of sustenance, a casting off from assured support to the tempest of market forces. In fact, institutions are the subject of the verb as much as they are the object. For postsecondary education in particular, privatization has as much to do with the desire of colleges and universities to secure and control their own destinies as it does with the reduced ability of government to fund all objectives in fulfillment of the public good in the same degree as before.

Privatization in postsecondary education is an old concept poured into a new mold, one that causes different kinds of institutions to behave in increasingly similar ways. For more than a century, American postsecondary education has been characterized by its mixed economy of public and private colleges and universities, but recently these two types of institutions have come into direct, increasingly undifferentiated competition for the same students and research dollars. Public funds have become pervasive enough that institutions once private are now commonly described as belonging to higher education's "independent" sector. Student financial aid serves as one example of this overlap. If school vouchers remain a divisive issue for public primary and secondary education, in postsecondary education Pell Grants and federally guaranteed loans—both forms of federal education "vouchers"—are commonly accepted as equitable programs for funding access to a broad range of public and private colleges and universities.

Public institutions have been quick to learn the benefits of private institutions' funding strategies as well. Public colleges and universities today expect their private constituencies—alumni, parents, current students, and friends— to contribute as much as their state toward the building of campuses and educational programs. According to the *Chronicle of Higher Education Almanac*, of the 20 top endowments held by institutions of higher education, eight belonged to public flagship universities. In 1995, the five most successful public institutions collectively raised more than $750 million in private funds to support their expanding ambitions;[1] and, as the vice president for development reminded his would-be speaker, it is simply accepted that development professionals are essential for the survival of public institutions.

If privatization is not exactly an idea whose time has come, it is a phenomenon whose presence is pervasive. It is not so much a question of what "privatization" means as of how it will change the functioning of colleges and universities that once looked to state legislatures as their primary patrons. Why have public agencies felt compelled to privatize their institutions? How was privatization transformed from implicit and occasional practice to explicitly stated policy for postsecondary education? What is behind this departure from a preceding era of public support? Most importantly, what challenges face postsecondary education institutions in dealing effectively with a rapidly transforming set of rules?

For most of the 1980s, the increasing privatization of postsecondary education's public revenue sources had proceeded largely in the absence of political debate or analysis. The cuts in postsecondary education budgets had been presented as practical necessities. Shortfalls in state funding coupled with increased spending on mandated federal programs had meant that everyone would have to learn to live on less. Institutional leaders had been assured that "it was nothing personal"—postsecondary education was still important, though for the short run the state's colleges and universities would have to rely more on their own and less on public revenues.

As the reductions have continued—as postsecondary education's share of public revenues has dwindled—the new distribution has required an explanation; absent anything else, the resulting explanations have become the basis for public policy. The first of these explanations holds that postsecondary education's lowered place in the queue for public funds derives from a sense that the enterprise's costs are out of control and from a feeling that public institutions, like their private counterparts, have become wasteful as well as expensive in pursuit of their own, as opposed to the public's, agenda. What a number of postsecondary education's political critics have come to believe is that reduced public funding will not only make public universities more efficient (almost by definition), but more accountable as well.

While colleges and universities have continued to claim societal purpose, legislative critics in particular have come to argue that, if left to their own devices, those institutions would continue to use public monies to insulate themselves from the rigors of public accountability. Persuaded that their colleges and universities have become arrogant in their self-directness, more than a few legislators have been heard to say, in effect, "We'll bleed them dead until they change."

This questioning of postsecondary education's commitment to public purposes, accompanied as it has been by reduced public funding, now erodes postsecondary education's credibility as an agent of public improvement. It makes the market, rather than public policy, the dominant shaper of the nation's postsecondary institutions—a concept that has become the guiding principle behind the privatization of postsecondary education. According to this frame of mind, the academy would come to reflect the individual choices of its customers more than the collective decisions made by government—except for government's decision not to substitute its own judgments for those of the market. From this perspective, privatization becomes another example of the trend toward smaller, less active public agencies. In part, this reaction against public initiative reflects a new wariness of government itself, a sense that it has grown too big, too cumbersome, and too concerned with serving its own as opposed to public ends. The result is a call for smaller government: reduced taxes, dismantled programs, fewer promises, and less inclination either to design or engineer a collective future.

It is these forces that in state after state have made the privatization of public postsecondary education so attractive to some and seemingly inevitable to others. If, as some suggest, privatization is an idea whose time has come, it is largely because state agencies lack the resources, the will, and, frankly, the insight necessary to reorder their systems of postsecondary education—to satisfy the rising demand for postsecondary education in an era of budget constraints and growing uncertainty as to what kinds of education best prepare a productive citizenry. Public officials have learned to accept, and in some cases celebrate, the market as the most practical arbitrator for matching individual needs and institutional offerings. What has been weakened—and perhaps abandoned—is the public consensus that both the individual and society benefit from the public investment in postsecondary education. It was once possible to assume that the ways in which colleges and universities defined their own futures overlapped with public goals and concerns to a greater degree than is the case today. How the rift between the aspirations and goals of institutions is bridged to the concerns and needs of the public will largely determine how the nation chooses to shape its system of postsecondary education in the future.

NOTE

1. *Chronicle of Higher Education Almanac* 43, no. 1 (September 1996), p. 27.

PART TWO

• • • • • • • • •

Financing Higher Education
in Five States: 1990–1995

CHAPTER

California

Financing Higher Education Amid Policy Drift

Mario C. Martinez and Thad Nodine

*T*his chapter on higher education in California draws on documents obtained from public offices and higher education institutions, publications germane to public higher education finance, and interviews with California public officials and higher education administrators. Interviews were conducted in the state between December 1995 and February 1996. Although this chapter focuses on fiscal years from 1990 to 1995, some data are included for fiscal years 1996 and 1997 as well.

In many ways, the financing of higher education in California during the first half of the 1990s provides the most dramatic narrative of any in this study. Beginning in fiscal year 1991, California fell into the longest and most severe economic downturn to hit the state since the Great Depression. The recession overwhelmed the state's public colleges and universities, which responded primarily by raising tuition sharply, reducing enrollments and services, and accelerating retirement of senior faculty. One consequence was reduced participation of high school students in the state's public colleges and universities.

Employment peaked in California in 1990, then fell sharply each year from 1991 to 1993. Falling state revenues and increasing spending pressures—combined with budget deficits carried over from previous years—created one fiscal crisis after another. Military base closings and natural disasters—including a drought, an earthquake, and several major fires—contributed to the budget shortfalls and to the "crisis" mentality. Moreover, whereas most other states were pulling out of the recession in 1993 and 1994, California's recovery was slower. State revenues only began increasing in 1995, and even by 1996, unemployment in the state was still higher than in 1990.

As the governor and legislators sought to bring spending in line with revenues during the first half of the 1990s, higher education did not fare well. State general fund appropriations to higher education in California dropped three years in a row, in 1992, 1993, and 1994. Only in 1997 did state appropriations to higher education reach 1991 levels (in current dollars). As a response to these cuts in state spending, the state's public colleges and universities raised tuition and fees sharply, thereby replacing much of their state revenues lost. The decline in state funding and increase in tuition and fees represent a significant shift in the burden—from the public to the individual—of paying for higher education in California.

As in most other states during this period, student borrowing increased dramatically. Institutional aid to students also increased, and by 1995, public universities were relying more on student fees to fund institutional aid. Of particular consequence to private colleges and universities, however, was the continuation of a trend in the use of Cal Grant awards, the state's major student aid program that was originally developed to enhance student choice in attending private institutions. By 1995, a significantly larger share of Cal Grant aid was going to students at public rather than private colleges and universities.

Student enrollment fell at all three public systems, while it increased at the private colleges and universities. From 1991–92 to 1994–95, enrollments at each of the three public systems dropped every year—while the number of qualified high school graduates was increasing steadily. Although enrollments finally rebounded during 1995–96, they remained below 1990–91 levels at all three public systems. Student enrollment in the private sector, on the other hand, increased about 3 percent from fall 1990 to fall 1995.

Beginning in fiscal year 1995, state general fund revenues began to rebound, and state appropriations to higher education began increasing significantly. In accepting increased state funding for fiscal years 1996 and 1997, colleges and universities entered into a "compact" with the state that guaranteed annual increases in state appropriations to higher education with a commitment to increase enrollments gradually and improve productivity.

State projections estimate a surge in demand for higher education in California of approximately 488,000 students during the next decade. The looming increases in enrollments will make it more difficult for California to provide the next generation of high school graduates with the opportunities for higher education that recent generations have enjoyed—and that Californians have come to expect.

STATE CONTEXT

California, with 31.5 million residents, is the most populous state in the country. The state's minority population stands at 31 percent, compared with an estimated national average of 20 percent. With a projected five million new non-whites by the end of the century, California's current "minority" populations are expected to comprise over 50 percent of the population within the next decade.[1] Compared to other states, California's residents are young. Although the state has a higher educational attainment level than the national average, it also has a large high school dropout rate and a high percentage of families living in poverty.[2] Per capita income in 1994 was $22,493, also above the national average, but this statistic shrouds a significant disparity—high-income families earn nearly 10 times more than low-income families make. Although median household income is one of the highest in the nation, California has the second highest rate of citizens on public assistance of any state.[3]

Beginning in fiscal year 1991, California's robust economy fell into the most severe recession the state has faced since the Great Depression. Employment peaked in 1990 at 14.5 million, then fell sharply each year from 1991 to 1993.[4] Unemployment, on the other hand, stood at 5.8 percent in 1990 and soared to 9.4 percent by 1993.[5] This downturn in the economy had dire consequences for state finances, which were already on shaky ground. As table 4.1 reveals, state revenues dropped in 1991, 1993, and 1994. In 1992, state revenues rose for two primary reasons: personal income and sales tax increases were implemented, and the state changed its accounting methods. Overall from 1990 to 1995, revenues failed to keep pace with inflation, as measured by the Consumer Price Index (CPI).[6]

TABLE 4.1

CALIFORNIA GENERAL FUND REVENUES (IN MILLIONS OF DOLLARS)

	1990	1991	1992	1993	1994	1995	% Change 1990–95
Revenues	38,750	38,214	42,027	40,947	40,095	42,710	10.2
% Change	7.8	(1.4)	10.0	(2.6)	(2.1)	6.5	
CPI*	5.4%	4.2%	3.0%	3.0%	2.6%	2.8%	16.6%

* The CPI figures are based on calendar rather than fiscal years.

Sources: California Department of Finance, interoffice communication, January 1997. The CPI figures are from the U.S. Department of Labor, Bureau of Labor Statistics, "Consumer Price Index for All Urban Consumers, U.S. City Average," October 1996.

Adding to the fiscal difficulties of the state in the early 1990s were the military base closings and other defense cutbacks in California, increases in the immigration of undocumented aliens in the state, and several natural disasters—including a drought, an earthquake, and several fires. During this period, California continued a long-term transformation from a high-tax, high-spending state, to more of an average-tax, average-spending state.[7] This transformation began with Proposition 13, a voter initiative passed in 1978 that established a ceiling on taxes on homes and other real estate properties. The immediate effect of Proposition 13 was that it reduced local property taxes by about $7 billion,[8] and the longer effect has been that it has not only limited revenue intake for local units of government, but has also increased budget pressures on the state.

Another voter initiative, Proposition 98 (along with an amendment passed in 1989), set aside a specified percentage of state general fund appropriations for public primary, elementary, secondary, and community college education (referred to as K–14) each year. With this new guarantee for K–14 education in place and with much of social service spending already composed of entitlements, legislators looking to balance the budget in lean years must look to higher education or corrections—the two largest "discretionary" spending categories in the budget.

Yet even corrections spending is losing its "discretionary" nature. In 1994, California voters passed an initiative that has since become known as the "Three Strikes" law. In effect, the statute mandates longer prison terms for repeat felons (and lifetime terms for those convicted of a third violent crime), thereby requiring higher appropriations levels to pay for the longer terms. Although this law was not passed until 1994, the growth rate in spending for corrections outpaced other categories of state spending even before "Three Strikes" was implemented. From 1985 to 1994, the annual growth rate in spending for corrections averaged 15 percent, far more than its nearest competitor, health care, and double that of higher education. By 1995, corrections' share of the budget had grown to equal that of the University of California (UC) and California State University (CSU) combined.[9]

Table 4.2, which provides data on state general fund appropriations, shows yearly trends in state spending priorities from fiscal year 1990 to 1995. In 1992, general fund appropriations reached $43.3 billion, a level that was not surpassed until 1996. During the entire period shown in table 4.2, state general fund appropriations increased 6.5 percent while inflation increased 16.6 percent (as measured by the national CPI). As table 4.2 also shows, state general fund appropriations to higher education were cut three years consecutively, in 1992, 1993, and 1994. From 1991 to 1994, state general fund appropriations to higher education were reduced by 20 percent. During the entire period shown in table 4.2, state general fund spending for higher education decreased by 8.5 percent, while spending for corrections increased by 47.9 percent.

TABLE 4.2

STATE GENERAL FUND APPROPRIATIONS (IN MILLIONS OF DOLLARS)

	1990	1991	1992	1993	1994	1995	% Change 1990–95
Legis./Jud./Exec.	1,403	1,346	1,617	1,355	1,268	1,338	(4.6)
Health & Welfare	12,478	13,377	13,680	13,084	13,282	13,957	11.9
Corrections	2,451	2,667	3,049	3,032	3,383	3,624	47.9
K–12 Education	14,682	14,265	16,416	16,266	14,481	15,533	5.8
Higher Education	5,576	5,833	5,831	4,920	4,681	5,102	(8.5)
Other	2,817	2,583	2,710	2,165	1,861	2,396	(14.9)
Total	39,406	43,177	43,303	40,824	38,956	41,951	6.5
U.S. CPI*	5.4%	4.2%	3.0%	3.0%	2.6%	2.8%	16.6%

* The CPI figures are based on calendar rather than fiscal years.

Sources: California Postsecondary Education Commission (CPEC), *Fiscal Profiles 1996* (Sacramento: 1996), display 1. The CPI figures are from the U.S. Department of Labor, Bureau of Labor Statistics, "Consumer Price Index for All Urban Consumers, U.S. City Average," October 1996.

Figure 4.1 shows the overall changes in general fund spending categories from fiscal year 1990 to 1995. Total appropriations for 1990, as shown in table 4.2, were just over $39 billion and increased slightly to almost $42 billion in 1995. Of the four major spending categories, only higher education saw a decrease in funding during this period.

While most other states were pulling out of the recession in 1993 and 1994, California's recovery was slower. State revenues only began increasing in 1995, when tax receipts ran about 3 percent above original estimates. Thanks to an employment explosion in the entertainment industry, in advanced-technology manufacturing, and in international trade, California's gross product ran at a healthy $900 billion in 1995. This ranks as the largest economy of the fifty states and seventh among the world's economies.[10] Nonetheless, the construction, aerospace, and defense industries remained sluggish. The housing market also remained shaky, with homes selling for 30 to 40 percent less than their value just five years earlier.[11] And even as late as 1996, the state unemployment rate was still higher than in 1990.

As state revenues picked up, appropriations increased as well. State spending for higher education reached $5.6 billion in 1996 and $6.0 billion in 1997, which represent 9.2 and 8.2 percent annual increases, respectively. The increase in 1997 brought state spending for public colleges and universities back to the level of support (in current dollars) they received in 1990–91.[12]

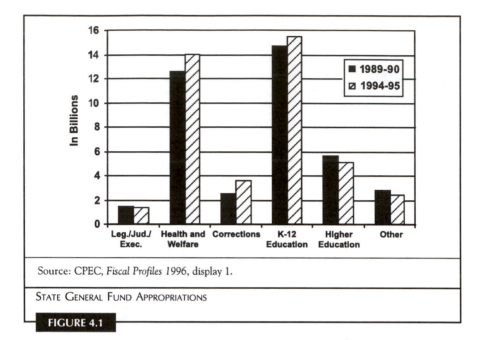

Source: CPEC, *Fiscal Profiles 1996*, display 1.

STATE GENERAL FUND APPROPRIATIONS

FIGURE 4.1

Kent Halstead has calculated several measures of public support of higher education that help in accounting for variables across states. Table 4.3 shows several of these measures for 1995–96, comparing California to national averages. State dollar amounts have been adjusted for inflation by the System Support Index (SSI). The SSI adjusts for two factors: the effect of cost-of-living on salary payment schedules, and differing enrollment mixes in different states due to the academic level of the state's students and the types of institutions in the state. The measures do not include dollars allocated to private higher education.

TABLE 4.3

STATE SUPPORT FOR PUBLIC HIGHER EDUCATION (IN DOLLARS)

	California		National Average	
	1990–91	1995–96	1990–91	1995–96
Tax Revenue Per Capita	2,212	2,685	2,011	2,535
Appropriation Per Public FTE*	4,713	4,798	4,364	4,801
% of Taxes Allocated to Public Higher Education	9.1	7.1	7.0	6.0

* FTE stands for "full-time-equivalent" student.

Source: Kent Halstead, *State Profiles: Financing Public Higher Education, 1978–1996 Trend Data* (Washington, D.C.: Research Associates of Washington, 1996), pp. 9–10.

As table 4.3 reveals, although California collects more taxes per capita than the average state, it was closer to the national average in 1995–96 than it was in 1990–91. Of more immediate consequence for California higher education, however, are the two other measures shown in table 4.3. California's appropriation per full-time-equivalent (FTE) student at public institutions has increased during the period shown, but is now below the national average. And the state's percentage of taxes allocated to public higher education has dropped faster than the national average. Likewise, figure 4.2 reveals that public higher education's share of the total California tax base (state and local) has slipped over the past decade, though it is still above the national average.

The trends represented in all of these measures reveal that California has slipped compared to the national averages shown. California's placement on each measure, however, is still relatively high for a state that has such an extensive community college system. States with large community college systems tend to rank poorly on these measures, since spending per community college student is much lower than spending per university student.

POLITICAL CONTEXT

California is classified as a "strong governor state," largely because of the governor's power over the state budget and the high number of appointments the governor makes.[13] In the budget process, the governor has line-item veto

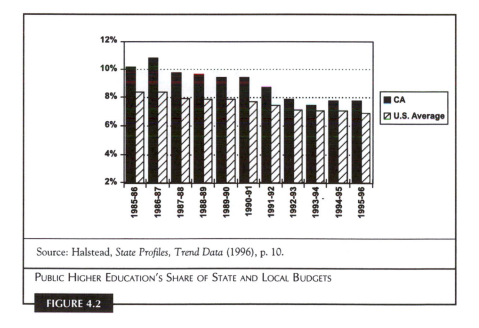

Source: Halstead, *State Profiles, Trend Data* (1996), p. 10.

PUBLIC HIGHER EDUCATION'S SHARE OF STATE AND LOCAL BUDGETS

FIGURE 4.2

authority, which Republican Pete Wilson has used regularly since becoming governor in 1991.

The state legislature is in session year-round. Members of the assembly serve two-year terms with a limit of three terms. Senators are limited to two terms of four years each. These term limits were imposed when Proposition 140 was instituted in 1990. After the 1994 elections, Republicans held a slim majority in the assembly for the first time in 25 years. In 1996, however, Democrats gained a 43-to-37 majority in the assembly and a 23-to-16 majority in the senate, with one independent. Also in 1996, 25 incumbent assembly members and 10 senators were "termed out," the first sweep as a result of Proposition 140.[14]

Many of those we spoke with in Sacramento agreed that terms limits, as one lawmaker said, "will shift power to lobbyists," since legislators will not have as long to build relationships and understand the intricate fiscal and other workings of state systems such as higher education. Many others, on the other hand, suggested to us that in the case of higher education, term limits will not have much effect. As one respondent told us, "the current system allows higher education administrators and the governor to bypass the legislature" anyway.

Gubernatorial Priorities

When Pete Wilson became governor early in 1991, California's economic problems consumed much of his attention. Although he has generally promoted tax cuts, his first budget depended upon significant fee and tax increases (both in income and sales taxes). This budget also cut expenditures from projected (though not previous) levels, shifted state funds, sought increased federal funding, and realigned responsibilities and revenues between state and local jurisdictions. During the rest of the recession, his subsequent budgets continued the latter three trends, while making deeper cuts in expenditures.[15]

The governor has promoted California as a "business friendly" state. He has also been a vocal advocate of the "Three Strikes" law, which he signed in 1994. During his 1994 reelection campaign, he strongly favored a proposition that declared undocumented immigrants ineligible for educational and social services. Voters approved that proposition. He has also been actively trying to recover funds from the federal government to help pay for state services spent on undocumented immigrants.

During his first years as governor, Wilson was not actively involved in issues relating to higher education. Many of those we spoke with said the governor showed a minimal interest in higher education, and gave the least attention to the community college system. As California pulled out of the recession, however, the governor began taking a more active role in negotiating with the state systems of higher education concerning issues such as enrollment levels and tuition freezes.

THE PROFILE OF HIGHER EDUCATION

California's historic priorities of higher education are outlined in the 1960 California Master Plan for Higher Education, which sought to make the benefits of college education available to every state resident motivated and capable of taking advantage of the opportunity.[16] This opportunity was offered through direct state support of three public systems of higher education: UC, CSU, and the California Community College system (CCC). Legislative actions supporting the Master Plan's commitments guaranteed tuition-free admission (meaning no charges for the cost of instruction) to (1) UC for students ranked in the top 12.5 percent of their high school class; (2) CSU for those ranked in the top one-third; or (3) any of the state's community colleges. Finally, the Master Plan called for—and the legislature provided—financial aid to support residents who choose to attend private institutions.[17]

Largely due to the priorities established through the Master Plan, California set a national standard for college opportunity for state residents. Particularly notable is the affordability and accessibility of the community college system. One community college administrator who came to California from another state said he had believed his former state was doing well in terms of access, but moving to California redefined what access meant to him. He was amazed at the furor that was caused when the CCC began charging $100 for tuition in the mid-1980s. He went on to say the CCC offers access like no other state he has seen. Although the UC system also has had a reputation for affordability compared to other flagship public institutions in other states, recent tuition increases have placed it above the national average.

Of the three public systems of higher education, the state's 106 community colleges serve the largest student population, including a significant number of minority and low-income students. The 22 CSU campuses—comprehensive institutions that focus on undergraduate and master's programs—serve the greatest number of baccalaureate-degree students. The nine UC campuses house the educational research function and award doctoral degrees. In total, the state has 318 institutions of higher education: 29 public four-year institutions; 106 public two-year colleges; and 183 private institutions.

The Role of Private Institutions

The independent sector in California serves about 13 percent of the state's higher education population, compared to a national average of about 22 percent.[18] Moreover, the influence of the privates in California has been described as "moderate."[19] Nonetheless, California is known for its high-quality independent institutions that range from universities like Stanford and the University of Southern California to small regional liberal arts colleges throughout the state. Several lawmakers we spoke with described the role of private colleges and universities as critical in providing greater choice for state residents and in enhancing the reputation of higher education in the state as a whole.

From fall 1990 to fall 1995, enrollments in public colleges and universities decreased while enrollments in private institutions increased about 3 percent (see table 4.4). Also, independent institutions in California award a high number of degrees relative to the percentage of the higher education population they serve. This is largely because of the high persistence rate of their students. Independents award about 66 percent of the professional degrees in the state, 12 percent of the doctoral degrees, almost 50 percent of the master's degrees, and about 25 percent of the baccalaureate degrees.

Enrollment Data

California's fall 1994 enrollment accounted for 12.9 percent of the higher education population of the nation, due mostly to the massive number of community college students the state serves.[20] Although California still enrolls more students than any other state, the state's public institutions have experienced significant enrollment decreases since 1990–91 (see table 4.4).

Rising tuition rates and decreasing state funds for higher education contributed to the decreases in enrollment in public institutions during the period shown in table 4.4. These declines in enrollment are particularly significant because the number of qualified high school graduates was increasing during

---

TABLE 4.4

ENROLLMENT IN CALIFORNIA HIGHER EDUCATION (IN THOUSANDS OF DOLLARS)

	1990–91	1991–92	1992–93	1993–94	1994–95	1995–96	% Change
UC*	155.9	156.4	154.3	152.3	152.1	153.0	(2)
CSU†	377.1	367.8	347.0	328.5	324.4	330.8	(12)
CCC†	1,505.4	1,515.3	1,500.4	1,376.6	1,357.6	1,344.0	(11)
Independents†	180.9	177.3	180.5	182.4	181.0	186.7	3

* Figures for UC are based on FTE students.

† Figures for CSU, CCC, and the independents are based on head count.

Sources: Data for the public institutions are from the department of finance, "Major Education Systems, Full Time Equivalents or Average Daily Attendance," spreadsheet, January 1997. Data for the independent institutions are from the Association of Independent California Colleges and Universities, "Enrollment by Level, Fall 1990 to 1996," facsimile dated 18 February 1997.

this period. Between 1990 and 1994, the number of high school graduates increased by 7.1 percent and the number of graduates who had completed a college preparatory curriculum increased even more—by 10 percent.[21]

Halstead offers two indicators that analyze a state's public higher education opportunities. The first, the participation ratio (the number of FTE public students divided by the number of new high school graduates), can be construed as measuring the size of the public system and the opportunity provided to high school students. A large participation ratio indicates that the state has a large public system relative to its source of resident high school students. Also, states that have a strong community college system tend to do well on this measure, as many high school graduates who do not want to attend a four-year institution (or do not yet qualify) have a readily available option of higher education. In 1995–96, California ranked fourth out of the 50 states in its participation ratio; but as figure 4.3 shows, California's participation ratio declined sharply from 1991–92 to 1994–95.

The second indicator, student enrollment, measures FTE public students per 1,000 residents. This measure can be interpreted a number of ways, from assessing opportunity available per capita to inferring the education level of the state's population. In 1995–96, California ranked eighth among the 50

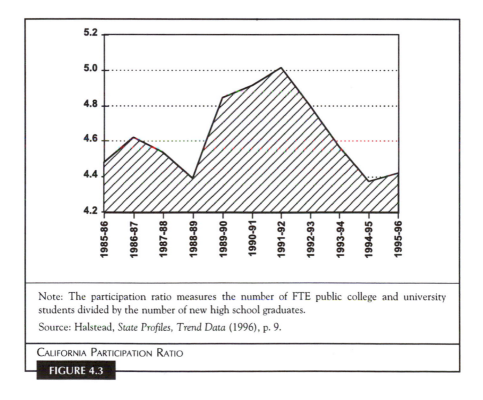

Note: The participation ratio measures the number of FTE public college and university students divided by the number of new high school graduates.

Source: Halstead, *State Profiles, Trend Data* (1996), p. 9.

CALIFORNIA PARTICIPATION RATIO

FIGURE 4.3

states on its student enrollment ratio. But figure 4.4 shows the steep decline in this measure since 1989–90.

Several projections have estimated that enrollment in California's colleges and universities will surge over the next ten years. This surge, called "Tidal Wave II" by Clark Kerr,[22] is expected to bring 488,000 additional students to California's colleges and universities during the next decade—assuming that the commitment of the 1960 Master Plan to provide educational opportunity to all qualified students remains intact.[23]

GOVERNANCE

The UC system's nine major campuses are governed by the board of regents. Eighteen of the 26 regents are appointed to 12-year terms by the governor. Seven others include the governor, lieutenant governor, president of the university, state superintendent of public instruction, speaker of the assembly, and the president and vice president of the UC Alumni Association. A student member serves a one-year term. While the university has constitutional autonomy, the regents in practice maintain constructive relationships with the governor and with legislators, largely due to their influence over the budget.[24] For instance, the university can set student fees without state

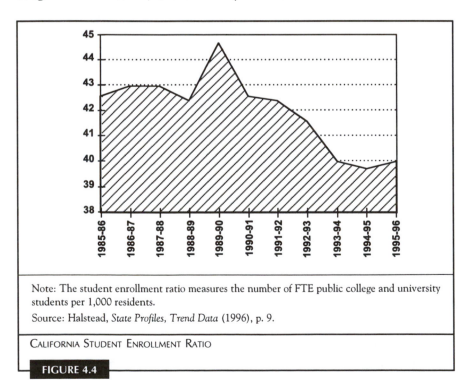

Note: The student enrollment ratio measures the number of FTE public college and university students per 1,000 residents.

Source: Halstead, *State Profiles, Trend Data* (1996), p. 9.

CALIFORNIA STUDENT ENROLLMENT RATIO

FIGURE 4.4

intervention, but in practice, fees are established with considerable sensitivity to the legislature and governor.

The 22-campus CSU is governed by the board of trustees, a 24-member body with 16 members appointed by the governor. Appointees serve eight-year terms. Trustees representing the alumni, faculty, and students serve two-year terms. Finally, there are five ex-officio members of the trustees, including the governor, lieutenant governor, speaker of the assembly, superintendent of public instruction, and the chancellor. The state *Education Code* stipulates that the trustees set student fees, but in actuality, the annual budget act or subsequent legislation usually specifies the student fee level for the year.

The CCC is coordinated through the statewide board of governors, which was created by the legislature in 1967. The 15-member board of governors has responsibility for selecting a system chancellor and providing leadership in developing the community colleges. Student fees at the community colleges are set by state law. Local colleges, however, maintain considerable autonomy.

The California Postsecondary Education Commission (CPEC) is an independent advisory agency to the legislature. The agency gathers statewide data, but has no formal coordination powers. As a result, the commission's influence has varied with its leadership and the political context within which that leadership has served. Several people told us that CPEC's effectiveness has been dependent upon the extent to which the governor and lawmakers have been willing to use the agency. One CPEC official added that the organization's influence has diminished over the years.

The Education Roundtable brings together the chief executive officers from the public systems, a representative from the independent sector, and the executive director of CPEC to discuss issues such as long-term financing and student eligibility. Barry Munitz, chancellor of CSU, now leads this voluntary forum. Several respondents told us that Munitz's leadership has strengthened the group. Several others also indicated that the roundtable represents an effort by the state systems to assure legislators that formal state coordination is not needed since leaders are coordinating voluntarily.

HIGHER EDUCATION SPENDING

The Budget Process

During the recession, California changed its methods for funding its three public systems of higher education. Until 1991, operational funding was largely based on enrollment levels. In 1991, however, just as the state entered the recession, the governor and legislature abandoned their enrollment-based funding formulas for UC and CSU. As state higher education spending dropped significantly from 1992 to 1994, the governor and legislature did not establish state higher education priorities but left each system largely to its own devices to adjust to the lower appropriation levels. The governor urged the governing boards to use fee increases to offset the decreases in state funding, and all three systems increased fees significantly. After funding was disconnected from enrollment levels, some CSU campuses decided, with legislative concurrence, to decrease enrollments.

The financing of the community colleges is complex because of the various propositions that affect the system. Proposition 13 distributes local property taxes through the state appropriations process, and Proposition 98 guarantees a minimum of general fund tax revenues and property taxes to K–14 education,[25] which includes the community colleges. This guaranteed minimum was at 37 percent during 1992–93, but is subject to change. The percentage of Proposition 98 funding provided to the community colleges has varied from a high of 11.8 percent in 1990 to a low of 9.9 percent in 1995.[26] In addition to directing the state controller in distributing general funds to the individual districts, the chancellor's office manages several categorical programs that usually account for 10 to 15 percent of the total appropriation.

In September all three systems submit yearly budget requests to the department of finance. The University of California and CSU requests provide some information by campus (such as enrollment), but otherwise the proposals are an aggregate of all system campuses. In November the chief executive officer of each system meets with the governor to discuss the budget proposals.

As state appropriations to higher education increased again for 1995–96 and 1996–97, UC and CSU have continued to receive lump-sum appropriations, but the governor has taken a more active role in negotiating state expectations concerning enrollment levels, appropriation increases for the future, and student fees. In his 1995–96 budget proposal, the governor made appropriations to the four-year systems based on a "compact" that covered many conditions: a guaranteed 4 percent annual general fund increase; an agreement that institutions could raise student fees by up to 10 percent; an agreement that institutions would increase enrollment by 1 percent; and several other conditions that included efficiency, articulation, salaries, and technology. After Democratic legislators who opposed the planned fee increases threatened to hold up the entire state budget, the governor acquiesced. As a result, rather than allow the institutions to raise fees, the state "bought out" the difference—appropriating to institutions the amount they would have received if they had increased fees. In their 1996–97 budget requests, the systems again requested to raise fees up to the 10 percent level, but the governor included in his budget sufficient funding to "buy out" the fee increases once again.

The community college budget request relies on a funding formula applied to each community college—based on enrollment and growth, but also accounting for other factors. The full cost of running the community college system is then calculated by the chancellor's office, approved by the state board, and submitted to the department of finance in August or September. The request also includes estimates of property taxes and student revenues. Like UC and CSU administrators, community college leaders meet with the governor in November to defend their request.

The governor's budget proposal is released in January. Discussions continue throughout the winter and spring, but not until May are key decisions made or revisions negotiated. These decisions are made primarily by two members from each chamber and a representative of the governor.

Legislators use three mechanisms to influence the public systems of higher education during the budget process, although each is limited in the case of UC, due to its constitutional status. The first is the use of control language in the budget, which can be stricken through a line-item veto. Governor Wilson has made it known that he will reject any such language that he considers inappropriate. The legislature also produces supplemental reports that accompany the budget and contain information concerning instruction, research, anticipated enrollment levels, etc. Although the reports do not have the force of law, they are useful in conveying legislative intent. Finally, lawmakers sometimes pass "trailer bills" that conform statutes to the budget act. Whereas control language can be deleted through a line-item veto, trailer bills must be vetoed in total.

State Funding Patterns for Higher Education

The last half of the eighties produced consistent state spending increases for higher education, but as the recession of the nineties hit California, state general fund appropriations to higher education were cut significantly. Figure 4.5 reveals how each of the three systems of public higher education fared in state appropriations during the last 12 years. University of California and CSU data represent state general fund spending only; data for the community colleges include state general fund spending and state appropriations from local property taxes.

State general fund spending for the UC and CSU systems remained flat from 1989–90 to 1991–92, then dropped in 1992–93 and 1993–94. In 1995–96, state funding for CSU finally returned to 1989–90 levels. State general fund appropriations to the UC system did not return to 1989–90 levels until 1996–97. Combined local and state funding for the community colleges remained flat during the early 1990s, dipped significantly in 1993–94, and increased steadily beginning in 1994–95.

The state lottery is also a source of funds for the three systems of public higher education. The community colleges receive the majority of this allocation, followed by CSU. The funds received from the lottery are small compared to general fund appropriations. In 1994–95, funds from the lottery were

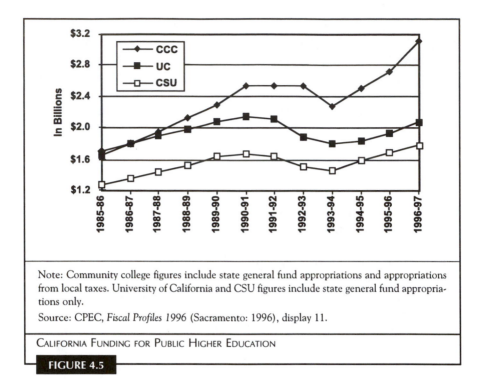

Note: Community college figures include state general fund appropriations and appropriations from local taxes. University of California and CSU figures include state general fund appropriations only.

Source: CPEC, *Fiscal Profiles 1996* (Sacramento: 1996), display 11.

CALIFORNIA FUNDING FOR PUBLIC HIGHER EDUCATION

FIGURE 4.5

estimated to be $92 million, $44 million, and $16 million for the community colleges, CSU, and UC, respectively. Over the last 10 years, the community colleges have received, on average, 66 percent of the lottery funds that are allocated to higher education, followed by 22 percent for CSU.[27] The community college system also receives some revenue from federal funds via the 1966 Federal Vocational Education Act.

Student Aid Funding

The 1960 Master Plan for Higher Education recommended processes that would enable students to choose among private as well as public institutions. In following up on this recommendation, the state instituted the Cal Grant financial aid program.[28]

Cal Grants, which are distributed by the Student Aid Commission, take three forms. Cal Grant A, the oldest and largest state financial aid program, provides aid to needy students on the basis of merit. Independent institutions and UC benefit primarily from Cal Grant A. Cal Grant B is for disadvantaged students. The majority of CSU and community college students who qualify for grants receive Cal Grant B. Cal Grant C is for vocational education and is the smallest of the three programs. The demand for Cal Grants far exceeds the supply, and only one in five eligible students receives a grant.

Approximately 90 percent of Cal Grant dollars went to students at independent colleges and universities at the commencement of the program. However, the distribution has shifted over the years. During 1990–91, students at private institutions received about 42 percent of Cal Grant funding, while students at public institutions accounted for over 51 percent. By 1993–94, 34 percent of the funding went to students at private colleges and universities, whereas 62 percent was awarded to students attending the public institutions.[29]

Funding for Cal Grants has increased significantly during the last few years. The maximum amount that Cal Grant A recipients could receive remained at $5,250 from 1990–91 to 1995–96, except for a dip to $4,452 in 1992–93. The 1996–97 budget increased the maximum Cal Grant amounts to $7,164, and the awards are estimated to increase again for 1997–98.[30]

Institutional aid has always been an important source of aid for students at private colleges and universities, and it is becoming an increasingly significant source of aid for public higher education as well. In 1990–91, institution-based aid for all postsecondary institutions exceeded state aid by approximately $350 million. By 1994–95, this form of aid exceeded state aid by $665 million (see figure 4.6).[31]

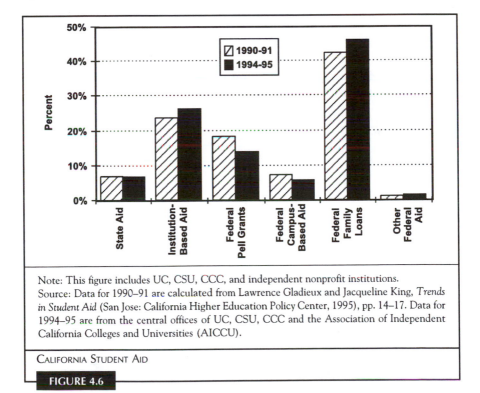

Note: This figure includes UC, CSU, CCC, and independent nonprofit institutions.
Source: Data for 1990–91 are calculated from Lawrence Gladieux and Jacqueline King, *Trends in Student Aid* (San Jose: California Higher Education Policy Center, 1995), pp. 14–17. Data for 1994–95 are from the central offices of UC, CSU, CCC and the Association of Independent California Colleges and Universities (AICCU).

CALIFORNIA STUDENT AID

FIGURE 4.6

The amount of institutional aid in public colleges and universities funded by student fees is known as "recycled dollars," since student fees are first collected and then used as financial aid for other students. In 1993–94, UC student fees funded 61 percent of the system's institutional aid compared to 41 percent in 1990–91. At CSU, student fees provided over 48 percent of this aid in 1993–94, compared to 43 percent a year earlier.[32]

From 1990–91 to 1994–95, total student aid increased from $2.2 billion to $3.4 billion. During this period, federal family loans increased 66 percent, from $0.95 to $1.58 billion.

TUITION AND EXPENDITURES

Tuition and Fees

Tuition and fee rates for public higher education in California are below and above the national average, depending on which sectors of higher education one is discussing. As one observer said, "Treating all systems together means that the community college defines the average. Even if one were just considering the four-year college fees, the average of UC and CSU indicates an amount that nobody pays." One trend, however, *has* been consistent regarding tuition and fees across *all* systems of higher education in California: As table 4.5 reveals, tuition and fees have increased sharply during the early 1990s. The increases in tuition and fees helped to replace the drop in state revenues at public colleges and universities, thereby shifting the burden of paying for higher education from the state to the individual. The tuition and fee increases also caused widespread public concern over access.[33]

TABLE 4.5

AVERAGE PUBLIC UNDERGRADUATE TUITION AND FEES (IN DOLLARS)

	National Average		California		% Increase for California
	1990–91	1995–96	1990–91	1995–96	
Universities	2,156	3,210	1,999	4,355	117.9
Colleges and State Univ.	1,735	2,534	929	1,900	104.5
Community Colleges	947	1,391	100	390	290.0

Note: The data in this table were compiled using surveys of state agencies or individual institutions or both and hence may vary slightly from tuition and fee rates reported by the UC and CSU systems.

Source: Washington State Higher Education Coordinating Board, *1994–1995 Tuition and Fee Rates: A National Comparison* (Olympia: 1995), pp. 4, 8, 12.

Although tuition and fees at the community colleges, which are set by the state, showed the most drastic increase (290 percent) from 1990–91 to 1995–96, these rates are still among the lowest in the country. Community colleges in California did not charge tuition until 1984, when the state set a rate of $100. This rate did not change until 1990–91.

Tuition rates at UC have accelerated well above the national average for public research universities, as shown in table 4.5. Although not represented in table 4.5, the average tuition levels for the private sector are also well above the national average for private institutions. *The Chronicle of Higher Education* reported California's private four-year tuition for 1993–94 to be $13,282, compared to a national average of $10,994.[34]

Kent Halstead calls resident tuition at public two-year colleges "access tuition," in part because large percentages of poor and underrepresented students have historically started their postsecondary education at such institutions. In 1993–94, California ranked first out of all reporting states with regard to the cost of access tuition. Measured in this way, the affordability of the state's community college system was the best in the nation. Halstead has calculated student financial aid in a way that measures state aid as a percentage of access tuition paid by all families in poverty with related youth under 18 years of age. Again, California ranks first, with aid paying for 109 percent of access tuition in the state compared to a 43 percent national average.[35]

The "family payment effort" is a more general measure that indicates the family burden of paying for a higher education. This measure indicates the percentage of median family income going toward tuition. The family payment effort in California has always been well below the national average because of the low fees charged by the community colleges. In 1995–96, California's family payment effort was 3.1 percent versus 6.9 percent for the national average.[36]

Since the family payment effort aggregates student tuition for all three public systems in California, it does not give a complete picture of each system. Table 4.6 displays the annual percentage change in tuition for UC, CSU, and CCC, and the annual percentage change in California personal income per capita from 1991–92 to 1995–96. (Community college tuition rose from $120 in 1991–92 to $390 in 1995–96. This increase, although small in dollar terms, produces a large percentage increase.)

The annual percentage changes in tuition were dramatic during the early nineties, while growth in personal income remained flat. Except for a negligible increase at UC, tuition did not increase in 1995–96 (and it remained frozen in 1996–97). The trends in table 4.6 reflect a paradox that one public official pointed out: "In good times the state buys out fees or pays for them when it isn't needed; and then in bad times tuition is raised when it is more difficult for students to pay."

| TABLE 4.6 |

CHANGE IN TUITION AND FEES, AND IN CALIFORNIA PERSONAL INCOME PER CAPITA (IN PERCENT)

	1991–92	1992–93	1993–94	1994–95	1995–96	Change 1991–92 to 1995–96
UC	36.6	22.4	22.4	10.3	0.7	66.5
CSU	17.4	34.8	10.4	7.9	0.0	60.6
CCC	20.0	75.0	85.7	0.0	0.0	225.0
Personal Income	0.5	2.9	0.9	2.7	4.7	11.7

Sources: Tuition changes calculated from CPEC, *Fiscal Profiles 1995*, pp. 28, 46. Personal income percentages calculated from CPEC, *A Capacity for Growth* (Sacramento: 1995), p. 106.

Table 4.7 illustrates the shifting revenue composition of the three higher education systems from state funding to a greater reliance on student fees. In each system, the student share of state and student revenues almost doubled from 1985–86 to 1995–96.

Expenditures

While revenues for higher education shifted significantly during the first half of the 1990s, expenditures did not. From 1990–91 to 1995–96, the share of expenditures spent on the segments' primary functions remained fairly constant.[37]

Although there is no direct relationship between state funding levels for each public system and the amount each system spends for instruction, there is a general understanding among public officials that the majority of state dollars to the public colleges and universities is provided to support instructional purposes. One observer said that as higher education administrators increasingly speak of weaning themselves from the public dole, it is important for them to consider not just revenue amounts and sources, but also the purpose of those revenues: "I suppose we could say the human heart is a very small proportion of the human body, but it provides a vital function. Likewise, if administrators think state appropriations are a small proportion of their total revenue sources, they must consider where these appropriations are expended."

INSTITUTIONAL RESPONSES TO UNCERTAINTIES IN FUNDING

Besides raising fees and decreasing enrollments, each system instituted wide-ranging, short-term efforts to cut costs. For instance, one university chancellor said that the fiscal challenges forced institutions to look for efficiencies. He

TABLE 4.7

STUDENT AND STATE REVENUES FOR UC, CSU, AND CCC (IN MILLIONS OF DOLLARS)

System	1985–86	1990–91	1995–96
University of California			
Student Revenues	313	490	850
State Gen. Fund Revenues	1,642	2,077	1,912
Student + State	1,955	2,567	2,762
Student Share	16.0%	19.1%	30.8%
California State University			
Student Revenues	235	375	598
State Gen. Fund Revenues	1,275	1,653	1,620
Student + State	1,511	2,028	2,217
Student Share	15.6%	18.5%	26.9%
Community College System			
Student Revenues	67	72	197
State Gen. Fund Revenues	1,293	1,897	1,350
Local Revenues	685	1,061	1,818
Student + State + Local	2,045	3,030	3,365
Student Share	3.3%	2.4%	5.9%

Source: Calculated from William Pickens, "Financing the California Master Plan: A Data Base of Public Finance for Higher Education in California, 1958 to 1996" (San Jose: The California Higher Education Policy Center, 1996 update), computer spreadsheet.

said that his institution collaborated with a local community college to use their buildings, and that these sorts of cost-cutting attempts were made throughout the state. He cautioned, however, that "once the money comes back, people tend to return to the old ways of doing business."

Community Colleges

An independent report on the community colleges questioned the system's ability to perform job-skills training and retraining during the heart of the recession. The report stated that the colleges have been "unable to meet their obligations for retraining the unemployed during the recession" because classes were cut and fees were increased.[38] Thousands also dropped out of the two-year system in the early nineties as the legislature increased—from $13 to $50 per unit—the charge to students who already held a bachelor's degree. The legislation that instituted this change had a sunset clause that eliminated the higher charge in December 1995.

Officials estimate the community college system reduced its curriculum offerings by 10 percent from 1991–92 to 1993–94. This occurred at the same time that approximately 2,800 part-time faculty were laid off. In addition, many full-time positions vacated by retirements remained unfilled. With reduced funding, increased fees, reduced courses, and reduced faculty, head-count enrollment dropped by over 170,000 students from 1991–92 to 1995–96.[39] Since the community college system represents a "loose confederacy," as one administrator put it, it is difficult to determine how many of these students would have enrolled in transfer or occupational courses versus courses that are of lower priority from a statewide perspective. The state chancellor's office did estimate, however, that more than half of the two-year enrollment drop was due to fee increases.[40]

California State University

Like the community colleges, CSU responded to the fiscal pressures of the early nineties through short-term solutions such as early retirements, reductions in class offerings and other services, increases in student-faculty ratios, salary freezes, and increases in student fees. While both the CSU and UC systems tried to protect academic programs and full-time faculty, CSU was less successful in protecting its programs, for state general funds accounted for almost 80 percent of its budget in 1993–94.[41]

Although student fees at CSU remain below the national average for state colleges and universities, the 100 percent rise in fees from fall 1990 to fall 1995—together with reductions in class offerings and other services—has had an impact on enrollment. California State University enrollment dropped four straight years (a loss of about 50,000 students) and finally recorded an annual increase in fall 1995.

University of California

The University of California probably weathered the recession better than the other systems because it is less reliant on state general funds. Unlike CSU, the UC system derives less than 30 percent of its budget from the state general fund. Like CSU and the community colleges, however, the UC system primarily sought short-term solutions to the fiscal crisis, such as encouraging early retirements of senior faculty and staff, reducing classes and other services, shifting to more part-time positions, foregoing maintenance, and raising fees. Former UC president David Gardner said that even in the midst of budget cuts, the priority was to protect the integrity of instructional programs, and many believe this goal was achieved.[42]

University of California officials estimate that about 5,000 full-time positions were eliminated or remained unfilled, including a few hundred temporary faculty positions. Over 6,600 faculty and nonacademic employees took advantage of early retirements, many of whom were hired back as consultants or lecturers. (The university was also able to fund these early retirements out of its own overfunded retirement system, partially mitigating the negative impact of this short-term response to state cuts.) Some upper-division and graduate classes were eventually discontinued as adequate faculty replacements were not found in time. While the UC system experienced declines in enrollment three years in a row, the decreases were modest compared to the other two public systems.[43]

University of California state general appropriations began to rebound in 1994–95, but vacillating state support has motivated many within the UC system to adopt strategies to bring in more private revenues. In 1994–95, UCLA raised $110 million in private gifts, the third largest year for private fund-raising in its history, as state contributions dropped to approximately 25 percent of the campus' $1.8 billion operating budget. The University of California at Berkeley raised a record $156 million in private gifts, a feat that continues to fuel belief in the value of diversifying revenue sources.[44]

STATE RESPONSES TO HIGHER EDUCATION

During economic upturns, the State of California has provided significant annual increases in funding to public colleges and universities. During the recession of the 1990s, however, higher education received the first and the deepest cuts in state general fund spending compared to other major funding categories. In 1991, just as the state entered the recession, elected officials broke the link between funding and enrollment levels, thereby diminishing their role in negotiating priorities for higher education. Only as the state's economic climate brightened did the governor and legislators begin to assert state priorities concerning student fees, enrollment levels, and ongoing state support.

One senator described the state's approach to higher education as "responding to fires" and "crisis management." He stressed that public higher education basically sets its own priorities and does not want legislative involvement. He also said that the state's long-term commitment to higher education was lacking, and this was part of the reason for the reactive behavior and fluctuating support.

Everyone we interviewed agreed that higher education is an important area that needs more attention in the capital, but, as one analyst said, "Hitching one's wagon to higher education will not make an aspiring politician a star." Although there is debate as to whether term limits help or hurt higher education, they certainly diminish the opportunity for lawmakers to understand the intricacies of the system.

Several administrators said the state's funding of and interest in higher education is dependent on the governor's commitment to higher education.

Administrators agreed that Governor Wilson favors other priorities and is particularly "disinterested" in the community colleges. A community college administrator said Jerry Brown was the last governor to make significant changes to the community college system. The administrator said, "Brown made us reevaluate what we were about; made us get rid of the so-called 'basket-weaving' courses. . . . He took an interest and he stimulated change."

CONCLUSION

As California fully emerges from the recession of the 1990s, the state's public institutions of higher education are at a crossroads. State funding has rebounded significantly, and the legislative and executive branches have agreed to tuition freezes and expect gradual increases in enrollments. Moreover, California's colleges and universities are still accessible and of top quality by national standards. But the trends established during the first half of the 1990s are not quickly forgotten: volatile state support to higher education, sharp increases in student fees, increased reliance on those fees by colleges and universities, significant reductions in services and enrollments when the number of qualified high school graduates was increasing steadily, and the accelerated retirement of senior faculty—to mention only a few. Many of these signposts suggest that as state fiscal pressures increased during the recession of the 1990s, California drifted away from the ideals of the Master Plan.

A projected surge of increasingly diverse students is expected to begin enrolling in California's colleges and universities over the next decade. Although state officials and higher education leaders are aware of the challenges that lie ahead, they have done little to find solutions that will enable the systems to adapt to these challenges. It remains to be seen if short-term reactions to annual funding levels give way to long-term strategic considerations in order for California's colleges and universities to preserve the attributes that have made them some of the top providers of postsecondary education in the country.

NOTES

1. Dan Walters, "State Saw Big Trend Changes," *Sacramento Bee* (7 January 1996), p. B1.
2. *Chronicle of Higher Education Almanac* 42, no. 1 (September 1995), pp. 6–9.
3. Gary W. Adams, "How California Can Maintain its Commitment to Higher Education," prepared for the California Senate, 23 August 1994, p. 2.
4. Jeffrey I. Chapman, "California: Enduring the Crisis," in *Fiscal Crisis of the States: Lessons for the Future*, edited by Steven Gold (Washington, D.C.: Georgetown University Press, 1995), p. 105.

5. U.S. Department of Labor, Bureau of Labor Statistics, "California Labor Force Statistics, Civilian Noninstitutional Population, Seasonally Adjusted," in *Faxstat* (1996).

6. Appropriations, revenue, and other budgetary data are presented in fiscal years, unless otherwise noted.

7. Chapman, "California: Enduring the Crisis," p. 105.

8. Ibid., p. 108.

9. *Three Strikes Law Could Undermine College Opportunity*, newsletter (San Jose: California Higher Education Policy Center, 1994), p. 3.

10. B. Drummond Ayres, Jr., "Recession Can't Keep a Golden State Down," in *New York Times* (18 December 1995), pp. A1+.

11. Ibid.

12. California Postsecondary Education Commission (CPEC), *Fiscal Profiles 1996* (Sacramento: 1996), display 11.

13. James Burns, J. W. Peltason, and Thomas Cronin, *State and Local Politics: Government by the People* (Upper Saddle River, NJ: Prentice Hall, 1990), p. 113.

14. MultiState Associates, Inc., "Multiple Perspective: Legislative Outlook, 1996" (Alexandria, VA: 1996), p. 6.

15. Chapman, "California," p. 114–118.

16. California Higher Education Policy Center, *Time for Decision: California's Legacy and the Future of Higher Education* (San Jose: 1994), p. 1.

17. Ibid.

18. *Chronicle of Higher Education Almanac* 43, no. 1 (September 1996), p. 9.

19. Task Force on State Policy and Independent Higher Education, *The Preservation of Excellence in American Higher Education: The Essential Roles of Private Colleges and Universities* (Denver: Education Commission of the States, 1990), p. 35.

20. *Chronicle of Higher Education Almanac* 43, no. 1 (September 1996), p. 9.

21. CPEC, *The Performance of California Higher Education, 1995* (Sacramento: 1995), pp. 38–45.

22. Clark Kerr, *Preserving the Master Plan: What Is to be Done in a New Epoch of More Limited Growth of Resources?* (San Jose: The California Higher Education Policy Center, 1994), p. 2.

23. David W. Breneman, Leobardo F. Estrada, and Gerald C. Hayward, *Tidal Wave II: An Evaluation of Enrollment Projections for California Higher Education* (San Jose: The California Higher Education Policy Center, 1995), p. iv.

24. William Trombley, "UC Regents: Lots of Pomp, Little Circumstance," in *CrossTalk* 3, no. 3 (San Jose: The California Higher Education Policy Center, October 1995), pp. 7–14.

25. CPEC, *Fiscal Profiles 1995* (Sacramento: 1995), p. 17.

26. Ibid., p. 26.

27. William Pickens, *Financing the Plan: California's Master Plan for Higher Education, 1958–1994* (San Jose: The California Higher Education Policy Center, 1995), pp. 8–9.

28. William Pickens, "The Master Plan for Higher Education: Access, Affordability, and Financing," Outline to the Assembly Committee on Higher Education, Berkeley, CA, 21 November 1995, p. 2.

29. Lawrence Gladieux and Jacqueline King, *Trends in Student Aid* (San Jose: The California Higher Education Policy Center, 1995), p. 22.

30. CPEC, telephone communication, 14 February 1997.

31. Figures for 1990–91 are calculated from Gladieux and King, *Trends in Student Aid*, pp. 14–17. Data for 1994–95 are from central offices of UC, CSU, CCC, and the Association of Independent California Colleges and Universities (AICCU). Includes UC, CSU, CCC, and independent nonprofit institutions.

32. Calculated from Gladieux and King, *Trends in Student Aid*, p. 27.

33. See John Immerwahr, *The Closing Gateway: Californians Consider Their Higher Education System* (San Jose: The California Higher Education Policy Center, 1993).

34. *Chronicle of Higher Education Almanac* 42, pp. 6–9.

35. Kent Halstead, "Quantitative Analysis of the Environment, Performance, and Operation Actions of Eight State Public Higher Education Systems," unpublished paper commissioned by The California Higher Education Policy Center, San Jose, p. 49.

36. Kent Halstead, *State Profiles: Financing Public Higher Education, 1978 to 1996 Trend Data* (Washington, D.C.: Research Associates of Washington, 1996), p. 11.

37. CPEC, *Fiscal Profiles 1995*, pp. 22, 24, 25, 47.

38. Jack McCurdy, *Broken Promises* (San Jose: The California Higher Education Policy Center, 1994), p. 2. All figures cited in this section are taken from *Broken Promises* unless otherwise noted.

39. Calculated from table 4.4.

40. McCurdy, *Broken Promises*, p. 6.

41. Jack McCurdy and William Trombley, *On the Brink* (San Jose: The California Higher Education Policy Center, 1993), p. 17–19. All figures cited in the CSU and UC sections are taken from *On the Brink* unless otherwise noted.

42. Ibid., p. 3.

43. Ibid., pp. 4–5.

44. All figures for UCLA in this section are taken from Amy Wallace and Ralph Frammolino, "Privatizing UCLA: Has The Time Come?" in *Los Angeles Times* (30 July 1995), pp. A1+.

CHAPTER 5

Florida

Protecting Access and Anticipating Growth

Yolanda Sanchez-Penley, Mario C. Martinez, and Thad Nodine

*T*his chapter synthesizes information gathered from interviews, relevant publications, and other sources to present the primary financial issues that faced Florida's system of higher education from 1990 to 1995. Interviews with state officials, educational administrators, faculty, and staff took place in November 1995.

Florida's state budget process was thrown into turmoil by the economic recession that hit the state in the early 1990s. State revenues stagnated in 1990, 1991, and 1992, and fell well below budget projections. At the same time, the demand for state services—in health care, social services, public education, and corrections—escalated sharply. Florida's legislators, mindful of voters' demands for no new taxes, refrained from major new tax increases—and were forced to drastically scale back budgeted spending increases during the first three years of the decade. In 1993 and 1994, the Florida economy began to slowly recover, but state revenues increased only incrementally. Although expenditure demands in social services and health care leveled off during these latter years, spending needs in corrections and public education continued to rise sharply and exerted continuing pressures on the state budget.

As actual revenues lagged behind budgetary projections during fiscal years 1990, 1991, and 1992, budgeted increases for public education (K–12, community colleges, universities, and student financial aid) were repeatedly whittled away during midyear fiscal negotiations. In each of these years, over half of the general fund spending cuts came from the education budget, even though education accounts for only about one-third of state appropriations. As a result, state funding for higher education remained stagnant during the first three years of the decade. From fiscal years 1994 to 1996, state funding for higher education increased slowly.

While state funding for higher education was stagnating, student enrollments continued to increase. From 1990–91 to 1995–96, student enrollment in public institutions of higher education (as measured by head count) increased by 7.5 percent.[1] As a result, appropriations per student dropped significantly in the early 1990s, and by 1995–96, appropriations per student still had not reached the 1990–91 level. Institutions of higher education responded to this reduction in per-student funding largely through short-term efforts such as reducing adjunct professors, freezing salaries, and foregoing maintenance.

As in other states during the first half of the 1990s, students in Florida became increasingly reliant on loans to fund their education. Unlike in other states, however, students in Florida did not face huge increases in tuition. This was due largely to tuition limits placed on universities and community colleges by the legislature, which historically has been active in issues regarding higher education. During the first half of the 1990s, the legislature was also active in limiting the number of credit hours per student and in setting up plans for performance-based budgeting for higher education.

With its open-door policies and low tuition rates, Florida has emphasized access in its system of higher education. Twenty-eight public and 15 private two-year institutions provide higher education within commuting distance of 99 percent of the state's population. The state also has nine public universities and 54 private four-year institutions, with a new public university scheduled to open in fall 1997 in southern Florida.

Although state revenues and state spending on higher education increased during the last few years, higher education in Florida faces important challenges in the years ahead. While state revenues are increasing slowly, demand for education and corrections spending—due to demographic conditions— are still at high levels. During 1996, a constitutional limit on the growth of state revenues will go into effect. This change is expected to intensify competition for state funds. Furthermore, the state is expecting a 29 percent increase in high school graduates over the next 10 years, along with a declining dropout rate. Despite these conflicting trends between funding and enrollment, Florida's legislators are hoping that by focusing on performance-based budgeting and other ways of improving productivity in higher education, the state can avoid large tuition increases and maintain its emphasis on access.

STATE CONTEXT

Demographics

With 14 million residents, Florida is the fourth most populated state in the nation. The percentages of African-American residents (13.6 percent) and

Hispanic residents (12.2 percent) are above the national averages. In 1994, Florida's per capita income of $21,677 was slightly below the national average. During the same year, the state's poverty rate was 17.8 percent compared to a national average of 15.2 percent.[2]

Much of the growth in population comes from the influx of retirees, immigrants, and young adults attracted to what has been—until the early 1990s—a robust economy. The fastest growing segment of the population is over 65 years of age, but the percentage of those under 17 years is also increasing rapidly. These two groups require more spending in education, health, and social services than other age groups.

Among all states, Florida has the highest proportion of its residents over age 65.[3] The vast majority of these retirees depend on property income and transfer payments as sources of income. One positive aspect of this is that transfer payments are typically less sensitive to the economy and act as stabilizing forces in weak economic times. The large proportion of persons on fixed incomes, however, usually translates into widespread political opposition to higher taxes.

Although tourists and part-time residents also provide the state with revenues and stimulate economic activity, they also place high demands on the state's infrastructure.

State Fiscal Challenges in an Antitax Climate

The economic recession of the 1990s affected Florida's budget process drastically. State revenues stagnated in 1990, 1991, and 1992, and fell well below budget projections during those years. At the same time, spending demands escalated sharply. The stalled economy created rising demands for entitlement spending in health care and social services. The number of recipients of Aid to Families with Dependent Children (AFDC), for instance, rose 109 percent between fiscal years 1989 and 1993. From 1990 to 1993, the share of state general fund spending devoted to Medicaid rose from 7 to 13 percent of the state budget. Due to demographic and other factors, spending demands for corrections and public education also increased dramatically.[4]

Although the state economy improved during fiscal years 1993, 1994, and 1995, the improvement has not been as pronounced as past economic recoveries. State revenues have increased only incrementally. And even though expenditure demands in social services and health care have leveled off as the economy improved, demographic changes have kept spending needs in corrections and public education at high levels.

State Revenues

Florida's governor and legislators responded to declining state revenues by closing tax loopholes, tightening exemptions, increasing some user fees, and "borrowing" money from the state's Working Capital Fund (rainy day fund) and other state trust funds. Lawmakers took these approaches to circumvent raising taxes and to minimize spending cuts. Despite these efforts, however, a minor tax increase was instituted as part of the budget negotiations for fiscal year 1993.

Since Florida does not have a state income tax, the vast majority of state general fund revenues derives from sales taxes (about 70 percent) and business taxes (about 25 percent). Although general fund revenues increased even through the worst years of the recession (from 1990 to 1992), these increases were small by comparison to previous years and they fell well below budgeted projections. Revenues from taxes were particularly flat, and, as table 5.1 reveals, revenues from sales taxes actually declined in 1991.[5] During 1990 and 1991, the total percentage of change from the previous year would have been lower were it not for the transfers from trust funds. During fiscal year 1993, the state's finances—and particularly its revenues from taxes—began improving.

♭ TABLE 5.1

FLORIDA'S REVENUE SOURCES (IN MILLIONS OF DOLLARS)

	1990	1991	1992	1993	1994	1995	1996	% Change 1990–96
Sales Taxes	7,037	6,950	7,636	8,380	9,007	9,578	10,456	49
Business Taxes*	2,403	2,562	2730	3,006	3,309	3,332	3,484	45
Licenses, Fees	151	199	303	352	353	358	326	116
Other Fees[†]	201	297	354	386	442	440	467	132
Interest	109	107	89	96	84	116	146	34
Transfer from Trust	150	150	0	0	0	0	0	(100)
Less Refunds	(148)	(150)	(201)	(162)	(152)	(185)	(227)	
Total	9,896	10,115	10,992	12,059	13,043	13,689	14,652	48
% Change	7.0	2.2	7.9	10.5	8.2	4.6	7.4	
U.S. CPI[§]	5.4%	4.2%	3.0%	3.0%	2.6%	2.8%	2.6%	20%

* This category includes corporate income and other business taxes.
[†] This category includes primarily medical and hospital fees, and automotive fees.
[§] CPI data are based on calendar rather than fiscal years. The CPI figure for 1996 includes data through October 1996.

Note: These figures exclude the state lottery and other trusts.

Sources: State of Florida, Executive Office of the Governor, Office of Planning and Budgeting, "Revenue and Economic Analysis," unpublished. The CPI figures are from the U.S. Department of Labor, Bureau of Labor Statistics, "Consumer Price Index for All Urban Consumers, U.S. City Average," October 1996.

State Appropriations

On the expenditure side, Florida's lawmakers were forced to drastically scale back budgeted spending increases in 1990, 1991, and 1992. In making their spending cuts, legislators targeted the three most heavily funded functions—education, human services, and transportation—but also made significant cuts in corrections.[6] In fiscal years 1990, 1991, and 1992, over half of the general fund spending cuts came from the education budget, even though education accounts for about one-third of state appropriations.[7] As a result, state funding for education—and higher education in particular—remained stagnant during the first three years of the decade (see table 5.2), so that from fiscal year 1990 to 1993, state appropriations to the community colleges increased only 1.6 percent and funding for the State University System (SUS) increased only 3.3 percent. Each of these increases represents an actual decline in constant dollars. Table 5.2 also shows that while state spending increased significantly from 1990 to 1996, at a rate well above inflation, spending increases for the universities and community colleges only kept pace with inflation, and they lagged well behind all other major spending categories.

During the first half of the 1990s, there was also a significant drop in the share of state spending going to higher education. Figure 5.1 compares Florida to the national average concerning the percentage of the state budget allocated for public higher education. The figure reveals that during the past 11

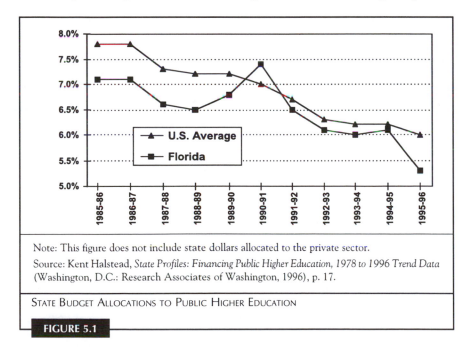

Note: This figure does not include state dollars allocated to the private sector.

Source: Kent Halstead, *State Profiles: Financing Public Higher Education, 1978 to 1996 Trend Data* (Washington, D.C.: Research Associates of Washington, 1996), p. 17.

STATE BUDGET ALLOCATIONS TO PUBLIC HIGHER EDUCATION

FIGURE 5.1

TABLE 5.2								
STATE APPROPRIATIONS (IN MILLIONS OF DOLLARS)								
	1990	1991	1992	1993	1994	1995	1996	% Change 1990–96
Education:								
Public Schools	5,393	5,700	5,467	5,812	6,303	6,825	7,230	34
Com. Colleges	563	588	569	572	613	647	671	19
Universities	1,405	1,454	1,408	1,452	1,555	1,606	1,714	22
Other Educ.[†]	1,467	1,626	1,560	1,903	1,853	1,871	1,514	3
Subtotal, Educ.	8,828	9,369	9,003	9,738	10,325	10,950	11,130	26
Gen. Govern.	7,097	9,198	10,009	10,418	11,531	13,198	13,534	91
HRS/Crim. Jus.*	7,022	8,812	9,744	11,706	13,628	14,611	14,455	106
Total	22,946	27,379	28,847	31,863	35,484	38,759	39,119	71
% Change, Educ.		6.1	(3.9)	8.2	7.5	6.0	1.6	
% Change, Total		19.3	5.4	10.5	13.6	9.2	0.9	
U.S. CPI[§]	5.4%	4.2%	3.0%	3.0%	2.6%	2.8%	2.6%	20%

* This line item includes human resources and criminal justice.
† This line item includes the department of education, various public schools like the Florida School for the Deaf and Blind, some financial aid appropriations, and several other education expenditures.
§ CPI data are based on calendar rather than fiscal years. The CPI figure for 1996 includes data through October 1996.
Sources: Florida Senate, Ways and Means Committee, A Statistical Review of Education in Florida, 1991–92 to 1996–97 editions (Tallahassee, FL). The CPI figures are from the U.S. Department of Labor, "Consumer Price Index for All Urban Consumers, U.S. City Average," October 1996.

years, Florida has been lower than the national average on this measure for all but one year (1990–91). It also shows that over the past five years, Florida's percentage allocation to higher education has dropped much faster than the national average.

Another important indicator of state support to higher education is its appropriations per full-time-equivalent (FTE) student. At the same time that state funding for higher education remained relatively flat, student enrollment increased steadily. As a result, whereas the appropriation per FTE student in 1990–91 was $5,586, this figure fell to $4,121 by 1995–96—a drop of 26 percent.[8]

Kent Halstead provides other measures, however, that suggest the state's commitment to funding public higher education is higher than the trends indicate. In 1995–96, for instance, Florida ranked just above the national average (23rd out of all states) in terms of educational appropriations per FTE student, and 12th in terms of per capita tax revenues used to support students.[9] During the same year, only five other states show families paying a smaller percentage of their median family income for tuition costs.[10]

An Antitax Electorate

Florida's voters have been active in the 1990s in placing limits on governmental taxing and spending. In November 1990, for instance, the public overwhelmingly approved a state constitutional amendment to limit the ability of the legislature to pass unfunded mandates. Another state constitutional amendment, which will go into effect in 1996, limits growth in state revenues to the average growth rate in Florida's personal income over the preceding five years. No one knows exactly how the new limit will affect state revenues over the long-term, but university officials have expressed concern that the limit will intensify competition for state funds, particularly between higher education and the criminal justice system.[11]

This voter dissatisfaction with tax burdens has also affected local governments. In November 1992, voters passed a state constitutional amendment limiting the growth of assessment on homestead property to either 3 percent or the inflation rate. Property taxes, along with fees and charges, are the most important revenue sources for local governments. Both younger and older voters disapprove of raising property taxes; the younger ones feel that property taxes make it more difficult for them to own a home, and the older voters recognize that increased taxes undermine their fixed incomes. The 1992 constitutional amendment leaves local governments with few revenue-raising options other than raising fees and charges, since most local governments have to obtain the voters' approval to tap new revenue sources or raise taxes—and that approval is usually not forthcoming.

Even though Florida is well below the national average in the tax burden placed on residents, there is widespread belief among Floridians that taxes are escalating rapidly in the state. A 1993 study by Florida Tax Watch found that between 1977 and 1993, the taxes paid by Floridians to federal, state, and local government grew 363 percent. During the same period, population and inflation, combined, increased only 271 percent. The study also reported that the average Florida family's effective buying power declined three years in a row, from 1991 to 1993.[12] These statistics have enhanced an already strong antitax, antigovernment sentiment among many voters.

POLITICAL ENVIRONMENT

Although Florida has traditionally been a Democratic stronghold, the Republicans have been steadily increasing their influence in statewide politics. This trend, which was enhanced by the state legislative reapportionment in 1992, has made Florida a competitive two-party state. In 1992, the state senate's political power was evenly divided between 20 Democrats and 20 Republicans. The party leaders agreed to rotate the senate presidency. Democrats controlled the house (by a 71-to-49 majority) and the governorship during 1993 and 1994.

The 1994 elections gave Republicans control of the senate for the first time since Reconstruction, with a 22-to-18 majority. The house maintained a Democratic majority, but lost eight seats in the election. The senate will almost certainly remain Republican; there are rumors that some Democrats may switch parties, which could produce a Republican majority in the house.

The governor and senators are elected to four-year terms, with the incumbent senators of even- and odd-numbered districts alternately facing the voters every two years. The governor and legislators are limited to eight-year terms. The legislature is constitutionally limited to 60 calendar days each year, but the session can be extended by a three-fifths vote of each chamber.[13]

The current governor, Democrat Lawton Chiles, defeated Republican incumbent Bob Martinez in 1990 and was reelected by a narrow margin in 1994. Florida has been referred to as a "weak governor state,"[14] primarily because the governor's cabinet is elected; as a result, his ability to implement his political agenda is limited. In the 1980s, former Democratic governor, Bob Graham, made higher education one of his top priorities and was able to accomplish most of his objectives because he worked with a legislature of the same party. Since the emergence of a more competitive political system in Florida, however, such gubernatorial influence has weakened significantly.[15] The seven-member cabinet for 1995 was made up of three Republicans, one of whom is the commissioner of education.

Three features make state government distinctive in Florida: (1) the initiative process (Florida voters may directly propose a law that will be enacted if approved by a majority of the voters at a subsequent election); (2) "sunshine laws" (all meetings where the public's interest is debated must be open and publicly announced); and (3) the existence of eight-year term limits.

The State Legislature and the Budget Process

The Florida legislature is the most influential political body in the state. The senate and house appropriations committees exercise considerable power in setting policy through the appropriations process. The governor is responsible for developing a state budget, but many of those interviewed described his budget as "unrecognizable" by the end of the legislative process. Prior to the development of the state budget, the governor, lieutenant governor, and cabinet and legislative leaders agree on "consensus estimates" or revenue estimates for the state. Consensus estimates establish the framework for budget development.

After the governor submits his budget to the legislature, the legislature then develops its own budget. House and senate leaders agree on lump-sum amounts to be provided to different areas of the state government. A conference process resolves disagreements over spending priorities between the two chambers. The house and senate usually support the outcomes agreed upon by conference committees. After approval by both chambers, the budget goes to the governor, who has line-item veto authority.

Florida lawmakers actively involve themselves in higher education issues and use the budget to exert influence on education policy. The chairs of the appropriations and education committees have strong influence over higher education funding and policy. Priorities change frequently since committee chairs change every two years. During the past five years, the house has focused on issues concerning access and accommodating the growing demand for higher education. It is the senate, however, that has the more active—and as one observer called it, "contentious"—relationship with the higher education community. In recent years the senate has focused on performance-based budgeting, time-to-degree issues, tuition and, most recently, the "deregulation" of higher education. Those interviewed agreed that the senate's activism in higher education is not the result of the recent political shift from Democrat to Republican control.

Although the community colleges and the SUS receive lump-sum allocations, their funding is accompanied by provisos to assure that the systems meet legislative requirements regarding important state policies. Lawmakers make frequent demands for information from colleges and universities. The legislature also initiates independent studies that frequently result in legislation. In the most recent example, the legislature conducted a study on student credit hours that resulted in a bill that capped the state-funded hours to earn a degree.

Higher education administrators, of course, do not necessarily see legislative involvement in matters of higher education policy as positive. Campus administrators complained about what they perceive as the legislature's micromanagement of higher education. One faculty member noted that legislative action does not come from a policy vision for higher education but evolves from specific issues. But state legislators contend that higher education, like any other state-funded operation, can and should be held accountable for state expenditures.

HIGHER EDUCATION

Institutions

There are 106 degree-granting institutions in Florida: 9 public universities, 54 private four-year institutions, and 28 public and 15 private two-year institutions. An additional public university is scheduled to open in fall 1997 in southern Florida. In fall 1994, the last year for which information on undergraduate enrollment is available, total undergraduate enrollment (measured by head count) in Florida's institutions of higher education was 562,961 (with about 83 percent of students attending public institutions).[16]

During the 1950s and 1960s, the priority for higher education in Florida was to improve access to colleges and universities for residents living throughout the state. During the 1960s and 1970s, legislators focused more on improving the quality of education, especially graduate education. Yet it is the early 1980s that are known as Florida's golden years for higher education. During those years, Democratic governor Bob Graham made access and quality a state priority for higher education, and the legislature largely supported his agenda. As the economic decline of the late 1980s reduced state revenues, however, the situation changed under Governor Martinez. And the 1990s have seen stagnant—and in some years, declining—state support for higher education while student demand has continued to grow.

State University System

Florida's public four-year institutions are part of one multicampus system, the SUS. The system includes two medical schools, two law schools, a dental school, a veterinary school, and the Institute of Food and Agriculture.

The University of Florida (UF) and Florida State University are the two public flagship universities supporting research activities and graduate education. The newer regional universities in the university system were developed to provide access to baccalaureate education in cooperation with the area's community colleges.[17]

The oldest and largest public universities are in northern Florida, which has been a source of great irritation to political leaders in central and southern Florida, where populations are swelling. The new campus at Ft. Myers, Florida's Gulf Coast University, was planned to create a university in southern Florida.

Community Colleges

In the late 1950s, the legislature established the Community College Council and in 1957 the council's first master plan recommended a comprehensive system of public community colleges in Florida. The plan called for the provision of post-high-school education at a reasonable cost within commuting distance of 99 percent of state residents seeking higher education.

Florida's "two-plus-two" policy promotes the public community colleges as the primary point of entry to postsecondary education. A statewide articulation agreement offers admission to the SUS for public community college transfer students who hold an associate in arts degree.[18]

Private Colleges

Florida's private sector includes small, church-affiliated colleges, large institutions like the University of Miami, and three historically black colleges. The private colleges of Florida enroll nearly 20 percent of the total higher education student enrollment and award 36 percent of the state's undergraduate degrees. Private colleges also enroll a higher percentage of minority students than do public colleges and universities in Florida.

Twenty-three private institutions belong to the Independent Colleges and Universities of Florida (ICUF), which has a strong voice in the state legislature. The state's commitment to its private institutions can be found in the many student grant and scholarship programs available to students who attend private institutions. Two such programs—the Private Student Assistance Grant and the Florida Resident Access Grant—are available exclusively to students attending private institutions. In addition, private colleges, with state support, make slots available in high-demand programs to accommodate Florida students, and the state pays the difference between public university tuition and private tuition to send students to these programs.[19]

Governance

The state board of education is the chief policy-making and governing body for all public education in Florida. The board is composed of the governor and seven elected cabinet members, including the commissioner of education, who also serves on the board of regents (for the SUS) and the state board of community colleges. Although the board of education has statutory responsibility for budgetary review and for giving budget recommendations to the governor for all boards, institutions, and agencies under its supervision, several state and university officials described this role as insignificant.

Governor Graham created the Postsecondary Education Planning Commission (PEPC), which advises the board of education on all postsecondary education matters. The major responsibility of the commission is to prepare and update a master plan for postsecondary education every five years. Several state officials mentioned PEPC's critical role in drawing the private institutions into the master plan for higher education. Additionally, PEPC reviews all contracts with the privates.

The SUS board of regents is a consolidated governing board that has governing and coordinating authority over the nine public universities in Florida. The board of regents is made up of 13 members, including one student regent and the commissioner of education. Members are appointed by the governor with the approval of the state board of education and subject to senate confirmation.

The regents' policy directives are carried out by a staff of about 200 headed by the chancellor, who reports to the regents. The regents' primary responsibility is to establish systemwide policies, plan for future needs of the system, and advocate system priorities to the governor and legislators in Tallahassee. The regents also review institutional programs and conduct contract negotiations with the SUS faculty union.

In 1968, the Florida legislature established independent, local boards of trustees for community colleges. The governor, after consultation with district representatives, appoints the trustees of the local community college boards. Although the state board of community colleges was originally chartered to coordinate, support, and oversee the 28 colleges, legal authority for maintaining and operating the individual community colleges remains at the local level.

Several state-level officials said that the SUS has high-quality data about the institutions and their students. Many legislative staff, however, said they were frustrated by the need to rely on the university system to produce the data. Systemwide data about the community colleges are even more difficult to collect, since no statewide data base on community college students exists. In order to learn more about specific issues at the university system or the community colleges—such as the number of excess credit hours students take—the legislature and other agencies dealing with higher education must undertake special studies and rely on the cooperation of the various sectors.

The state board of independent colleges and universities represents the private colleges and universities, and the state board of independent postsecondary vocational, technical, trade, and business schools, established in 1974 by the legislature, represents independent vocational, technical, trade, and business schools.

Current and Projected Enrollments

Although public community colleges enroll over half of the students who attend an institution of higher education in Florida, student enrollment in community colleges increased only 3 percent from academic year 1990–91 to 1995–96, as shown in table 5.3. The community colleges also saw enrollment declines in half of these six years, and they reached their peak enrollment in 1993–94. The SUS, on the other hand, experienced steady yearly increases in enrollment and produced the largest enrollment growth from 1990–91 to 1995–96: a 15.6 percent increase. Institutional size varies widely throughout the SUS, from about 4,400 students enrolled at the University of West Florida to about 35,000 at UF.[20]

Overall, head-count enrollment in all public institutions of higher education increased 7.5 percent from 1990–91 to 1995–96. While this modest increase is significant in the midst of an economic recession, enrollment levels in public institutions had increased by 16 percent from 1988–89 to 1990–91 alone, revealing that enrollment growth during the economic downturn slowed significantly.

Table 5.3 also shows that enrollment in the private sector increased modestly by 5.9 percent from 1990–91 to 1995–96, but dropped in 1993–94 and 1994–95. Although enrollment in private institutions increased again in 1995–96, the total number of students still fell short of the peak level of 1992–93.

TABLE 5.3

FALL HEAD-COUNT ENROLLMENT BY SECTOR

	1990	1991	1992	1993	1994	1995	% Change 1990–95
Comm. Colleges	312,345	308,376	324,302	325,043	324,813	321,566	3.0
SUS	175,960	181,889	182,896	188,928	197,931	203,478	15.6
Independents	97,311	103,054	108,115	104,405	101,147	103,046	5.9
Total	585,636	593,319	615,313	618,436	623,891	628,090	7.2

Note: These totals include graduate students.

Sources: Florida Community Colleges, *The Fact Book*, 1990 to 1995 editions. State University Systems, *Fact Book for SUS*, 1990 to 1994 editions; and the Florida Board of Independent Colleges and Universities. The 1995–96 head-count enrollment figures come from the segment offices, and are not yet published.

Twenty-eight percent of the enrollments in Florida are minority students, with private institutions accounting for a greater proportion of minority students than public institutions. The strong minority representation in the private sector is largely attributable to the presence of several private, historically black colleges and universities in the state.

The PEPC projects that the SUS and the Community College System (CCS) will continue to experience steady growth in terms of student demand as immigration into the state remains high, and as more educated adults return for job training or retraining. PEPC also projects a 20 percent growth in the 0-to-17 age group by the year 2000. Within this age group, the number of high school graduates is expected to increase by 28 percent over the next 10 years, and the number of students in grades nine through 12 is projected to grow by 37 percent during the same period.

These trends in population translate into more demand for higher education. Figure 5.2 shows the continuous growth projections for the SUS and the CCS between the years 1994 and 2004. Growth for this 10-year projection is 33 percent and 32 percent for the SUS and CCS, respectively.

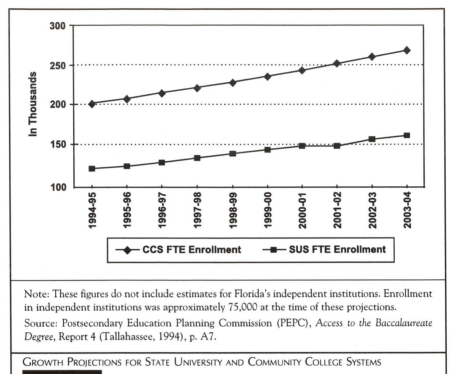

Note: These figures do not include estimates for Florida's independent institutions. Enrollment in independent institutions was approximately 75,000 at the time of these projections.

Source: Postsecondary Education Planning Commission (PEPC), *Access to the Baccalaureate Degree*, Report 4 (Tallahassee, 1994), p. A7.

GROWTH PROJECTIONS FOR STATE UNIVERSITY AND COMMUNITY COLLEGE SYSTEMS

FIGURE 5.2

Kent Halstead reports two indicators that focus on public higher education enrollment. The first is the participation ratio, which measures the number of FTE students in public institutions divided by the number of new high school graduates. According to Halstead, the participation ratio measures "the degree to which a state provides attractive and accessible opportunities for higher education students relative to the number of high school graduates."[21] Higher ratios indicate a larger public system with more opportunity for high school students.

Florida's participation ratio has increased steadily over the time period shown in figure 5.3. Florida has a very low number of high school graduates per capita (7.1) combined with a large public higher education system. The result is a high participation ratio that has remained above the national average since 1991–92, indicating that high school graduates have more access to public higher education in Florida than do graduates in most other states. The Florida CCS contributes to its high participation ratio, for states with large community college systems tend to rank well on this measure. As demographic

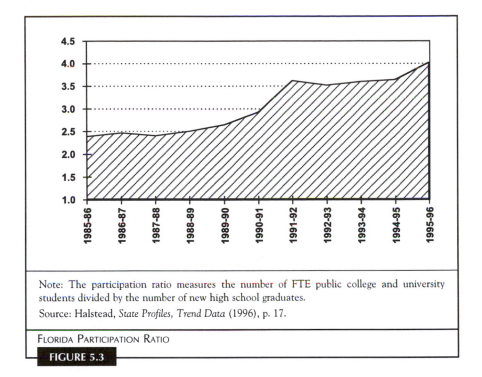

Note: The participation ratio measures the number of FTE public college and university students divided by the number of new high school graduates.

Source: Halstead, *State Profiles, Trend Data* (1996), p. 17.

FLORIDA PARTICIPATION RATIO

FIGURE 5.3

projections indicate, the Florida higher education system will be challenged to provide the same level of opportunity to future high school graduates of the state.

The second indicator, student enrollment, measures the number of FTE students in public institutions of higher education per 1,000 state residents. The measure can be interpreted similarly to the participation ratio, but is applied to the general population of the state rather than just to high school graduates. Figure 5.4 reveals that Florida's enrollment ratio, except for a period of stagnation during the recession, has been increasing steadily over the past 10 years.

Unlike Florida's participation ratio, its enrollment ratio falls below the national average. In 1995–96, for instance, Florida ranked sixth in the nation on the participation ratio and 38th on the student enrollment ratio.[22] Florida's population is older than the national average, which means that a significant portion of the population is either already educated or not currently in the public system. This can partly explain Florida's lower enrollment ratio relative to the general population.

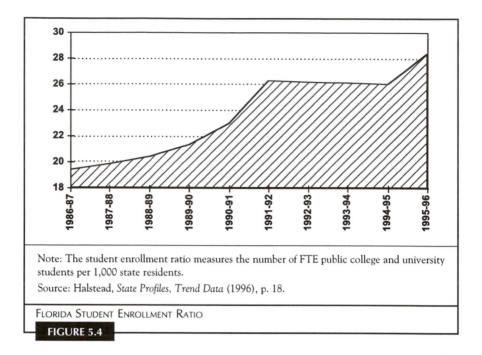

Note: The student enrollment ratio measures the number of FTE public college and university students per 1,000 state residents.
Source: Halstead, *State Profiles, Trend Data* (1996), p. 18.

FLORIDA STUDENT ENROLLMENT RATIO

FIGURE 5.4

FINANCING HIGHER EDUCATION IN THE STATE OF FLORIDA

State Funding

The State University System

The SUS compiles individual campus budgets into one system budget and submits it directly to the governor and the legislature. The budgets are based on historical allocation, changes in institutional mission or in enrollment, and system priorities. While the board of education is responsible for submitting the SUS budget, university and state officials described their involvement in the process as a "rubber stamp." The SUS receives a lump-sum appropriation from the legislature, with five or six major categories. Individual campuses then receive a lump sum from the system office.

Prior to 1991, the budget process did not grant as much flexibility to the system. A line-item budget was submitted to the legislature and a detailed line-item budget was approved. Some state leaders have expressed concern about dropping the line-item budget process. For instance, one observer stated, "We should not have given them the flexibility without some accountability mechanism in place."

A second concern on the part of many legislators has centered on the formula used to arrive at the system's budget request. The regents work from a formula that highlights the previous year's base funding, while the legislature uses a formula that places less emphasis on base funding. The legislature is attempting to remedy this situation.

In a related development, PEPC has recommended that the funding formula for the university system be altered to reflect only the cost for lower-level instruction for first-time students. State University System officials have expressed concern about this possibility, and have commented that campuses would be reluctant to take on more students without full funding. The legislature has not yet acted on PEPC's recommendation.

As table 5.4 shows, the SUS receives more of its funding from state general revenues than from all other sources combined. State general fund revenues, which comprised 66 percent of total funding in fiscal year 1991–92, comprised 70 percent in fiscal year 1995–96—a trend that is the reverse in most states during this period. The growth in the general revenue funds also accounts for the majority of the 16 percent growth in the total funding over this period. Student fees, which have remained below 20 percent of total funding during each of the last five years, comprised 17 percent in 1992 and 1996.

TABLE 5.4

STATE UNIVERSITY SYSTEM APPROPRIATED FUNDING (IN MILLIONS OF DOLLARS)

	1991–92	1992–93	1993–94	1994–95	1995–96	% Change 1992–96
State General Fund	956.0	921.6	991.2	1,079.6	1,166.7	22.0
Lottery	127.0	125.2	120.5	139.9	124.4	(2.0)
Student Fees	246.3	283.6	308.6	276.3	286.6	16.3
Other Trust Funds	111.8	104.8	103.2	87.8	93.2	(16.6)
Total Funds	1,440.1	1,435.2	1,523.6	1,583.6	1,670.9	16.0

Note: 1991–92 represents the first year that data are available. These figures differ somewhat from the ones in table 5.2, largely because these figures include the state's employee budget fund.

Source: Florida Senate, Ways and Means Committee, *Education Funding Summary* (Tallahassee, FL: 1991–92 to 1995–96 editions).

During the early years of the decade, when state funding remained stagnant, the SUS responded by reducing adjunct professors and teaching assistants, thereby increasing teaching loads and foregoing lower priorities such as maintenance of facilities. In addition, faculty salaries were frozen for one year.

The Community Colleges

The legislature appropriates funds directly to the state's 28 community colleges through the Community College Program Fund. Although the formula that determines funding levels emphasizes enrollment as the primary factor, it also accounts for the base budget from the previous year, the costs to continue operations, the need for new facilities and new programs, and other factors.

Each local board of trustees is expected to develop priorities for programs that meet local needs. These boards of trustees are also given the flexibility and responsibility to set local policies on salary increases. The legislature establishes an average student fee charge each year. Local boards then have the flexibility to set their fees within 10 percent above or below this average. The legislature also provides funding for special projects or state priorities. These funds are restricted in purpose.

The legislature does not penalize the community colleges for enrollment losses, especially if the declines are due to an improving economy or a decline in the high school graduating classes. This has produced some differences in funding levels per student at various colleges.

According to a number of state officials, the community colleges are moving toward performance-based budgeting. Beginning in 1997, budgeting will be based on measures of effectiveness in the associate of arts degree, the associate of science degree, and student transfers. One recent legislative practice encouraged the colleges in this direction. The legislature challenged the community colleges and area technical centers to dedicate 5 percent of their budgets to augment a $30 million, state-funded incentive program. To participate in this voluntary program, the colleges had to trim 5 percent from their budgets and commit to the program for three years. Twenty of the 28 community colleges agreed to participate in this program. The 5 percent and more could be earned back by demonstrating successful outcome results in areas such as completion, graduation rates, and placement. One legislator said that the program has prompted the majority of community colleges to focus on outcomes. This incentive program has eased the community colleges into the performance-based budgeting process being pushed by the legislature and the governor as part of "reinventing" government.

Like the SUS, the community colleges receive over half of their revenue from the state general fund (see table 5.5). Community colleges in Florida do not receive local funds unless a local referendum has passed that allows the district to tax for the community colleges. The success rate of such referendums is quite low. FTE student enrollment figures are established for each community college every funding session and are instrumental in determining the level of general revenue funds appropriated.

As in the university system, revenues from the state general fund increased as a percentage of total revenues from 1991–92 to 1995–96. State general revenues increased from 59 percent of total funding in fiscal year 1992 to 61 percent in fiscal year 1996. Student fees comprised 24 percent of total funding in 1992 and almost 26 percent in 1996.

Some community colleges responded to stagnant funding during the first few years of the decade by approving tuition increases up to the 10 percent cap, while others actually decreased tuition in hopes of attracting more students.

TABLE 5.5						
FUNDING FOR COMMUNITY COLLEGES (IN MILLIONS OF DOLLARS)						
	1991–92	1992–93	1993–94	1994–95	1995–96	% Change 1992–96
State General Fund	441	438	472	497	528	19.7
Lottery	128	122	124	126	117	(8.6)
Student Fees	176	178	210	223	224	27.3
Total Funds	745	738	805	846	869	16.6

Note: Sums may not total due to rounding. The year 1991–92 represents the first year that data are available. These figures differ somewhat from the ones in table 5.2, largely because these figures include the state's employee budget fund.

Source: Florida Senate, Ways and Means Committee, A Statistical Review, 1991–92 to 1995–96 editions.

The Independent Sector

The independent sector receives funding primarily from tuition and fees, foundations, private donations, and the state. The independent sector's involvement in the budgetary process largely takes the form of lobbying for increased funding for the various state programs that support private institutions. The state funds several grant and scholarship programs exclusively for students who attend private colleges or universities (see "Financial Aid"). In addition, private colleges, with state support, make slots available in high-demand programs to accommodate Florida students, and the state pays the difference between public university tuition and private tuition to send students to these programs.

Tuition

Unlike in most states, students in Florida's public colleges and universities did not face huge increases in tuition rates during the recession of the early 1990s—largely due to limits placed on the SUS and on the community colleges by the legislature. As a result, tuition levels in Florida—as is reported in the sections that follow—still remain below national averages in all sectors of higher education.

Compared to other states, Florida also has a low tuition factor, which measures the proportion of a public institution's funding that comes from tuition (relative to state appropriations plus tuition). A low tuition factor generally means that, compared to other states, the state leans more toward public rather than individual and family financing of public higher education. Florida's tuition factor stood at 20 percent before the recession, rose to 24 percent at the height of the recession, and fell to 23.5 percent in 1995–96. The national average for the tuition factor was 31.6 percent in 1995–96.[23]

Although there are occasional rumblings among lawmakers concerning the need for students to contribute more toward the cost of their education, the legislature has generally taken an active role in *preventing* large tuition increases. When tuition rates increase, however, state officials and campus leaders try to ensure that the additional funds remain on campus.

State University System

In 1991, the legislature passed a bill authorizing the following tuition indexing policy: by December 1 of each year, the board of regents sets the resident undergraduate fees for the subsequent fall term at no more than 25 percent of the prior year's cost of undergraduate programs, with an overall tuition increase cap of 10 percent per year; graduate tuition may be increased by the same percentage as undergraduate education, except that it is capped at an overall level of 25 percent increase per year. Currently, the board of regents cannot act unilaterally on setting tuition for the system. Legislative approval for appropriating tuition dollars is required.

SUS fees for in-state students are shown in table 5.6. As this table reveals, tuition increases for in-state undergraduate students in Florida exceeded the state cap in 1991–92 and 1992–93. Nonetheless, the tuition increase from 1990–91 to 1995–96 was 36 percent—a very modest increase compared to many other states. As of 1995–96, tuition at the SUS ranked as the sixth lowest in the nation.[24]

TABLE 5.6

STATE UNIVERSITY SYSTEM FEES FOR IN-STATE STUDENTS (IN DOLLARS)

	1990–91	1991–92	1992–93	1993–94	1994–95	1995–96	Total % Change
Undergraduate	839	965	1,109	1,142	1,142	1,142	36.2
Graduate	1,773	2,039	2,549	2,626	2,626	2,626	48.1

Source: Florida Senate, Ways and Means Committee, *A Statistical Review*, 1990–91 to 1995–96 editions.

Community College Tuition

Student fees for the community colleges are set by the legislature, but individual colleges can vary their fees by as much as 10 percent above or below this state level. Full-time annual student fees at the community colleges rose from $766 in 1990–91 to $1,052 in 1994–95, about a 35 percent increase. In 1994–95, Florida ranked 31st in the nation in the fees charged at community colleges.

Independent Institutions

Tuition at the independent institutions, which increased 38 percent from 1989–90 to 1993–94, averaged $9,000 in 1993–94. This is still well below the national average for private institutions, although charges have continued to rise.[25]

Financial Aid

The Office of Student Financial Assistance is housed in the Florida Department of Education, and the executive director reports directly to the commissioner of public instruction. In 1995–96, the office administered aid for 32 programs totaling $119 million. The appropriated funding levels for the four largest state aid programs are shown in table 5.7. In terms of dollars, the Undergraduate Scholars Fund has experienced the most growth over the four years shown ($14 million). State programs such as these have continued to receive increases in funding and are widely viewed in the legislature as essential in providing students with access and choice. It is important to note, however, that during 1992–93, the state's two need-based programs, the Public Student Assistance Grant and the Private Student Assistance Grant, received cuts in funding at a time when enrollments and tuition were increasing.

TABLE 5.7

FINANCIAL AID PROGRAM FUNDING (IN MILLIONS OF DOLLARS)

	1990–91	1991–92	1992–93	1993–94	1994–95	1995–96
Undergrad. Scholar's Fund	19.3	22.9	23.0	25.0	30.7	33.2
Public Assistance Grant	16.0	20.2	18.5	21.0	22.3	27.6
Private Assistance Grant	7.3	7.4	6.1	6.9	7.1	7.3
Resident Access Grant	16.1	17.0	17.4	16.6	18.5	19.9

Sources: Consolidated from PEPC, *State Student Financial Aid Report* (Tallahassee, FL: 1996); and Florida Council of Student Financial Aid Advisors, *The Annual Report on State Financial Aid Programs, 1993 to 1995* (Tallahassee, FL).

The Undergraduate Scholar's Fund is Florida's oldest and largest merit-based scholarship program. Since legislators and others believed that Florida was losing talented students to out-of-state institutions, merit aid enjoyed steady annual increases since the late eighties. The Scholar's Fund provides support to encourage residents with strong academic records to attend either a public or private institution in the state. As of 1994, Florida's merit program represented over 30 percent of all state-funded merit aid nationwide.[26] Funds are provided to all eligible students. The maximum annual award in 1995–96 was $2,350.

The Florida Student Assistance Grant (FSAG) is divided into two major components: the Public Student Assistance Grant and the Private Student Assistance Grant. The public program provides need-based financial assistance grants to full-time public students at any two- or four-year institution. The private program is for students who attend an eligible independent, nonprofit Florida institution offering a four-year degree.

Each year, the actual FSAG award levels are determined not just by the appropriation level, but also by the number of recipients. If the actual number of qualified students applying for the award exceeds projections, the award level is reduced proportionately. In 1994–95, the average award amount was $646 for public community college students and $1,030 for state university students. The Private Student Assistant Grant maximum, which was $1,020 in 1994–95, increased to $1,230 in 1995–96.[27]

There is some concern among legislators and education officials about the widening difference between the cost of tuition and fees and the maximum available FSAG award. In 1993–94, tuition and fees exceeded the maximum award by more than 71 percent at the state universities and by 51 percent at the public community colleges. This differential may increase as more students participate in the program, and thereby drive award amounts down.[28]

The third largest financial aid program is the Florida Resident Access Grant (formerly called the Tuition Voucher Program). This program is neither need- nor merit-based; it provides tuition assistance to almost any full-time undergraduate student registered at an accredited independent, nonprofit college or university. Tuition voucher awards can range from a minimum of $1,150 to a maximum 40 percent of the state's cost per academic year for an undergraduate student in a state university. In 1995–96, the program received $19.8 million and the maximum award was $1,200. A higher education official said that 1996–97 will be an "interesting" year for the private sector; funding for the program is slated to increase nearly 50 percent to $28.8 million. In addition, the maximum award will increase from $500 to $1,800.

Some state officials feel that there is a need to consolidate the number of grant programs. Others believe, however, that legislative resistance to altering the programs would be very strong, since each program has the support of vocal and influential constituents.

Although the state has several financial aid programs, the federal government is by far the largest provider of student aid in Florida. While loan data are
somewhat incomplete for higher education as a whole in Florida, the SUS
financial aid picture (table 5.8) provides a good indication of where aid is
coming from. As this table reveals, total financial aid to the SUS has increased
by $273 million from 1990–91 to 1994–95. The bulk of this increase was due
to federal loans.

TABLE 5.8						
FINANCIAL AID AWARD SOURCE FOR STATE UNIVERSITY SYSTEM (IN MILLIONS OF DOLLARS)						
	1990–91	1991–92	1992–93	1993–94	1994–95	Total % Change
Federal	174.4	215.6	256.3	347.5	403.1	131
State	33.1	37.8	35.5	41.1	47.1	42
Institutional	29.6	36.0	41.9	47.6	49.2	66
Private	9.2	11.6	13.1	14.7	20.4	122
Other	0.05	0.05	0.04	0.04	0.14	180
Total	246.6	301.0	346.8	450.9	519.9	111

Source: Florida Senate, Ways and Means Committee, A *Statistical Review*, 1991–92 to 1995–96
editions.

As in other states during the first half of the 1990s, students in Florida have
become increasingly reliant on loans to fund their education. Of the $247
million in SUS financial aid in 1990–91, loans accounted for 52 percent of the
total, grants 27 percent, scholarships 18 percent, and student employment 3
percent. By 1994–95, loans were nearly 65 percent of the total, grants 19
percent, scholarships 15 percent, and student employment just over 1 percent.[29]

Financial aid information concerning the private sector and the public
community colleges is not as readily available. Aggregated data from the
department of education summaries, however, reveal that the private sector
received approximately $30.6 million through indirect state funding mecha-
nisms in 1991–92. By 1994–95, this amount grew to $32.4 million (esti-
mated), a meager growth rate that was impacted by the increased participation of the public sector in many of these programs. Public community colleges
received $10.8 million and $17.8 million for 1991–92 and 1994–95, respectively.[30]

Florida students also contribute to financial aid through "recycled" tuition
revenue. The state authorizes the board of regents to charge a financial aid fee
equal to 5 percent of matriculation fees. The legislature also authorizes
community colleges to collect 5 percent of matriculation fees to be used for
financial aid. One respondent said this percentage has not changed very much

over the years, although there was an unsuccessful proposal during the last legislative session to remove the 5 percent limit. In 1994–95, the student aid generated from student fees was about $16 million for the SUS and $11 million for the community colleges.[31]

Student and Family Resources

Trends in Family Income

A recent study undertaken by PEPC on student income reveals that higher education in Florida, like some other of the case study states, is divided along lines of family income. According to this study, the median family income for dependent students attending public community colleges is about $37,000, while the median family income for dependent students at private and public four-year institutions is about $46,000 and $50,000, respectively. Sorting by student income within the public four-year institutions, which include regional universities and flagship research universities, was not completed. State officials did mention, however, that increasingly, the state's flagship institutions have tended to enroll higher proportions of students from upper-income families, while the regional public universities generally have higher proportions of students from middle-income families.

These findings concern some state officials who would like to see more student financial aid dollars targeted for needy students and for those students who attend private institutions, rather than subsidizing middle- and upper-income students at state universities.

Trends in Family Savings

According to state officials, the likelihood of saving for college rises dramatically with family income, but even among families with incomes above $60,000, slightly less than half have saved for college. In order to encourage parents to save for their children's education, Florida has initiated the Florida Prepaid College Program, which allows parents in Florida to contract with the state for two or four years of tuition in either a lump-sum amount or installment payments over as many as 18 years. The program also provides a dormitory contract option. Contracts may be transferred to siblings and the contract may be transferred to any independent nonprofit institution. If a child decides to enroll in an out-of-state college, the program will transfer either an amount equaling the value of Florida state tuition at the time of college enrollment or the amount paid in, plus 5 percent interest, whichever is less. If the beneficiary attends a community college instead of a state university, the difference in tuition is refunded.

The money is invested in a trust fund set up by the state and administered by the seven-member Florida Prepaid Postsecondary Education Expense Board.

The program is guaranteed by the State of Florida. Sixteen percent of the families in Florida who save for their children's education use the program. Currently, the Florida Prepaid Tuition program has more than 192,000 active accounts with projected future benefit payments in excess of $1.5 billion.[32]

THE 1990s AND BEYOND

Most respondents referred to five primary challenges that face Florida's system of higher education in the years to come: (1) growth and access; (2) productivity; (3) accountability; (4) the "deregulation" of higher education; and (5) higher education's role in economic development.

Growth and Access

Perhaps the most formidable challenge facing higher education in Florida during the next decade will be accommodating increasing student demand in the face of uncertain state support. Public universities and community colleges are each anticipating growth rates of over 30 percent into the year 2000, and much of the growth in enrollment is expected to be in the southern part of the state. The number of high school graduates is also projected to increase dramatically.[33]

One strategy for accommodating growth proposed by the SUS Board of Regents would allow 20 percent of Florida's high school graduates to enroll as first-time-in-college (FTIC) students at state universities, as opposed to the current policy of 15 percent. The commissioner of education convened a special council that endorsed this proposal and recommended further study to determine appropriate policy into the next century. Many others in the state, on the other hand, believe that community college and vocational offerings should be expanded to accommodate the additional students.

Partly in reaction to the regents' proposal, PEPC recommended that the legislative funding formula for the university system include a new allocation process designed to fund FTIC students for lower-level instruction costs only. PEPC summed up its position by stating that "the commission recognizes and supports the importance of public service and research in the state universities but believes that these functions should not be components of undergraduate enrollment funding."[34] This proposal drew negative reactions from university officials, and the legislature has not yet acted on it.

Another attempt to expand access was the recent action of the Florida legislature to limit the state-funded credit hours to 60 hours for an associate degree and to 120 hours for the baccalaureate degree. Before establishing this limit, the legislature embarked on a study that revealed that excess hours often exacerbate articulation problems and limit course availability. One legislator summed up how this relates to access when he said, "the purpose of the new initiative is to save money through reducing the number of excess credits the students take and to use this money to fund the new students who are coming down the pike."

Opening the new campus in the southern part of the state will also help to accommodate future enrollment growth. The Florida Gulf Coast University is scheduled to open in 1997 with a projected enrollment of about 1,000 FTE students, and it is predicted to grow to 4,000 FTE students by 2003. A 10-year enrollment cap of 8,100 students was recommended by PEPC, with enrollment expected to double to over 16,000 in 25 years.[35]

Expanding capacity at existing institutions is also being encouraged. A challenge grant program was initiated to encourage public institutions to seek funding from private sources for capital development.

Surveys are underway to gather information about the availability of capacity in the private sector as well. State officials frequently mentioned their interest in "buying" spaces in independent institutions. The independent sector has even offered to provide graduate programs at the new Gulf Coast University, thereby saving the state this investment. One representative of the independent sector stated that the University of Miami could provide most, if not all, of the graduate programs for the new university.

Productivity

Legislation to limit the number of hours for an associate and baccalaureate degree has been the legislature's major effort to improve productivity in higher education. The legislature allowed the board of regents to make exceptions to the caps for programs that demand more time.

Although discussed less frequently, an equally important aspect of the legislative cap is the limit of 36 credit hours for general education courses. A legislative staff member stated that the limit exists simply to get faculty to make sure that students are not taking more classes than they need. The state also is trying to improve teaching quality by offering up to $5,000 increases in base salaries for exemplary teachers.

One legislator noted that tenure is also an issue and will be a topic of upcoming legislative sessions. The board of regents has planned a "retreat" to talk about tenure and alternatives to it in early 1996. As one newspaper editor noted, "Tenure will be under fire in 1996." A university observer said, however, that tenure is one of the last issues that the legislature wants to tackle. Florida Gulf Coast University, the new public campus, is hiring professors on multiyear contracts instead of offering tenure. These multiyear contracts, which are the result of a negotiated agreement between the board of regents and the union, are being tested on the new campus.

Accountability

All state agencies in Florida have or are in the process of moving toward performance-based budgeting, a result of Governor Chiles' efforts to "reinvent" government. According to the governor's office, each state agency will be required to identify goals over a specified time period. In exchange for specifically identifying goals (and measures to assess progress toward them), agencies will be given funding in lump sums, with increased management flexibility.

Both the SUS and the CCS have been asked to submit accountability plans, the first step in implementing performance-based budgeting in higher education in the state. The community colleges will be the first to submit a performance-based budget in 1996–97. The university system will also be required by the legislature to produce a performance-based budget, but the implementation year for this requirement has not yet been established.

Deregulation

Early in 1995, after the legislature proposed a 25 percent cut to the SUS, the chancellor responded by submitting a "deregulation" plan requesting a lump-sum appropriation with no strings attached. While many discussions were held about the plan, no legislative action was taken and the system actually received an increase in funding rather than the proposed decrease.

In the last few months of 1995, talk about "deregulation" surfaced again, this time in a controversial proposal by UF president John Lombardi. As a result of Lombardi's close work with the legislative leaders on credit-hour issues, discussions were being held about how to reduce the costs of higher education over the long term. Lombardi wrote a draft proposal, "Improving Efficiency and Accountability: Deregulating University Instructional Funding," which called for providing a maximum number of educational "credits" to Florida students admitted to any Florida college or university. The credits would be transferable from institution to institution. Students would choose where to use their educational credits, based on institutional programs and a host of other market-related factors. Since institutions would then be free to set tuition according to the market value of their programs and services, tuition rates would vary within the university system. Lombardi's proposal also described incentives provided to students and institutions through this model.

State University System regents were infuriated that Lombardi shared his proposal with legislative leaders before engaging in a full discourse with system leaders, and they let him know it. The animosity from all sides has since cooled, but some legislators, still angered by the system's response to Lombardi's letter, introduced a bill that significantly weakens the authority of the system office and changes the chancellor's title to executive director. The legislature has not acted on this legislation, and most higher education observers said the controversy had already died. According to one respondent, "It vanished as quickly as it arose." Nonetheless, the concept of deregulation, so long as it is accompanied by greater accountability, does seem to interest many state lawmakers.

Economic Development

While not mentioned with the same frequency as other key issues, several legislators spoke about higher education as a tool for economic development in the state. Respondents discussed the importance of vocational education and school-to-work programs as a critical strategy for economic development. A legislative committee chair said the connection between education and work is crucial, not just for individuals, but also for the state.

The Florida Department of Labor and Employment Security expects that the services and trade industries will generate more than 60 percent of new jobs between 1991 and 2005. Since most of the jobs those sectors generate will require a bachelor's degree, higher education in Florida will play a critical role in the state's economy in the foreseeable future.[36]

CONCLUSION

From 1990 to 1995, increases in state funding for the community colleges and for the SUS lagged behind all other major state spending categories. During this period, state funding per FTE student dropped significantly. Despite this fiscal tightening, however, Florida's public system of higher education has steadily enrolled more students year after year. The system is in the process of building a new university along the Gulf Coast. Unlike most other states, increases in tuition rates have remained moderate. Meanwhile, enrollments have continued to increase, though at slower rates than before the recession. All of these factors suggest that Florida, in spite of its recession, has been able to maintain its emphasis on access in higher education.

Yet Florida faces, as the chair of the state board of regents said, a "difficult budgetary future." The state's narrow tax base and its antitax electorate are likely to limit revenue growth. At the same time, projected demographic trends will most likely place rising demands on expenditures, especially in corrections and K–12 education. With the number of high school graduates expected to increase by almost 29 percent over the next 10 years, elected officials and higher education administrators will be faced with difficult choices concerning *how* and *whether* tomorrow's qualified high school graduates will have adequate opportunity to enroll in the state's institutions of higher education.

Historically, the Florida legislature has been very active in higher education issues, and it appears such involvement will continue. It remains to be seen how well the legislature's incentive program will prompt community colleges to establish and meet outcome measures. It is uncertain how well the new limits on state-funded credit hours will improve productivity concerning time-to-degree; and it is unclear whether the newly required accountability plans will press the community colleges and the SUS to begin moving toward performance-based budgeting. One thing is certain, however; many states will be watching.

NOTES

1. Calculated from table 5.3.
2. *Chronicle of Higher Education Almanac* 42, no. 1 (September 1995), p. 46.
3. Susan A. MacManus, "Florida: Reinvention Derailed," in *The Fiscal Crisis of the States: Lessons for the Future*, edited by Steven D. Gold (Washington, D.C.: Georgetown University Press, 1995), p. 202.
4. Ibid., p. 198.
5. Appropriations, revenue, and other budgetary data in this chapter are presented in fiscal years, unless otherwise noted.
6. MacManus, "Florida: Reinvention Derailed," pp. 224–25.
7. Calculated from MacManus, "Florida: Reinvention Derailed," pp. 224-25, and table 5.2 in this chapter.
8. Kent Halstead, *State Profiles: Financing Public Higher Education, 1978 to 1996 Trend Data* (Washington, D.C.: Research Associates of Washington, 1996), p. 18.
9. Kent Halstead, *State Profiles: Financing Public Higher Education, 1996 Rankings* (Washington, D.C.: Research Associates of Washington, 1996), pp. 22–23.
10. Ibid., p. 25.
11. *Chronicle of Higher Education Almanac* 42, p. 45.
12. MacManus, "Florida: Reinvention Derailed," p. 208.
13. MultiState Associates, Inc., "Florida," in *Multistate Perspective: Legislative Outlook 1996* (Alexandria, VA: 1996), p. 12.
14. James Burns, J. W. Peltason, and Thomas Cronin, *State and Local Politics: Government by the People* (Upper Saddle River, NJ: Prentice Hall, 1990), p. 113.
15. MultiState Associates, Inc., "Florida," p. 5.
16. *Chronicle of Higher Education Almanac* 43, no. 1 (September 1996), p. 50.
17. Florida Postsecondary Education Planning Commission, *Access to the Baccalaureate Degree in Florida*, Report 4 (Tallahassee, FL: 1994), p. 6.
18. Ibid., p. 9.
19. Ibid., p. 12.
20. Florida State Senate, Ways and Means Committee, *A Statistical Review of Education in Florida, 1994–95* (Tallahassee, 1994), p. 136.

21. Kent Halstead, *State Profiles: Financing Public Higher Education 1978 to 1994* (Washington, D.C.: Research Associates of Washington, 1994), p. 57.
22. Halstead, *State Profiles, Rankings* (1996), pp. 18–19.
23. Ibid., p. 19.
24. Washington State Higher Education Coordinating Board, *Tuition and Fee Rates, 1995–96: A National Comparison* (Olympia: 1996), p. 5.
25. Florida State Department of Education, *State of Florida Financial Aid Programs Legislative Report* (Tallahassee: 1994), p. 17.
26. Ibid., pp. 8–9.
27. State of Florida, Department of Education, *Financial Aid Programs Legislative Report* (Tallahassee: 1994), p. 2, with an update from department of education staff.
28. Ibid., p. 3.
29. State University Systems, *Fact Book for SUS, 1994–95* (Tallahassee: 1995).
30. State of Florida, Department of Education, Office of Student Financial Aid, *State Student Aid Expenditures Report* (Tallahassee: 1991–92 to 1994–95 editions).
31. Florida Senate, Ways and Means Committee, *A Statistical Review of Education in Florida, 1995–96* (Tallahassee, FL: 1995).
32. The Florida Prepaid College Program, *The Florida Prepaid College Program: How You Can Be Ready for College When Your Kids Are* (Tallahassee: 1995), p. 2.
33. Florida Postsecondary Education Planning Commission, *Access*, p. A7.
34. Ibid., p. iv.
35. Ibid., p. 6.
36. Ibid., p. A4.

CHAPTER 6

Michigan

Fiscal Stability and Constitutional Autonomy

Mario C. Martinez and Thad Nodine

T his chapter focuses on the primary fiscal issues affecting Michigan's system of higher education from 1990 to 1995. Interviews with public officials and higher education administrators were conducted in the state from September through November 1995. Data were collected through December 1996.

While the recession of the early 1990s hit Michigan hard, the economic slowdown was not nearly as deep or as prolonged as the recession that hit the state in the late 1970s and early 1980s. During the early 1990s, state revenues increased slowly each year except for fiscal year 1991, which saw a slight decline in revenues. At the same time that state revenues were increasing slowly, however, expenditures were increasing dramatically. The state carried a budget deficit (that was balanced on paper) until a new governor instituted spending cuts and accounting changes that brought state expenditures in line with revenues.

During this period of slow economic growth, state funding for higher education increased in Michigan, both in real and nominal terms. In fact, appropriations for higher education increased every year from 1992 to 1995, and would have increased in 1991 as well, if not for a shift in the fiscal year. From 1990–91 to 1995–96, enrollments in postsecondary institutions declined, causing state funding per student to increase even more than it would have if enrollments had remained steady.

Despite this increase in state funding per student, tuition increased significantly in Michigan's public colleges and universities from 1991 to 1996. This increase in tuition, which reflects a nationwide trend, has been particularly troubling for Michigan's elected officials because the state's public institutions have some of the highest tuition rates in the country. Since Michigan also ranks high in state appropriations per student, there is ongoing public concern about the affordability of Michigan's public system of higher education—both in terms of cost to the state and cost to students and families. For instance, several public officials expressed concern about whether qualified students with limited financial resources will be priced out of the college market.

Although the constitutional autonomy of public colleges and universities in Michigan limits the power of the legislature in influencing enrollment patterns and tuition levels, it cannot adequately account for the fiscal, enrollment, and tuition patterns in Michigan during the early 1990s. The legislature can influence institutional behavior through budget negotiations, yet during the severe recession in Michigan in the early 1980s, lawmakers chose to abandon the state's budget formulas for public four-year institutions of higher education. Since then, budgets have been disconnected from enrollment levels and other factors, and based instead on the previous year's allocations. This approach values past decisions about base funding levels at the expense of current policy decisions or future state needs. It also inadvertently rewards institutions that experience decreases in enrollment. Perhaps most importantly, however, it replaces long-term budget strategies with short-term, incremental negotiations.

A recent event has contributed an unpredictable quality to the budget process as well. In the past, university presidents always consulted with each other as a group and arrived at a consensus concerning the budgetary increases that each institution would seek from the legislature that year. The 1995 process saw a break in this tradition, however, as the president of Michigan State University negotiated with legislators and secured a significant increase in state funds without the consensus of fellow presidents. This event provides an example of the indirect influence that the legislature can wield through the budget process—despite the united front that the colleges and universities attempt to maintain. Some people in Michigan saw this as an attempt by the state—and an institution of higher education—to respond to priorities, particularly around the technology agenda. Others (mostly at institutions), however, thought it was an attempt to increase the political power of Michigan State University (MSU) and thereby undermine the consensus process of the presidents.

Since constitutional autonomy provides public colleges and universities with the power to set their own tuition levels, legislators must use the budget process and other means if they wish to influence tuition rates. Discussions about tuition levels are part of annual budget negotiations, but growing concern about high tuition rates recently led legislators to implement statewide savings mechanisms. Legislators also recently implemented tax break incentives to individuals who enroll in an institution that has limited its tuition increases. While these means of influencing tuition appear to be having some effect on institutional behavior, they have also caused significant controversy over who has the right to control tuition in Michigan's public institutions. Officials from colleges and universities claim that indirect means of controlling tuition through tax incentives violates the institutions' constitutional autonomy. Elected officials are split on this issue, and several have backed away from their previous support of the tax credit.

At the same time that enrollments in Michigan's 15 public four-year institutions and 29 public community colleges have been declining, enrollments in the state's 52 private institutions have been slowly increasing. Although the numbers served by the private sector are dwarfed by comparison to the public sector, the private sector fulfills a necessary—and growing—role, particularly in serving nontraditional and minority students. Unlike most other states, Michigan has a higher percentage of minority enrollment in its private colleges than in its public institutions. The state provides direct grants to independent institutions based on the number of Michigan residents who graduate from them. Several state-sponsored scholarship and grant programs are also tailored exclusively for students attending private institutions.

In spite of the controversies over the budget process and the setting of tuition, Michigan's state leaders appear satisfied that their system of higher education provides quality education to Michigan residents. Critics of constitutional autonomy contend that it is responsible for high tuition rates and for insulating institutions of higher education from greater accountability for their use of state funds. Yet voters have not clamored for lower tuition rates. Michigan's legislators have not demanded outcome data from public colleges and universities. And the governor and state lawmakers seem satisfied with the incremental budget process for funding public institutions of higher education. Within this political context, state resources and tuition revenues over the past five years have been sufficient to meet the growing costs of Michigan's public colleges and universities. As long as this continues to be the case, the state appears willing to let the "market" determine how Michigan's public colleges and universities meet the higher education needs of Michigan's residents.

STATE CONTEXT

Michigan, with nearly 9.5 million residents, ranks fourth in size among the five study states, and eighth in the United States. About 17 percent of Michigan's population is comprised of minority groups compared with about 20 percent nationally. Michigan residents are relatively young and about average in terms of wealth and disposable income. Educational attainment is slightly below average, although the percentage of the population receiving an associate's degree is higher than the national average. The percentage of families living in poverty and the percentage of 18-year-olds who are high school graduates are also close to national averages. The state has a low high school dropout rate and a low percentage of families who do not speak English in the home.[1]

Because of the decline in the automobile industry, the late 1970s and early 1980s were more traumatic for the Michigan economy than the recession of the early 1990s. Real personal income, for instance, dropped much more dramatically from 1979 to 1982 than it did during the early 1990s, when it fell both in 1990 and 1991. Beginning in 1992, real personal income began growing significantly.[2]

During the early 1990s, state revenues increased slowly each year except for fiscal year 1991, which saw a slight decline in revenues. In each of the fiscal years from 1990 to 1993, however, state revenues fell short of budgeted projections, with the worst years being 1991 and 1992. At the same time that state revenues were increasing slowly, however, expenditures were increasing dramatically. Like many states, Michigan experienced dramatic increases in caseloads and spending commitments for social services. Increases in corrections spending were even more dramatic, causing appropriations to corrections to reach unparalleled levels both in overall amounts and in percentage increases. Although in 1990 most of the budgetary shortfall was "balanced" by shifting funds and making other accounting adjustments, in fiscal year 1991, with a new Republican governor at the helm, the state began making significant long-term cuts in spending, many of which came in midyear negotiations. The cuts in spending, combined with accounting changes and increased federal payments, brought state expenditures in line with revenues by fiscal year 1993. By 1994, a strong economic recovery was in full swing in Michigan.[3]

Although Michigan's economy is still intricately tied to automobile manufacturing, the state is not as dependent on the automobile industry as it once was. The automobile industry traditionally supplied Michigan residents with a large number of manufacturing jobs, offering starting wages to high school graduates that were higher than typical starting salaries offered to college graduates in service industries. For the first time in Michigan's history, however, service jobs now outnumber manufacturing jobs. As these lower paying service jobs have become a larger part of the economy, the standard of living has dropped slightly. In 1993, Michigan's income per capita was 2 percent below the national average, compared to 8 percent above the national average in the late 1970s.[4]

Another economic transformation that took place in the early 1990s involves the state's revenue structure. Compared to national averages, the state in 1991 relied excessively on property and personal income taxes (see table 6.1). By 1995, however, the state reduced the share of revenues generated by property and personal income taxes, while raising the share generated by sales taxes.[5]

TABLE 6.1

REVENUE BY SOURCE (IN PERCENT)

	1991 Michigan	U.S. Average	1995 Michigan
Property Tax	35.7	31.0	29.0
Personal Income Tax	26.3	21.1	23.3
Sales Tax	16.6	24.2	24.4

Source: Robert J. Kleine, Public Sector Consultants, Inc., Lansing, Michigan, personal communication, 29 February 1996.

The Michigan state budget is divided into three major funds: general fund or general purpose (commonly referred to as the general fund), special purpose, and special revenue. Although the general fund has historically reflected the state's major transactions, the other funds have grown in importance. For example, a key recipient of the special revenue fund is the K–12 system, which receives much of its money through the state school aid fund. The school aid fund receives restricted allocations from sources such as revenues from the taxes on cigarettes and liquor. In addition, as general fund spending for social services was drastically cut during the fiscal shortfalls of the early 1990s, other funding sources, such as the special fund and the special revenue fund, became increasingly important in meeting state needs.

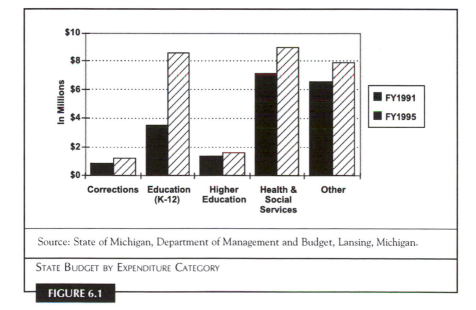

Source: State of Michigan, Department of Management and Budget, Lansing, Michigan.

STATE BUDGET BY EXPENDITURE CATEGORY

FIGURE 6.1

Since large amounts of K–12 education and health-care–related spending draw from several state funding sources, it is instructive to look at state expenditure categories to understand the contextual climate of Michigan's budget. Michigan's total 1991 and 1995 state budgets (for all three funds) are compared in figure 6.1, with expenditure categories simplified to avoid unnecessary detail.

As figure 6.1 shows, the increase in education (K–12) spending represents the most significant change from 1991 to 1995. This increase is attributed to school finance reform, which replaced a large share of local property taxes with state-level taxes, mainly in the form of an increase in the sales tax rate and a statewide school property tax.[6]

Since public institutions of higher education receive virtually all of their state funding from the general fund, it is also helpful to examine the general fund in isolation. Table 6.2, in providing the major spending categories for the state general fund only, shows the annual percentage increases and decreases over the last five years. The last column shows the percentage change from fiscal years 1991 to 1995. The national Consumer Price Index (CPI) is also provided.

TABLE 6.2

CHANGE IN GENERAL FUND SPENDING CATEGORIES (IN PERCENT)

	1991	1992	1993	1994	1995	Change 1991–95
Corrections	7.2	10.9	11.9	8.1	11.8	50.1
Education (K–12)*	29.2	(13.3)	28.1	(34.0)	(4.8)	(30.2)
Higher Education	(3.5)†	13.4†	0.9	0.3	3.3	18.4
Health and Social Services	(5.6)	(11.4)	1.0	3.6	5.1	(2.6)
U.S. CPI§	4.2	3.0	3.0	2.6	2.8	11.9

* The education (K–12) general fund category does not include the state school aid fund, which accounts for the decrease in funding shown in this category. See figure 6.1 for a more comprehensive picture of K–12 funding over the past five years.

† A shift in the timing of the fiscal year for higher education accounts for most of the discrepancy between these figures for 1991 and 1992. Actual state-appropriated funds available to universities for spending during these years grew about 4 percent in both 1991 and 1992.

§ CPI figures are for calendar rather than fiscal years.

Sources: State of Michigan, Department of Management and Budget, Lansing, Michigan. The CPI data are from the U.S. Department of Labor, Bureau of Labor Statistics, "Consumer Price Index for All Urban Consumers, U.S. City Average," October 1996.

Despite competition for state dollars and unprecedented increases in funding for corrections, higher education fared well. Higher education's growth from 1991 to 1995 outpaced inflation by almost 6 percent. This level of funding is particularly impressive when considering that many other states were decreasing appropriations to higher education during the same period.

In addition, even during the worst years, when legislators were making significant cuts in appropriations as a result of midyear fiscal shortfalls, higher education fared much better than most state services in Michigan. For instance, from fiscal year 1991 to 1993, state services such as agriculture, commerce, social services, and K–12 education received double-digit percentage reductions from budgeted general fund appropriation levels. Higher education, on the other hand, received only a 2.7 percent reduction from budgeted appropriations levels during this period.[7]

Kent Halstead, of Research Associates of Washington, offers some useful measures to assess state support of public higher education. Table 6.3 provides several of these measures comparing Michigan to national averages for fiscal years 1991 and 1996. State dollar amounts have been adjusted for inflation by the System Support Index (SSI). The SSI adjusts for two factors: (1) the effect of the cost of living on salary payment schedules, and (2) the effect of differing enrollment mixes in different states due to the academic level of the state's students and the types of institutions in the state.

TABLE 6.3

STATE SUPPORT FOR PUBLIC HIGHER EDUCATION (IN DOLLARS)

	Michigan		National Average	
	1991	1996	1991	1996
Tax Revenue Per Capita	2,063	2,638	2,011	2,535
Appropriations Per FTE Student*	4,194	5,163	4,364	4,801
% of Taxes Allocated to Higher Education	7.3	6.5	7.0	6.0

* FTE stands for full-time-equivalent.

Source: Kent Halstead, *State Profiles: Financing Public Higher Education, 1978 to 1996 Trend Data* (Washington, D.C.: Research Associates of Washington, 1996), pp. 45–48.

In 1990–91, Michigan was slightly above the national average for two of the three measures shown in table 6.3. By 1995–96, the state had moved above the national average for the third measure as well: appropriations per full-time-equivalent (FTE) student. Taken together, these three measures point to the higher cost to the state—compared to national averages—of Michigan's public colleges and universities. They can also be seen as evidence of higher fiscal commitment by the state to its system of higher education.

Several factors caused the increases in the measures for Michigan in table 6.3. Most importantly, Michigan's appropriations to higher education increased while many other states' appropriations were decreasing. The result was that the national average either decreased (see the last measure in table 6.3) or did not grow as fast as the Michigan measure (see the appropriation per FTE student). Second, Michigan's public student enrollment (measured by FTE) declined from 334,443 in 1990–91 to 316,400 in 1995–96.[8] A decline in student enrollment combined with increasing state appropriations for higher education produced a higher appropriation per FTE student during this period. Finally, Michigan would be expected to show a higher appropriation per FTE student than most other states because its community college system accounts for a smaller proportion of enrollments than in some other states. Full-Time-Equivalent students in the community college system lower the appropriation per FTE measure because community colleges are less expensive per student than four-year institutions. Yet one of the interesting features of table 6.3 is that it shows that in 1991, Michigan's appropriation per FTE student, in spite of the state's relatively small community college system, was well below the national average. By 1996, it was significantly above the national average.

It is important to note that Halstead's measures do not account for state dollars that go to private institutions or students who attend private institutions; Michigan has several state programs that support the private sector.

Another way to measure a state's fiscal commitment to higher education is to look at the percentage of state and local taxes allocated to public higher education. Figure 6.2 compares Michigan with national averages in this area over a six-year period. On a percentage basis, higher education's share of the state and local budget declined slightly in Michigan, but still remains well above the national average.

POLITICAL CLIMATE

Michigan has been characterized as a strong governor state, largely due to the influence of the governor in creating the budget and exercising line-item veto authority.[9] In fact, several state officials mentioned that the governor's budget provides the foundation for state spending levels; subsequent adjustments by the legislature are usually minor. State officials also noted that the governor's veto power is taken quite seriously.

Governor John Engler, a Republican in his second term, has worked with a Republican-controlled house and senate since the 1994 elections. Although Governor Engler received national attention for his refusal to rely on tax

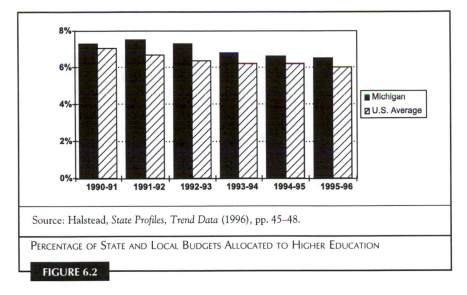

Source: Halstead, *State Profiles, Trend Data* (1996), pp. 45–48.

PERCENTAGE OF STATE AND LOCAL BUDGETS ALLOCATED TO HIGHER EDUCATION

FIGURE 6.2

increases to balance the budget, this had been standard practice in Michigan since 1983. The recession of the early 1990s, however, highlighted the governor's strategy both within Michigan and on a national level, since other states were implementing tax increases to balance their budgets. His campaign commitments also included downsizing government, reducing social services, revitalizing the economy, improving K–12 education, and shifting the burdens of the tax system by reducing property taxes and increasing sales taxes.

Some experts in the state speculate that although the Republicans do appear to be in ascendancy in the state, term limits may be the wild card in the state's political future. For the first time, representatives have term limits of six years, senators have eight years, and the governor has 12 years (or three consecutive terms). Although the effects of these term limits are not yet known, they could shift power from the legislature to the governor's office (due to the longer time in office allowed for the governor), and they could enhance the influence of the administrative branch generally and of institutions of higher education, since cabinet, career, and university officials could have longer tenures in office than legislators.

GOVERNANCE AND THE POLITICS OF CONSTITUTIONAL AUTONOMY

Michigan differs from the other study states in that it has no statewide agency responsible for the coordination or governance of higher education. Moreover, Michigan's public colleges and universities are constitutionally autonomous, which means that their governing boards have exclusive management responsibility for their institutions.

Michigan's three largest public universities (University of Michigan, Michigan State University, and Wayne State University) have governing boards that are elected. The board of regents for the University of Michigan (UM) also has responsibility for the three branches of the university (Ann Arbor, Dearborn, and Flint). Although the governor appoints the remaining 10 university boards, Governor Engler has made public comments indicating his preference for appointed boards throughout the system. Public two-year community colleges have governing boards elected from the region they serve.

Although constitutional autonomy dates to 1850 when UM became the first institution in the country to be extended such status,[10] the tradition has evolved over time. Michigan's constitutional language regarding institutional autonomy was refined in 1963.[11] Also, institutions periodically "remind" the state of their autonomy through legal means. One president said he expected the number of lawsuits to increase due to term limits and the accompanying need to preserve constitutional autonomy in light of new members of the legislature who may want to challenge it. While this comment may indeed reflect a need to preserve constitutional autonomy, it also reflects the political realities of term limits: law suits can last longer than legislators' tenures in office.

The autonomy that the public system enjoys is both revered and criticized. Opponents contend that autonomy is responsible for high tuition rates and for insulating higher education from greater accountability for the spending of tax dollars. Proponents argue, on the other hand, that constitutional autonomy is largely responsible for the high quality of Michigan's system of public higher education. Proponents also argue that constitutional autonomy allows the market to establish tuition rates and determine program offerings as well. In relation to programs, for instance, Western Michigan University recently set up and marketed an evening MBA program in Lansing since MSU was not offering an evening MBA program there. The success of the program eventually prompted MSU to reconsider offering evening MBA courses. "Now, because MSU wasn't responsive at first, we have two program offerings in Lansing," said a public official.

Although the autonomy of the public system of higher education is both revered and criticized, there is widespread agreement among state officials and university presidents that constitutional autonomy has served the state well, particularly during times of economic difficulty. One president said, "The advantage of the Michigan system is that each board can make knowledgeable decisions with regard to its institution that a centralized board could not—especially during hard times. This is how we survived the deep budget cuts in the early eighties."

State Information on Higher Education

The governor and legislators receive information about higher education through three primary sources: the Michigan Department of Management and Budget (DMB), the house and senate fiscal agencies, and the institutions themselves. The DMB prepares the governor's budget. The DMB and the house and senate fiscal agencies collect financial and statistical information on institutions electronically and use it as their primary source of information for lawmakers. The Higher Education Institutional Data Inventory (HEIDI) is the state data base and is housed at the DMB. HEIDI primarily contains information on institutional revenues and expenditures, but also includes salary and enrollment data. The house and senate fiscal agencies create profiles of each public institution based on HEIDI information. Analysts also use the federal Integrated Postsecondary Education Data System (IPEDS) data base when necessary.

The fact that HEIDI is housed at the DMB is the result of a strategic effort by higher education officials. Administrators feel there is less political intrusion with HEIDI located at DMB, rather than at the Michigan Department of Education.

HEIDI is not a data-rich source of information. Rather than providing performance or outcome data, it reports input data. Yet legislators appear satisfied with the kinds of information they receive through HEIDI, for they have not requested more strenuous outcome measures. "With the level of analysis actually requested by state officials," a budget manager said, "it is hard to get a true sense of efficiency in the system."

The governor and the chairs of the house and senate appropriations committees communicate frequently with university presidents, both as a group and individually. Presidents and other administrators appear before committees to testify regarding funding requests. In addition, almost all universities have a vice president for governmental affairs and have substantial lobbying presence in Michigan. In general, the senators and legislators we interviewed said that administrators are cognizant of legislative priorities. Most ascribed this to good rapport between the legislature and the higher education community—and the threat of reduced funding.

University presidents also communicate with lawmakers through a voluntary association called the Presidents Council. The council is composed of presidents of public four-year institutions. Although the council meets regularly to discuss issues relating to funding, enrollment, capital projects, or other concerns of public institutions, its most important role has been to seek to present its members' budgetary needs to the legislature in a united front. Several public officials, however, used words like "highly symbolic" to describe the council.

Although some state officials offered criticisms of the public higher education sector, there is also widespread belief in the state that it is one of the finest in the country. Senators and representatives told us that people think the public system is doing a fine job of providing quality education. While some legislators expressed concern about rising tuition rates and low minority retention, most of those interviewed expressed the belief that the system is working, improving, and growing in prominence.

Those working in state offices that deal with appropriations data, however, suggest that legislative satisfaction is not based on solid evidence. Several budget staff members described the system as sound, but said there is no comparative data to substantiate comments about overall quality. A representative confirmed this when he said, "The legislature is generally satisfied with higher education in Michigan, but not really very well equipped to evaluate it."

The Debate over Tuition

The legislature is not, however, satisfied with tuition rates in Michigan. Almost every state official we spoke with expressed ongoing concern about high tuition. Since constitutional autonomy allows the public institutions to set their own tuition rates, legislators can voice displeasure and can indirectly try to influence tuition through budgetary and other means, but they cannot dictate tuition rates. University presidents describe this as "allowing the market" to set tuition.

The two primary means that lawmakers have to influence tuition rates are through the budgetary process and the creation of new laws. Discussions about tuition rates are part of annual higher education budget negotiations, and have had some impact on institutional behavior in the setting of tuition. As far back as 1986, legislators also tried to institute a prepaid tuition program to help families cope with the cost of college. The plan became mired in a legal fight with the Internal Revenue Service (IRS), however, which was settled only recently, when a federal court ruled against the IRS in 1995.

In another attempt to provide an "incentive" for institutions to hold back on tuition increases, lawmakers passed a bill that provides tax incentives for individuals who enroll in an institution that caps its tuition increase at the previous year's inflation rate. Governor Engler signed the bill into law in March 1995. During 1995–96, only four of the state's four-year institutions met the criteria to offer the tax credit. Many higher education officials cried foul as allegations against the state ranged from attempting to control tuition to trying to score political points for lawmakers.[12] A state senator offered a different opinion when he said, "The tax credit let people decide to get a break at one institution if another wasn't keeping its costs down." In the aftermath, however, several legislators have suggested that the tax credit be reconsidered.

Many state employees view the furor over the tax credit as one example of higher education's excessive influence over the state whenever the state suggests its own priorities or attempts to monitor quality. One public official said there are many examples of the state attempting to establish programs or funding for assessing performance in some area, only to have the resources taken away. He believes the public higher education community successfully ended funding for two recent programs: an office to assess minority and women student retention and graduation rates, and a public opinion poll on higher education. An administrator in the independent higher education sector said the state board of education put some planning programs in place for public higher education, only to have the Supreme Court decide that the board had no such authority.

Although tuition is the dominant state concern regarding higher education, there are others. One administrator said, "The state cannot control growth at the institutions," and believes this is problematic from a statewide perspective. Several respondents who characterized duplication as a worrisome side effect of the Michigan system claimed that the state produces five times as many teachers as it needs. Defenders of constitutional autonomy for Michigan's colleges and universities counter that the higher education community is more in tune with state needs regarding higher education than is the legislature. The defenders are also quick to assert that the market provides the best controls for both enrollment levels and program development. If a program is not in demand, they claim, it will eliminate itself. And for the time being at least, they appear to have the ear of legislators.

CHARACTERISTICS OF HIGHER EDUCATION

In terms of overall enrollment, Michigan's system of higher education is dominated by public institutions. The state has 15 public four-year institutions, 29 public community colleges, and 52 private two-year and four-year institutions, but almost 85 percent of students are enrolled in public institutions.

The Role of Private Institutions

Although the numbers served by the private sector are dwarfed by comparison to the public sector, the private sector fulfills a necessary—and growing—role in the state. Some studies even classify the state's private sector as playing a "major" role relative to other states.[13] In fact, while enrollments in Michigan's public system of higher education declined from fall 1991 to fall 1995, enrollments in private colleges and universities increased during the same period.

The state's commitment to its private institutions can be found in several state grant programs that provide direct funding to private colleges and universities, based on the number of graduates who are Michigan residents. One state tuition grant program provides support exclusively to Michigan residents who attend private institutions in-state. And several other grant and scholarship programs can be used by students at private colleges and universities. The president of a public institution expressed little concern when asked about public money going to private institutions and their students: "Some people are troubled by public dollars going to privates, some aren't. I believe the privates provide a liberal arts education that some students need and that we can't provide."

Several respondents mentioned that many private colleges and universities, particularly the newer ones, are quite sensitive to meeting the needs of nontraditional and minority students. Unlike most other states, Michigan has a higher percentage of minority enrollment in its private colleges than in its public institutions (see table 6.4). A member of the Independent College Association emphasized the importance of private higher education when he stated that 85 percent of the students in private colleges are state residents, and a large percentage are minorities (mostly African Americans).

TABLE 6.4

MINORITY ENROLLMENT IN PUBLIC AND PRIVATE INSTITUTIONS, FALL 1994 (IN PERCENT)

	Michigan	U.S. Average
Public 2-Year Institutions	15.4	27.7
Public 4-Year Institutions	15.8	21.3
Private 2-Year Institutions	19.4	25.8
Private 4-Year Institutions	20.0	19.3

Source: *Chronicle of Higher Education Almanac* 43, no. 1 (September 1996), p. 9.

Enrollment Data

In fall 1994, Michigan had the sixth largest higher education population in the nation, serving over 551,000 students. In fall 1993, Michigan actually served over 568,000 students, but, like many other midwestern states, the state experienced a decline in its fall 1994 student enrollment.[14] Only the private sector experienced an increase in student enrollment over the last five years. From fall 1991 to fall 1995, while enrollment at public community colleges decreased 6.7 percent and enrollment at public four-year institutions decreased 1.2 percent, enrollment at private institutions increased 2.9 percent.[15]

In relation to the future, higher education administrators used words like "moderate" and "steady" to describe enrollment levels over the next decade. Michigan has about an average number of high school graduates per capita (9.6),[16] and does not expect a dramatic change over the next several years. The Western Interstate Commission for Higher Education (WICHE) has likewise projected a moderate increase in high school graduates of less than 20 percent by 2009.[17]

Kent Halstead offers two indicators that provide insight into the access of a state's system of higher education. The first, the participation ratio (FTE public students in relation to new high school graduates), measures the size of the public system and the opportunity it provides to high school students based on this size. A large participation ratio indicates that the state has a large public system relative to its resident high school student source. Figure 6.3 shows that high school graduates have experienced a relatively stable level of opportunity to enroll in Michigan's public institutions since 1991–92.

Halstead's second indicator, student enrollment, is more broad and measures FTE public students per 1,000 residents. This measure can be interpreted a number of ways, from inferring opportunity available per capita to statewide educational achievement. Figure 6.4 reveals that Michigan's public

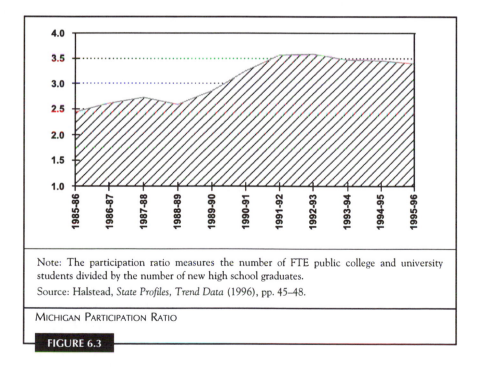

Note: The participation ratio measures the number of FTE public college and university students divided by the number of new high school graduates.

Source: Halstead, *State Profiles, Trend Data* (1996), pp. 45–48.

MICHIGAN PARTICIPATION RATIO

FIGURE 6.3

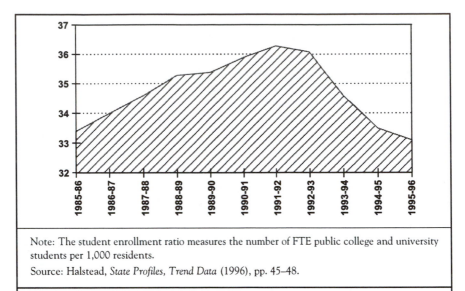

Note: The student enrollment ratio measures the number of FTE public college and university students per 1,000 residents.

Source: Halstead, *State Profiles, Trend Data* (1996), pp. 45–48.

MICHIGAN STUDENT ENROLLMENT RATIO

FIGURE 6.4

college and university student enrollment, relative to overall population, has been declining modestly since 1991–92.

From fall 1993 to 1996, the drop from 36 to 33 FTE students per 1,000 residents is a particularly moderate drop when considering that the main student source, high school graduates, actually dropped 9.2 percent from 1990–91 to 1995–96.[18] In 1995–96, Michigan ranked 18th (of all states) on the participation ratio and 23rd on the student enrollment ratio.[19]

STATE HIGHER EDUCATION SPENDING

The Budget Process

Public four-year institutions have not received allocations based on an enrollment-driven formula since the severe recession of the early 1980s, when the formula-driven methodology was abandoned. Public institutions receive state appropriations in a lump sum. The state does not exercise line-item control largely because of the constitutional status of four-year colleges and universities. The state does use a formula for allocation to the community colleges, however, and this formula takes enrollments into account.

The formal budget process begins in August and September. Although the DMB solicits yearly requests for funding from the public institutions, according to one employee, they are "not even really looked at because they are totally unrealistic." To develop a working budget for the governor, the DMB considers higher education in the context of the requests from other publicly funded functions. Discretionary dollars from the general fund are allocated to urgent areas first. Then the previous year's appropriations to each institution of higher education is considered in relation to higher education's revenue growth. The increase in higher education appropriations for each institution is best described as "incremental."

Capital outlay requests, which are considered separately, are sporadic and are not usually funded during times of economic difficulty. A senate aide told us that the 1994 session was the first time in a while that any institution received a significant capital project. According to this aide, the senator he worked for believed that each institution would eventually get a project, and that this would be equitable.

In February, after reviewing DMB recommendations, the governor submits an executive budget that the legislature considers through a series of appropriations bills. The house and senate make their adjustments and meet in joint committees to arrive at budgetary agreement. During this process, fiscal analysts are asked to look for additional information—in higher education as well as other areas—that might help the legislature make decisions. After the house and senate have jointly produced their budget it is sent back to the governor, who has line-item veto authority.

Unlike many other states, Michigan provides direct appropriations to independent institutions. These grants are based on the number of Michigan residents who graduate from the institution. The Mercy Dental School of the University of Detroit, for example, was given a block grant of about $4 million during 1994–95.[20] The Allied Health program also provides direct funding based on the number of Michigan graduates. Several other state programs provide funding for students at Michigan's private colleges. These include tuition grants, work-study grants, competitive grants, need-based grants, and part-time grants. A member of the Michigan Association of Private Colleges and Universities suggested that the legislature funds programs exclusively for the private sector because it "recognizes that for every student going to public institutions, the subsidy from the state is about $5,500. The independent sector makes the argument that they can serve students through these grants at a much lower cost than the state subsidy to the public institutions."

Although the budget process is largely an individual exercise for each institution, members of the Presidents Council usually present their needs collectively. The Presidents Council, composed of the presidents of Michigan's public four-year colleges and universities, encourages consensus on institutional budget requests. The collegiality of the Presidents Council was challenged in the 1995 budgetary process, however, when the budget for MSU was augmented by $10.4 million for technology—an increase above the budget increases for all 15 four-year campuses. Michigan State University proponents argued that the university had effectively communicated to the legislature its proven commitment to state priorities. Opponents raised issues of political favoritism and behind-the-scenes maneuvering. Either way, the normal protocols of the Presidents Council were upset, and some predict an increase in institutions jockeying for position to obtain favorable appropriations.

Yet, it is by no means evident that the MSU incident represents the first time that legislators have reacted more favorably to one institution than another. In fact, one representative told us that during the years an influential Democrat was operating in the house appropriations committee, Wayne State University (located in Detroit) received "significant budget increases."

In the absence of a funding formula that accounts for enrollment, there seems to be little policy basis for budgetary decisions regarding higher education in Michigan—except for the overall health of the economy, the previous year's funding level, and the ability of universities to make their case on the margin. When an institution's enrollments increase, the increase is quickly used as a justification for higher funding. Yet when enrollments have declined, appropriations have not reflected the decrease in students served. As an example, questions have recently arisen about Northern Michigan University, which maintained its funding levels despite substantial enrollment declines. In addition, the incremental budgetary approach values past decisions about base funding levels at the expense of pressing state needs as defined by the legislature. As one state worker said, "The incentive [for universities] is to increase the base as much as possible. In the past, schools were including as many things as possible under this base . . . that perhaps didn't belong there."

Nonetheless, legislators seem content with their budget process. With no huge increases in enrollment projected for the foreseeable future, it could be that legislators do not see budgetary incentives relating to enrollment as nearly as important as, for instance, those relating to tuition.

State Funding Patterns for Higher Education

Even during the state fiscal shortfalls of the early 1990s, Michigan's governor and legislature continued to support higher education. Michigan's economy also fared better than the economy of most other major states in the early 1990s. As a result of these two conditions, higher education escaped many of the cuts that systems in other states experienced during this time. From 1990 to 1993, for example, California's and New York's systems of higher education reported state spending cuts of 9.7 percent and 13.2 percent, respectively.[21] Michigan's public colleges and universities enjoyed a 10 percent increase during these years, which represents a slight increase even after factoring in inflation.

Virtually all of Michigan's state support of higher education comes from the general fund, with only a small portion of financial aid coming from other sources. Figure 6.5 shows the three general categories reported in the Michigan budget for higher education: community colleges, colleges and universities, and financial aid. Higher education spending in the state grew 18.4 percent from 1991 to 1995. The national CPI grew 11.9 percent.

Table 6.5 shows Michigan's higher education categories and the corresponding percentage growth from 1991 to 1995. The percentage growth in the national CPI is also provided. It is important to note that during this period,

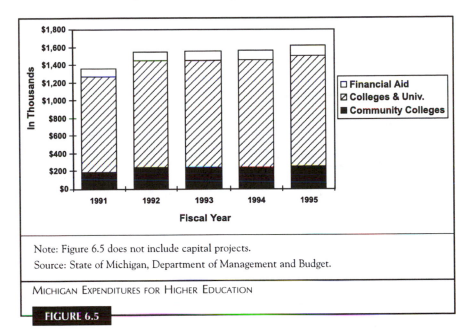

Note: Figure 6.5 does not include capital projects.
Source: State of Michigan, Department of Management and Budget.

MICHIGAN EXPENDITURES FOR HIGHER EDUCATION

FIGURE 6.5

public community college enrollment fell 6.7 percent and college and university enrollment fell 1.2 percent, according to the Michigan Department of Education, which received its data from the IPEDS data base. (Fall enrollment for community colleges was 223,578 in 1991 and 208,695 in 1995. Public four-year enrollment was 262,146 in 1991 and 258,996 in 1995.)

Most higher education administrators acknowledged that they were spared "the budget knife" over the last several years. Although some have also claimed that real growth was minimal, and in some years slightly negative, table 6.5 shows that from 1991 to 1995, colleges and universities experienced real growth of state support at almost 6 percent over the CPI.

Public institutions account for over 75 percent of state allocations to colleges and universities annually, and UM and MSU together make up almost half of the allocation to public colleges and universities. Table 6.6 provides detailed information about appropriations for fiscal year 1996.

TABLE 6.5

GROWTH IN MICHIGAN'S SPENDING FOR HIGHER EDUCATION, FISCAL YEARS 1991–1995 (IN PERCENT)

Community Colleges	30.7
Colleges and Universities	16.2
Financial Aid	19.5
Total Appropriation	18.4
U.S. CPI	11.9

Sources: State of Michigan, Department of Management and Budget. The CPI data are from the U.S. Department of Labor, Bureau of Labor Statistics, "Consumer Price Index for All Urban Consumers."

TABLE 6.6

STATE TAX-FUND APPROPRIATIONS FOR OPERATING EXPENSES, 1996 (IN MILLIONS OF DOLLARS)

University of Michigan	326
Michigan State	306
Other Universities & Colleges	674
Community Colleges	249
Grants and Scholarships:	
To Students at Public Institutions	50
To Students at Private Institutions	71
Total	11,676

STATE APPROPRIATIONS TO STUDENTS ATTENDING PRIVATE INSTITUTIONS

Private Tuition Grants	53.5
Private Dental Grants*	4.1
Private General Degree*	4.7
Private Allied Health*	0.8
Competitive Scholarships[†]	6.7
Part-time Students[†]	0.6
Total	71.0[§]

* These programs are institutional programs, so the dollars flow directly to the institutions and do not go to the student.

[†] National Association of State Student Grant and Aid Programs (NASSGAP), *NASSGAP 25th Annual Report* (Washington, D.C.: 1994), p. 44, estimates that 22 percent and 25 percent of Michigan residents who receive competitive scholarships and part-time grants, respectively, attend private institutions. The dollar figures were calculated based on these percentages.

[§] The figures do not add up to exact amounts due to rounding.

Sources: Edward R. Hines, *State Higher Education Appropriations, 1995–96* (Denver: State Higher Education Executive Officers, 1996), p. 30; and *NASSGAP 25th Annual Report*.

Community colleges receive their funds from three primary sources (tuition and fees, local support, and state aid), and each source contributes approximately 33 percent of the total. As figure 6.6 shows, local support, which is raised through property taxes, has been steadily rising, reaching almost $218 million in 1995–96 compared to about $159 million in 1990–91. During this period, local support to community colleges increased 37 percent compared to a 13 percent increase in state support.

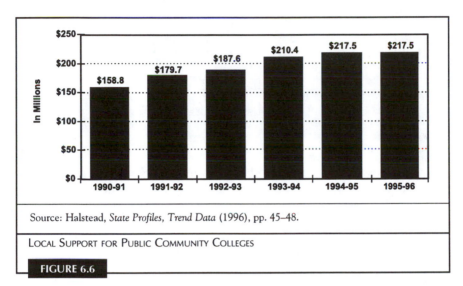

Source: Halstead, *State Profiles, Trend Data* (1996), pp. 45–48.

LOCAL SUPPORT FOR PUBLIC COMMUNITY COLLEGES

FIGURE 6.6

Student Aid

State agencies that deal with higher education issues in Michigan do not maintain comprehensive information on student aid for all sectors of higher education. As a result, the data in table 6.7 were consolidated from information provided by the senate fiscal agency and the house fiscal agency. The table presents several major categories of student aid for the last two years available, along with 1989–90 to give an indication of change.

Table 6.7 demonstrates that federal loans have quickly become the dominant category in funding students. From 1989–90 to 1993–94, public four-year fall enrollment actually decreased 0.1 percent.[22] State financial aid programs increased moderately during this same time frame, but appear to be leveling off, as the 1994–95 total shows. Institutional aid has grown, but not nearly as fast as guaranteed student loans. The senate fiscal agency reports that the number of guaranteed student loans awarded over the last two years grew by 19 percent (101,517 loan awards in 1993–94 compared to 120,284 in 1994–95), while the dollar amount borrowed increased by more than 27 percent.

TABLE 6.7

FINANCIAL AID IN MICHIGAN (IN MILLIONS OF DOLLARS)

	1989–90	1993–94	1994–95
Federal Programs			
Pell Grant Amounts	64.0	64.3	60.7
Supp. Educ. Opportunity Grants	8.0	9.4	10.9
National Direct Student Loan	18.9	18.9	20.9
Guaranteed Student Loan	111.7	308.5	393.0
Work Study	12.4	12.4	11.1
State Programs	24.6	27.2	27.2
Institutional Aid	90.2	142.4	147.9

Note: All data are for public four-year institutions only.

Source: Data for institutional aid were obtained from State of Michigan, House Fiscal Agency. All other information was obtained from State of Michigan, Senate Fiscal Agency, HEIDI data base, facsimile dated 4 March 1996.

Institutional financial aid is funded primarily through tuition (student fees) and state appropriations. Since aggregated state data are not available, the following discussion of institutional aid focuses on the general fund for UM and MSU.

According to MSU officials, MSU does not report how much institutional aid comes from student fees versus state appropriations because all the general fund revenues are pooled together and then allocated to the various categories. As a result, the only way to measure the extent to which student fees may have become a more significant source of operating funds for institutions, including funding for institutional financial aid, is to look at the changes in the primary sources of general funds. Figure 6.7 compares UM and MSU data regarding the dollar increase from 1990–91 to 1994–95 for state appropriations, student fees, and institutional aid.

In 1994–95, UM student fees comprised 57 percent of combined student fee and state appropriation general fund revenues, compared to 52 percent in 1990–91. In 1994–95, MSU student fees were 45 percent of combined student fee and state appropriation general fund revenues, compared to 41 percent in 1990–91. These data reveal that both universities are heavily reliant on student fees to provide overall revenues, and that this reliance has increased during the period shown. Since these funds are pooled together and then allocated, and since institutional aid also increased significantly during the same period, it is reasonable to infer that students are paying for an increasing share of institutional aid. University accounting mechanisms, however, cannot substantiate this.

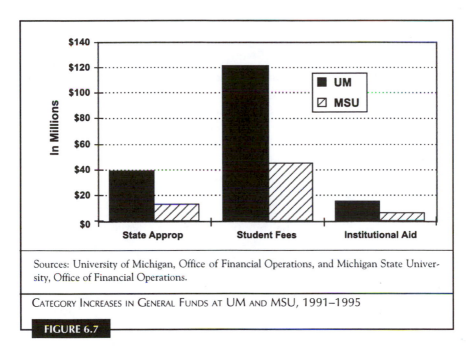

Sources: University of Michigan, Office of Financial Operations, and Michigan State University, Office of Financial Operations.

CATEGORY INCREASES IN GENERAL FUNDS AT UM AND MSU, 1991–1995

FIGURE 6.7

INSTITUTIONAL REVENUES AND EXPENDITURES

Revenues

Since Michigan ranks relatively high in both state appropriations per student and in tuition, there is an ongoing public concern in Michigan regarding the affordability of higher education. Table 6.8 reveals that tuition in Michigan's public institutions of higher education is well above the national average.

TABLE 6.8

AVERAGE PUBLIC UNDERGRADUATE TUITION AND FEES (IN DOLLARS)

| | Michigan | | United States | |
	1990–91	1995–96	1990–91	1995–96
Universities	3,688	5,842	2,156	3,210
Colleges and State Universities	2,172	3,213	1,735	2,534
Community Colleges	1,020	1,505	947	1,391

Source: Washington State Higher Education Coordinating Board, *1995–96 Tuition and Fee Rates: A National Comparison* (Olympia: March 1995), pp. 4, 8, 12.

Although student tuition in every sector of public higher education in Michigan is above the national average, the private sector's tuition levels are

below the national average. *The Chronicle of Higher Education* reported
Michigan's private four-year average tuition for 1993–94 to be $8,300, com-
pared to the national average of $10,994.[23]

Halstead has termed the tuition rate for residents at public two-year
institutions "access tuition" because large percentages of poor and underrepresented students have traditionally started their postsecondary education
at these institutions. In 1993–94 Michigan ranked as the 18th most expensive
state out of 49 reporting states with regard to the cost of access tuition. In
current dollars, the state ranked as having the sixth most expensive tuition
among public four-year institutions.[24] Halstead has calculated a student financial aid measure for aid as a percentage of access tuition paid by all families in
poverty with children under 18 years of age. Student financial aid pays for 30.6
percent of access tuition in the state of Michigan compared to 43.2 percent
nationwide.[25]

The percentage that public students pay in tuition relative to total revenues
(state and local appropriations plus student tuition) has been steadily rising in
Michigan. Halstead calls this the "tuition factor." The Michigan tuition factor
for public institutions was 34.4 percent in 1985–86 and rose to 43.0 percent in
1995–96. The national average for the tuition factor in 1995–96 was 31.6
percent.[26] Figure 6.8 shows Michigan's tuition factor along with what Halstead

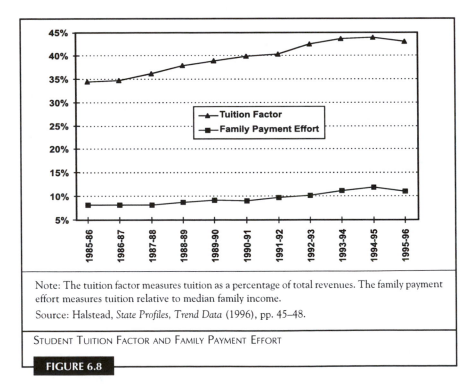

Note: The tuition factor measures tuition as a percentage of total revenues. The family payment
effort measures tuition relative to median family income.

Source: Halstead, *State Profiles, Trend Data* (1996), pp. 45–48.

STUDENT TUITION FACTOR AND FAMILY PAYMENT EFFORT

FIGURE 6.8

calls the "family payment effort." The family payment effort indicates the proportion of median family income that is going to tuition. Higher percentages indicate that Michigan families are using more income for tuition. The family payment effort, like the tuition factor, has been rising and is well above the national average (11.0 percent for Michigan in 1995–96 versus 6.9 percent nationwide).[27] A high tuition factor coupled with a high family payment effort could be an indicator that affordability may be a problem in the future.

While the family payment effort in Michigan is well above the national average, the increase in the state's disposable income per capita has tempered the upward slope in figure 6.8. If the tuition factor continues to climb, however, the family payment effort will probably continue its gradual increase.

Many higher education officials feel that tuition increases are necessary to maintain quality. In the face of rising state costs in other areas (such as corrections), these officials have indicated that institutions must diversify their revenue structure. In addition, administrators are well aware that general fund appropriations to higher education are discretionary. One state employee explained, "We look at where discretionary funds absolutely have to go, and then we figure out what is left over for higher education."

At UM, tuition and fees provide more revenue than state appropriations. Such diversification makes the institution less vulnerable to state fluctuations, but an increasing burden is shifted from the state to the student each time tuition and fees are raised. Legislators worry about locking potential students out of higher education if tuition is raised, and higher education administrators worry about covering rising costs. From the legislative perspective, incentives such as the savings plan and the tax credit have been marginally successful—at best—in dealing with rising tuition. Institutional respondents, on the other hand, talked about the publicly unpopular option of increasing the percentage of nonresident students if state support were cut. (In the past, Michigan's colleges and universities have generally held nonresident enrollment at or below what has been characterized as a "politically acceptable" level of 30 percent.)

At UM, where out-of-state tuition is equivalent to private rates, nonresidents pay three times as much as residents. This not only increases revenues, but also lessens the university's dependence on state funding. The university claims that private giving and nonresident tuition already contribute more revenue than the state.

The house fiscal agency calculates the revenue structure of public higher education for four-year institutions annually. The selected years shown in table 6.9 show past data as well as the most recent available year. The line items "Tuition and Fees" and "State Appropriations" reveal the most significant changes in the revenue structure of these institutions. This table reveals that even though state appropriations increased from 1990 to 1995, the increases in tuition and fees were so dramatic that state appropriations, as a share of total revenues, declined for the period.

TABLE 6.9		
TOTAL REVENUES FOR PUBLIC FOUR-YEAR INSTITUTIONS (IN PERCENT UNLESS OTHERWISE INDICATED)		
	1990	1995
Tuition and Fees	35.4	41.1
State Appropriations	52.8	46.3
Interest Earnings	1.3	0.7
Indirect Cost Recovery	3.9	4.1
Other	1.5	1.6
Ending Fund Balance	5.2	6.1
Total in billions (in current $)	2.0	2.6
Total in billions (in 1990 $)*	2.0	2.2

* The national CPI was used to adjust 1995 dollars to constant 1990 dollars. Real revenue growth has actually taken place as measured by this inflation factor.
Source: State of Michigan, House Fiscal Agency.

The University of Michigan's main campus alone comprises nearly 30 percent of the total revenue dollars shown in table 6.9. Institutions like MSU and Wayne State University do not rely on tuition as much as UM. The University of Michigan is sufficiently large to affect the statewide percentages given in table 6.9. The University of Michigan's revenue structure is given in table 6.10 for comparison. (Tables 6.9 and 6.10 report general fund revenue sources only.)

The University of Michigan enjoys a reputation within Michigan as the flagship university. The president of UM has described the university as a multibillion dollar corporation and pointed out that it would be 200th on the Fortune 500 if it were counted. When asked about the various revenue sources, the president replied, "The Golden Rule applies: the one with the gold makes the rules. State appropriations make up some 10-percent-plus of all of our total revenues. Tuition is now a larger source of revenue than state appropriations." University administrators like to think of their revenues in terms of the general fund, the designated fund, the auxiliary activities fund, and expendable restricted funds. When viewed in this way, state appropriations in 1994 made up 13.7 percent of the revenue pool. The state, on the other hand, prefers to exclude revenues from such activities as the hospital on campus and the athletic department. When we asked a manager at the house fiscal agency about the university's revenue structure, which excluded sales and services, he countered, "They [UM] like to say state support is only a small percentage of their total revenue, but it depends on what numbers you look

TABLE 6.10

General Fund Revenue Sources for the University of Michigan, Ann Arbor (in Percent Unless Otherwise Indicated)

	1990	1995
Tuition and Fees	42.3	49.2
State Appropriations	43.5	36.8
Federal Appropriations	0.1	0.1
Interest Earnings	1.1	0.4
Indirect Cost Recovery	8.0	7.8
Other	1.1	1.1
Ending Fund Balance	3.9	4.6
Total in millions (in current $)	576	761
Total in millions (in 1990 $)*	576	632

Note: All figures are based on state calculations.

* The national CPI was used to adjust 1995 dollars to constant 1990 dollars. Real revenue growth has actually taken place as measured by this inflation factor.

Source: State of Michigan, House Fiscal Agency.

at." According to the state's view, state appropriations account for about 38 percent of revenues at UM.

Expenditures

In Michigan, many close to higher education argue that expenditures have received less attention than revenues because revenues raise questions about tuition, which legislators are keen to address. Others have suggested that expenditures have escaped attention because higher education remained relatively unscathed in the fiscal crisis of the early nineties, even though the legislature cut many other areas. Still others have suggested that the spending habits of higher education have escaped scrutiny because so many people believe that the system works and provides a quality education. For instance, one respondent told us that business leaders in Lansing wanted to make sure that a local tax cut was not going to come at the expense of the local community college.

The national issues of faculty productivity, tenure, graduation rates, and job placement tend to define the context when one speaks of "accountability" in Michigan. Yet Michigan, like most other states, does not gather and compile the data that could support a relevant discourse about these issues. The constitutional autonomy of public colleges and universities may make it more difficult to gather this data in Michigan, but state legislators have not been particularly persistent in seeking this kind of information. It is perhaps for all of these reasons that "cost-cutting," as one budget manager said, "has not fully hit higher education—yet."

The state calculation of expenditures for all public four-year institutions is given in table 6.11. As with the revenue structure, data for two time periods are provided. The research percentage should be interpreted with care because it is calculated from the general fund and excludes other sources. In Michigan, large sums of research money come from private sources and appear in the expendable restricted fund. In 1993–94, for example, UM's expendable restricted fund contained over nine times the amount of research expenditures as the general fund.

TABLE 6.11

EXPENDITURES FOR MICHIGAN'S PUBLIC FOUR-YEAR INSTITUTIONS (IN PERCENT UNLESS OTHERWISE INDICATED)

	1989–90	1994–95
Instruction	46.2	47.2
Research	3.8	3.3
Public Service	0.8	0.8
Academic Support	12.8	12.2
Student Services	5.5	5.7
Institutional Support	11.0	11.2
Physical Plant	12.4	6.1
Financial Aid	4.8	6.4
Auxiliary Enterprises	1.4	0.8
Transfers	1.4	6.2
Total in billions (current $)	1.9	2.3
Total in billions (in 1990 $)*	1.9	1.9
Expenditures per FYES[†] (current $)	9,010	11,198
Expenditures per FYES[†] (in 1990 $)	9,010	9,294

* The national CPI was used to adjust 1995 dollars to constant 1990 dollars. Real expenditure growth has actually taken place as measured by this inflation factor.

[†] FYES stands for fiscal-year-equated student.

Source: State of Michigan, House Fiscal Agency.

MAINTAINING A "MARKET-DRIVEN" APPROACH

Unlike some states, Michigan is not expecting an enrollment surge over the next 20 years. Enrollment growth is projected to be slow, and the growth that does occur will probably take place in urban institutions. In spite of these projections for slow enrollment growth, Michigan's public colleges and universities are wary of the state's ability to increase funding to accommodate even these additional students. Several college and university administrators suggested that a primary objective in upcoming years will be to anticipate possible stagnation in state funds by attempting to become weaned from the state dole. Although a few described strategies to decrease costs, such as outsourcing auxiliary services at MSU or adopting responsibility-centered budgeting at UM, almost all referred to revenue-enhancing activities such as raising more private funding. Almost all of the administrators also emphasized the need to preserve constitutional autonomy.

In fact, some university officials mentioned that they could run their institutions more effectively if the state had less control. A scenario that was mentioned by one president would shift state appropriations from institutions to each student, thereby cutting the direct ties between state appropriations and institutions of higher education. Under this plan, institutions would compete on the "open market" for students, who would bring with them state funding as well as their own tuition and fees. While there appears to be little support for such a plan currently, it reveals the extent to which market forces are portrayed as an alluring model for many public colleges and universities in Michigan.

Michigan State University has gone so far as to purchase and operate a "private" institution, the Detroit College of Law. Although legislators had made it clear before the purchase that no new public law schools were needed in the state, MSU took over the Detroit College of Law, saying that the college would not receive state money and would remain fully private. A member of the state board of education, skeptical that this would be the case, hinted that money could be distributed across various line items in many different ways. Michigan State University has since been criticized for duplicating the services of state law schools and ignoring legislative input. Nonetheless, MSU is now offering a "private" educational service through the Detroit College of Law.

While representatives from the higher education community sound confident when they talk of preserving constitutional autonomy, state officials are quite cautious in addressing how state priorities can better be communicated to institutions of higher education. Michigan's legislators generally take a hands-off approach to how institutions run their educational services, and they appear to have little incentive to challenge the status quo.

For instance, even when state legislators have effectively influenced the actions of public colleges and universities through the budget process or other incentives, they have not necessarily held firm in their resolve. Early in the 1990s, when UM's nonresident population surpassed the politically acceptable rate of 30 percent, legislators inserted language into appropriations bills that required the rate to remain at or below 30 percent. That language held until 1994–95, when legislators allowed the language to slip. In 1994–95, the nonresident population at UM again surpassed the 30 percent level, but this time there were no major responses from lawmakers. A second example concerns the tax break that legislators have provided to individuals who attend institutions that keep tuition rates below a specified percentage. This tax break has met with strongly negative reactions from the higher education community, and although it has provided an incentive for colleges and universities to refrain from steep tuition hikes, several state legislators appear to be backing away from its support.

A third example also sends mixed messages about legislative intentions. As discussed earlier, MSU received an additional $10.4 million in appropriations in fiscal year 1995. The lesson that some people take from this example is that the state *will* support institutions that are effective in meeting state priorities, as defined by the legislature. Others maintain, however, that this example shows that the state responds to those who have political connections or who are particularly adept at communicating the achievements of their institutions.

CONCLUSION

In general, many political leaders, educational administrators, state workers, and residents in Michigan consider the state's public colleges and universities to be some of the best in the nation. The constitutional autonomy of Michigan's colleges and universities, although it complicates the way in which elected officials can achieve state policies regarding higher education, is also highly regarded within the state.

During the first half of the 1990s, higher education in Michigan fared well in receiving state funding, particularly compared to other major states. At the same time enrollments declined modestly, state funding for higher education increased, both in real and nominal terms. The steady increases in state revenues, combined with public satisfaction with institutions of higher education in Michigan, have so far precluded any widespread efforts at cost cutting in colleges and universities during this decade.

Despite an increase in state funding per student, however, tuition increased significantly in Michigan's public colleges during the first half of the 1990s, as it did in most states. Since Michigan ranks relatively high both in state appropriations per student and in tuition, the most controversial long-term issue regarding higher education in Michigan concerns affordability. As a result, the primary challenge facing Michigan's legislature and its institutions of higher education concerns whether or not the state—given high tuition rates—can continue to provide its residents with adequate access to its colleges and universities. Although the legislature has provided incentives to keep tuition levels down, these efforts have not been particularly successful to date. At what level is tuition too high? As long as state resources and tuition revenues continue to be sufficient to meet the growing costs of Michigan's public colleges and universities—and as long as Michigan's residents do not clamor for lower tuition rates—the legislature appears willing to let the "market" determine the answer to that question.

NOTES

1. *Chronicle of Higher Education Almanac* 42, no. 1 (September 1995), pp. 6–9.
2. Robert J. Kleine, "Michigan: Rethinking Fiscal Priorities," in *Fiscal Crisis of the States: Lessons for the Future*, edited by Steven Gold (Washington, D.C.: Georgetown University Press), p. 301.
3. Ibid., pp. 305–310.
4. Ibid., p. 302.
5. Appropriations, revenue, and other budgetary data are presented in fiscal years, unless otherwise noted.
6. Kleine, "Michigan: Rethinking Fiscal Priorities," p. 297.
7. Ibid., p. 310.
8. Kent Halstead, *State Profiles: Financing Public Higher Education, 1978 to 1996 Trend Data* (Washington, D.C.: Research Associates of Washington, 1996), table 2, p. 8.
9. James Burns, J. W. Peltason, and Thomas Cronin, *State and Local Politics: Government by the People* (Upper Saddle River, NJ: Prentice Hall, 1990), p. 113.
10. L. A. Glenny and T. Daglish, in *Public Universities, State Agencies and the Law: Constitutional Autonomy in Decline* (Berkeley: Center for Research and Development in Higher Education, 1973), report that in 1850, the University of Michigan was the first institution in the country to be accorded constitutional status. This was largely due to years of political interference in university operations, including legislative and gubernatorial involvement in the hiring and firing of faculty.
11. The Michigan Constitution, Article VIII, Section III, reads: "The power of the institutions of higher education provided in this constitution to supervise their respective institutions and control and direct the expenditures of the institutions' funds shall not be limited to this section." Language adopted in 1963.
12. Patrick Healy, "Power of the State," in *Chronicle of Higher Education* 41, no. 49 (18 August 1995), p. 30.
13. Task Force on State Policy and Independent Higher Education, *The Preservation of Excellence in American Higher Education: The Essential Roles of Private Colleges and Universities* (Denver: Education Commission of the States, 1990), p. 35.
14. *Chronicle of Higher Education Almanac* 43, no. 1 (September 1996), p. 9.
15. State of Michigan, Department of Education, facsimile dated 4 March 1996, regarding "Fall Term Enrollment History for the Various Segments of Higher Education." This information is tracked by the department and drawn from the IPEDS system.

16. Kent Halstead, *State Profiles: Financing Public Higher Education, 1978 to 1995* (Washington, D.C.: Research Associates of Washington, 1995), p. 38.
17. Western Interstate Commission for Higher Education, *High School Graduates: Projections by State 1992 to 2009* (Boulder: 1993), p. 25.
18. Halstead, *State Profiles: 1978 to 1996 Trend Data*, appendix, p. 8.
19. Kent Halstead, *State Profiles: Financing Public Higher Education, 1996 Rankings* (Washington, D.C.: Research Associates of Washington, 1996), pp. 18–19.
20. Edward R. Hines, *State Higher Education Appropriations, 1995–96* (Denver: State Higher Education Executive Officers, 1996), p. 30.
21. Calculated from California Postsecondary Education Commission, *Fiscal Profiles, 1994* (Sacramento: 1994), p. 83.
22. State of Michigan, Department of Education, internal memorandum titled "Michigan Public Universities: Trends in Fall Enrollment," table 7, drawn from IPEDS data base, sent to Mario Martinez 4 March 1996.
23. *Chronicle of Higher Education Almanac* 42, no. 1 (September 1995), p. 66.
24. Calculated from *Chronicle of Higher Education Almanac* 42, no. 1 (September 1995), pp. 6–9.
25. Kent Halstead, *The Workings of Public Higher Education* (Washington, D.C.: Research Associates of Washington, 1994), pp. 46–51.
26. Halstead, *State Profiles, Rankings* (1996), p. 24.
27. Ibid., p. 25.

CHAPTER 7

Minnesota

Uncertainty in a Time of Constrained Resources

Joan E. Sundquist

T *his chapter, which addresses higher education funding in Minnesota from 1990 to 1995, is based on relevant data gathered from publications and state sources. It also draws upon conversations conducted with state higher education leaders and policy makers during the last week of October 1995. It tries to faithfully represent opinions that were expressed at the time but that may have changed in the interim in response to shifting factors.*

Minnesota's high level of commitment to financial support of public higher education eroded somewhat during the early 1990s. This erosion is evident from a number of key indicators: postsecondary spending as a percentage of state general fund spending declined every year from 1987 to 1996; state appropriations for higher education declined in constant dollars between fiscal years 1992 and 1995; and tuition revenues as a percentage of instructional revenues increased during that same period. Given fluctuations in the state economy, a gradual shift in state budget priorities, and the added impact of expected federal budget cuts, Minnesota appears likely to experience an ongoing period of stagnation in public financial support for higher education.

It is still unclear whether these changes will give rise to an era of reform in the state's funding of higher education, or whether the existing method of subsidizing public higher education systems will continue. Although sufficient legislative support for changing the finance system does not currently exist, an important dialogue about alternative financing strategies for postsecondary institutions has begun in the state. This conversation has been initiated by citizens outside the public higher education community.

A bill was introduced in the state senate and house of representatives in 1991 to dramatically alter the nature of public subsidies to higher education. The bill would have reduced the direct appropriation for the public postsecondary systems from 67 to 33 percent of the total cost of instruction, as specified in law. Public postsecondary institutions would have found it necessary to replace lost state revenue with tuition to meet their instructional costs. Since the state's savings would have been directed into financial aid, the overall effect would have been to create a high-tuition and high-aid financing policy.

This legislation, developed and promoted by the Minnesota Private College Council, produced a strain between advocates of public and private higher education in the state. The Private College Council cast the need for this financing approach as a means of improving access for low-income students in the state. Representatives of the organization believe that their research demonstrates that under the current system, access has already eroded for Minnesotans with lower incomes,[1] and projected increases in the numbers of Minnesota youth from low-income families will only exacerbate the problem of access in the decade ahead. Currently, however, there is not wide agreement on whether access is even a problem in Minnesota. The clear improvement in the competitive position of the private colleges under the proposal—which would increase tuition dramatically in the public sector—makes the messenger suspect to many in the public higher education community.

In spite of the vehement opposition that the proposal generated in 1991, some in the higher education community in Minnesota believe that a gradual shift to a competitive, market-oriented approach to funding is inevitable. Others suggest that some measure of state deregulation is more likely than changes in the method of subsidization. Some of those interviewed for this study indicated that any changes would be the natural outcome of the competition provided by increasing numbers of private sector, for-profit educational vendors entering the higher education market. Others saw change as the unintended consequence of competition for state funds and a continued shifting of state budget priorities away from higher education.

In 1995, the debate on funding strategy reignited. Governor Arne Carlson appointed two influential Minnesotans—former Republican congressman Vin Weber and former Democratic state senator John Brandl—to address the state's chronic budget imbalance and propose ways to cope with expected cuts in federal funding without raising taxes. Brandl and Weber made their recommendations to the governor in November 1995.[2] Their recommendations suggest that the current method of funding public higher education does not provide the right incentives to impel institutions to respond efficiently to the educational needs of the citizens of the state.

Brandl and Weber rely upon three concepts in their restructuring plan for public services: competition, community, and concentration. They believe that the state needs to shift from supporting providers to supporting students, thereby creating a more competitive market for providing public higher education. The state also needs to allow local institutions, like schools, to function according to values and needs defined locally without much top-down interference from government bureaucracies. Finally, public funds must be spent on those most in need, rather than providing subsidies for those who can afford to pay. In maintaining this framework, Brandl and Weber propose that:

- Thirty percent of the total state funds appropriated to higher education should continue to subsidize the state's two public higher education systems, the University of Minnesota (UM) system and the Minnesota State Colleges and Universities (MnSCU) system.
- Sixty percent should be directed to Minnesota citizens to allow them to choose the public or private institution that meets their educational or training needs. An unidentified portion of this amount would be for "lifetime learning grants," with the rest budgeted for need-based financial aid.
- Ten percent of funds should support research and statewide programs like interlibrary loans and telecommunications.

The Brandl-and-Weber proposal has generated criticism from a number of quarters. One criticism is that it is fundamentally anti-middle-class. Since this proposal would drive up tuition at the state's public postsecondary institutions, especially at UM, the legislature would be responsible for severely reducing a public good that middle-class citizens have come to regard as inviolable—quality public higher education at an affordable cost. Others are concerned that financial aid is a vulnerable item in the state budget, easily raided in times of deficit or shifting budget priorities. Another concern is whether funding levels for state-sponsored research at UM would be adequate. The proposal also generates worries in rural communities concerning whether local institutions would be able to compete for students and remain viable.

The legislature is not expected to act on these recommendations in the biennial legislative session. But Governor Carlson has expressed interest in approaches that shift public higher education subsidies away from the institutions to the consumer, and may opt for such an approach in the budget he submits to the 1997 legislature. Even if no radical reform takes place, however, state and institutional higher education leaders have begun to establish mechanisms to improve the efficiency and productivity of public institutions of higher education, a movement that acknowledges that public higher education is going to have to make better use of the resources it receives from the state.

THE STATE CONTEXT

Minnesota is the smallest of the five case study states in terms of population. With almost 4.6 million residents in 1994, it ranks 20th in the nation in population. Only 5.6 percent of the state's population is non-white. Thirty-six percent of the population is below the age of 24. The high school dropout rate in 1990 was extremely low at just 6.4 percent; only North Dakota had a lower rate. The state's 1993 poverty rate was 11.6 percent.[3]

The state obtains its non-dedicated revenue primarily from four major taxes: individual income taxes (50.3 percent of 1996–97 estimated biennial revenues), sales taxes (36.8 percent), corporate income taxes (8.3 percent), and motor vehicle excise taxes (4.6 percent).[4] Property taxes collected in the state are returned to local communities and are thus not available as a source of general fund revenue.

According to a respected source of national comparative data on higher education financing,[5] Minnesota ranks very high among the 50 states in its willingness to tax itself for the provision of public services. As of fiscal year 1996, Minnesota ranked seventh in its "state tax effort"—that is, the ratio of collected state and local tax revenue to tax capacity.[6]

When this high level of tax effort is compared to student enrollment, however, Minnesota's funding capacity for higher education is much closer to the average among the states. The state has a larger-than-average number of students in public higher education institutions relative to its population size, and therefore its "tax wealth relative to enrollment load" ranked just slightly above the national average in fiscal year 1996.[7]

Minnesota began the 1990s with a strong economy and a large budget reserve. While the state experienced a decrease in employment at the beginning of calendar year 1991, the overall economic recession was relatively mild compared to other states.[8] Increases in state revenues on a yearly basis ranged from about 4 to 7 percent during fiscal years 1991, 1992, and 1994. In fiscal year 1993, revenues increased almost 10 percent, and in fiscal year 1995, they increased sharply at an annual rate of over 17 percent.[9]

Despite these steady increases in revenues, budget deficits plagued Minnesota lawmakers during the first few years of the decade. This was largely due to increases in appropriations for entitlement programs (largely because of increases in the numbers of school-age children and citizens over the age of 65). In the early years of the decade, lawmakers balanced state budgets primarily through a tax increase (sales and income) and by shifting dollars from the state reserve fund, largely depleting the fund by the end of 1992. Increased revenues in 1993, however, brought an unexpected surplus that once again augmented state reserves. Forecasts are projecting an $824 million budget surplus for the 1996–97 biennium.

State budget forecasts do not factor in the impact of any federal cuts the state may be facing as a result of efforts to balance the federal budget. The greatest impact in Minnesota is expected to be felt in the area of health care spending. Estimates of the impact of federal actions have been projected to be as high as $3.2 billion over seven years, a significant portion of which may be due to changes in the Medicare and Medicaid programs.[10] But until the final federal legislation is approved, estimating the impact of the federal cuts is little more than guesswork. In fiscal year 1995, the state received about $3.4 billion from the federal government.[11] Social Security and Medicare are the largest federal expenditures in Minnesota.[12]

The prospect for state higher education funding is also dimmed somewhat by an anticipated reduction in the systems' base-level funding during the next biennium. When the legislature adopted the 1996–97 biennial budget, it specified that new money appropriated above the base was to be considered a one-time increase. Thus, the recurring base for the 1998–99 biennium will be less than the systems received in the 1996–97 session.

As in all states, higher education in Minnesota competes for state resources with other public services. And as table 7.1 reveals, it appears that higher education funding lost out to other programs in the state budget—namely, health care and family support programs like welfare—from fiscal year 1991 to 1995.[13] Table 7.1 tracks growth in general fund spending for certain public services and provides data on the Consumer Price Index (CPI) for comparison. As this table shows, increases in funding to higher education failed to keep pace with inflation during the period shown.

TABLE 7.1						
CHANGE IN SELECTED FUNDING ITEMS IN STATE BUDGET (IN PERCENT)						
	1991	1992	1993	1994	1995	Change 1990–95
Higher Education	5.6	(0.8)	(0.5)	4.4	3.4	12.6
K–12 Education	3.9	3.6	5.9	5.0	13.8	36.3
Health Care	13.1	26.4	7.8	14.0	9.9	93.1
Family Support	33.1	38.9	(3.1)	0.2	(13.9)	54.5
U.S. CPI*	4.2	3.0	3.0	2.6	2.8	16.6

* CPI figures are for calendar rather than fiscal years.

Sources: Minnesota Department of Finance, "History-Summary," p. 1. The CPI data are from the U.S. Department of Labor, Bureau of Labor Statistics, "Consumer Price Index for All Urban Consumers: U.S. City Average," October 1996.

Figure 7.1 divides the state budget for 1996 into six major spending categories: aid to school districts, postsecondary education, property tax aids and credits, health care, family support, and other (which includes the operation of state agencies, debt service, and other spending items). Elementary and secondary education is the largest component of the state budget, while criminal justice is the fastest growing. Spending for prisons, however, still comprises only 2 percent of the total state general fund budget in Minnesota.[14]

As shown in figure 7.2, postsecondary education's share of the budget is down from a high of 15.5 percent in fiscal year 1987 and has slipped every year since. During this period the overall state budget has nearly doubled. State expenditures have increased from about $5 billion in fiscal year 1987 to an estimated $9.3 billion in fiscal year 1997.

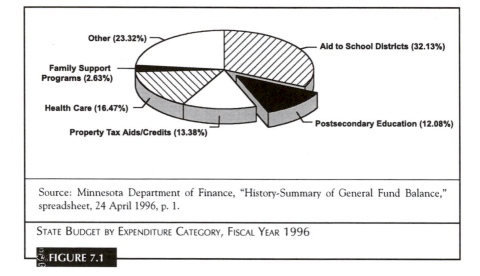

Source: Minnesota Department of Finance, "History-Summary of General Fund Balance," spreadsheet, 24 April 1996, p. 1.

STATE BUDGET BY EXPENDITURE CATEGORY, FISCAL YEAR 1996

FIGURE 7.1

National comparative data suggest that higher education's decline as a state budget priority is a national phenomenon. Indeed, Kent Halstead editorializes in the 1994 edition of *State Profiles*: "This shift in budget priority is the single greatest cause of the declining role of government support to higher education, not declining tax revenue."[15] The measure Halstead uses to compare the states in this area is "state payment effort," which gauges the percentage of tax revenue allocated for public higher education relative to the overall state budget. As figure 7.3 shows, Minnesota has consistently ranked higher than the national average in the percentage it allocates to public higher education, but the percentage has declined precipitously from its high in 1987.

In terms of allocations per student in public institutions, however, state funding shows a moderate increase that is just over the rate of inflation. The

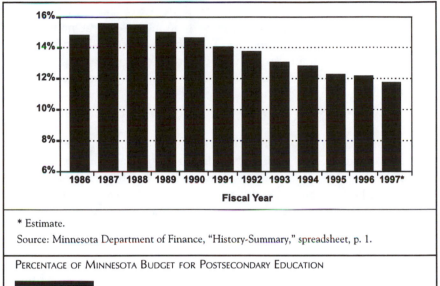

* Estimate.

Source: Minnesota Department of Finance, "History-Summary," spreadsheet, p. 1.

PERCENTAGE OF MINNESOTA BUDGET FOR POSTSECONDARY EDUCATION

FIGURE 7.2

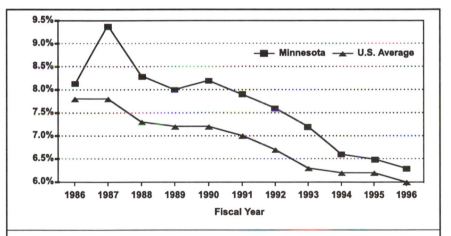

Note: State payment effort measures the percentage of tax revenue allocated to public higher education relative to the overall state budget.

Source: Kent Halstead, *State Profiles: Financing Public Higher Education, 1978 to 1996 Trend Data* (Washington, D.C.: Research Associates of Washington, 1996), pp. 46, 102.

STATE PAYMENT EFFORT

FIGURE 7.3

allocation per student rose from $4,444 in 1990–91 to $5,355 in 1995–96, an increase of about 20 percent (compared with an increase in the national CPI of about 16 percent during this period).[16] This increase is due primarily to increases in state funding to higher education that were just below the inflation rate, combined with a decrease in enrollments during the period.

POLITICAL CHANGES IN THE STATE

Minnesota has a bicameral legislature, with both the house of representatives and senate controlled by the Democratic-Farmer-Labor (DFL) party. Aside from a two-year term in the mid-1980s when the Republicans controlled the house, the DFL has maintained dominance in the state legislature for the past two decades. However, the DFL majority over the Independent-Republican (IR) party in the house of representatives is slim (69 DFL seats compared to 65 IR seats). The legislature's relationship with the state's Republican governor, Arne Carlson, has generally been contentious.

It is difficult to generalize about the politics of the state. Although Minnesota is perceived by many to be a Democratic stronghold given the candidates it has sent to run for the presidency, a significant segment of the population, particularly in rural areas, has a strong socially conservative outlook. And while many in the state have taken pride in the progressive public policies for which the state is nationally known, relatively high levels of taxation and government regulation are sources of continual public debate.

Governor Carlson won his first election in 1990 and reelection in 1994. He is perceived to be both a fiscal conservative and a social liberal, but neither of his two elections to office has been characterized by high levels of public debate over his political agenda or ideology. The governor's staff describes his approach to higher education as favoring initiatives that enhance performance and productivity. He approves of policies that provide incentives for institutions to meet statewide objectives. He is strongly in favor of a deregulation agenda that reduces the level of bureaucracy at the institutional and system levels. And he favors increased reliance on technology to deliver improved higher education services in the state.

Until recently, there has been strong philosophical agreement between members of the two parties on higher education policy. The reigning political wisdom was that Minnesota is a state that provides high quality and broad access to public higher education. Higher education funding bills routinely passed the legislature with nearly unanimous votes. But the introduction of proposals to leverage state funds through increased reliance on tuition has undermined to some extent this tradition of cooperation on higher education policy.

HIGHER EDUCATION GOVERNANCE AND DEMOGRAPHICS

Minnesota currently operates two public systems of higher education: the UM system and the MnSCU system.

The University of Minnesota is governed by a 12-member board of regents elected by the legislature. This board consists of one representative of each of the eight congressional districts in the state and four at-large members, of which one is a student voting member. Chartered before the birth of the state, UM has constitutional autonomy, which confers upon it the powers to manage its own affairs, including setting tuition rates. The system is comprised of four campuses with varied missions: a four-year "polytechnic" program at Crookston; undergraduate and graduate programs (through the master's level) at Duluth; undergraduate, graduate, and professional programs (through the doctoral level) at the Twin Cities campuses; and a four-year liberal arts program at Morris. The University of Minnesota, Twin Cities, is the state's land-grant institution.

The MnSCU system began operation on 1 July 1995, as a result of the merger of three previously existing systems: the technical colleges, the community colleges, and the state universities. The MnSCU system is governed by a 15-member board of trustees appointed by the governor. Before the merger, the three systems maintained 62 campuses, of which 7 were state universities, 21 were community colleges, and 34 were technical colleges. However, the MnSCU system administrators have begun the process of reducing the number of institutions by combining community and technical colleges.

The creation of MnSCU resulted from a bill proposed by the senate majority leader that passed in 1991. Although many house members bitterly opposed the merger and voted to repeal the legislation every year until the new system began operation, the frustration of other house members concerning excessive costs and duplication in the three systems, and concerning campus administrations that were perceived as unresponsive ultimately led to passage of the legislation. Duplication of services between community colleges and technical colleges—often located within the same town—was perhaps the most influential issue.

The problems that the new system faces are daunting. They include merging three different cultures and administrative practices, bringing the technical colleges (formerly locally administered by school districts) onto the state's administrative systems, and resolving significant differences in pay and employment contracts.

Minnesota also has a robust private postsecondary sector, and many of the state's four-year liberal arts institutions are noted for their high quality. In 1994–95, private colleges enrolled 36.5 percent of all high school graduates from the previous spring who enrolled in baccalaureate colleges in Minnesota.

Sixteen of the state's private four-year liberal arts colleges and universities belong to an association called the Minnesota Private College Council, which has assumed an active role in the state's public policy debate over higher education finance.

A central factor of higher education in the state is faculty unionization. State university, community college, and technical college faculty are all unionized. In addition, the faculty of the Duluth campus of UM is also unionized. Bargaining is legally the responsibility of the state department of employee relations, although system board representatives are involved. Many of the faculty and staff contracts include work regulations that are very favorable to members, but the contracts limit institutional flexibility in staffing and programming.

Geographic access has also played an important role in the development of many institutions in the state.[17] Rural legislators have advocated in favor of students being able to attend an institution without having to relocate, and they have valued the contribution of colleges and universities to the local economy. As a result, Minnesota has almost 15 campuses per million residents, compared to about eight campuses per million for other states in the Midwest.[18]

Halstead confirms that the state is in the "business" of public higher education to a greater extent than many other states. In Minnesota, full-time-equivalent (FTE) student enrollment in public postsecondary institutions per 1,000 population was above the national average in 1995–96, ranking 17th among all states, and second only behind California among the five case study states.[19]

Table 7.2 reveals a moderate decrease in students enrolled (as measured by head count) during the first half of the 1990s. But whereas enrollments declined overall in the public sector during this period, they increased in the private sector. In fall 1995, students from public institutions comprised 78 percent of the total enrollment, while students from the private sector comprised 22 percent.

TABLE 7.2

FALL HEAD-COUNT ENROLLMENT IN PUBLIC AND PRIVATE POSTSECONDARY INSTITUTIONS

	1990	1991	1992	1993	1994*	1995*	% Change 1990–95
Public	220,366	210,386	212,364	212,523	216,009	211,097	(4.2)
Private	55,425	55,007	60,818	60,716	61,809	59,482	7.3
TOTAL	275,791	265,393	273,182	273,239	277,818	270,579	(1.9)

* Technical college data are estimated for 1994 and 1995.

Source: Minnesota Higher Education Services Office, *Report to the Governor Fact Book* (St. Paul: January 1996), p. 8.

Part of the decrease in enrollments can be explained by looking at the pool of new high school graduates during this period. Whereas there were 52,562 new public high school graduates in 1990–91, that number dropped to 51,406 in 1995–96, a decline of just over 2 percent.[20] However, even though high school graduates declined during this period, the number of FTE students enrolled in public higher education per new high school graduate also declined steadily from 1990–91 to 1995–96.[21] This measure suggests that, on the aggregate, high school graduates experienced a somewhat decreasing level of opportunity to enroll in Minnesota's public institutions of higher education during the first half of the 1990s.

The Minnesota Higher Education Services Office (known before 1996 as the Minnesota Higher Education Coordinating Board) collects enrollment data from the various sectors to provide demographic analysis on higher education in Minnesota. Table 7.3 illustrates some characteristics of the 1995 postsecondary population. Over three-fourths of the students are state residents. Less than 9 percent of the students describe themselves as members of a racial minority. (The figures do not include students whose race or ethnic group was not reported.)

TABLE 7.3

Minnesota Head-Count Enrollment by Residency and Race, Fall 1995

	Head Count	Percentage
State residents	176,147	76.0
Out-of-state residents	37,482	16.2
Foreign	6,762	2.9
Unknown Residency	11,249	4.9
White	188,315	91.3
Black, Non-Hispanic	5,893	2.9
Amer. Indian, Alaskan Native	2,127	1.0
Asian & Pacific Islander	7,124	3.5
Hispanic	2,803	1.4

Source: Data compiled by the Minnesota Higher Education Services Office.

The number of minority students in Minnesota has been increasing gradually—up from 5.3 percent in 1985 to 8.7 percent in 1995—and is largely due to the growth in the state's non-white population. By the year 2020, 19 percent of the state's 15-to-24 year olds are projected to be non-white.[22]

Projections of high school graduates suggest that colleges and universities in Minnesota can expect greater numbers of traditional-age applicants in the immediate future. Based on an analysis by the higher education coordinating board issued in November 1993, the number of high school graduates in Minnesota reached a low of 49,241 in 1992, and is projected to increase by 30 percent to 63,831 by the year 2000.[23] This growth will continue at least until the year 2009, when the number of high school graduates is expected to reach 64,481, a 60 percent increase over the number in 1992 but still below the state's 1978 peak.

While the number of high school graduates is expected to increase statewide until the year 2000, after that date the number of high school graduates in the Twin Cities metropolitan area is projected to increase while greater Minnesota (the non-metropolitan area) will most likely experience a declining number of high school graduates. By the year 2009, 56 percent of the state's high school graduates will be residents of the metropolitan area.[24] This population shift may create a discrepancy between where students live and the location of higher education institutions.

STATE SPENDING FOR HIGHER EDUCATION

State spending on higher education is allocated to the two public systems of higher education, the state Higher Education Services Office (which administers financial aid), and the Mayo Medical Foundation.[25] Allocations to the public systems are made to the system governing boards in Minnesota; they in turn allocate funds to the campuses based on their own internal methodology. Local funds are not used in the financing of higher education in Minnesota. The only state funds going to support private postsecondary institutions are state financial aid grants that students apply toward their tuition.

Minnesota has allocated state higher education funds by formula since the early 1980s, but began to drift away from this method in the 1990s. The "average cost funding" formula used during much of the 1980s was replaced in 1994 by a formula that recognizes fixed and variable instructional costs as well as noninstructional costs for research and public service. This "base plus" formula still exists in statute, but was not used to calculate funding levels for higher education in either the 1995 or 1996 legislative sessions, and is essentially moribund.

The discussion over allocating state higher education monies has shifted to how much state funding should be considered base-level funding in future years. An agreement made in 1995 between the governor and legislature stipulated that spending increases above an agreed-upon base level would be recognized as nonrecurring. From a state perspective, this agreement to cap appropriations provides some limits on the extent to which budget decisions made one biennium encumber state funds in future bienniums, while still providing one-time increases for investments in quality. From the perspective of administrators within the postsecondary systems, capping has limited the dependability of a portion of state revenue, and their flexibility in using it.

The $1.1 billion appropriated for higher education in fiscal year 1996 was allocated as shown in figure 7.4. The breakdown of funding is as follows:

$491.7 million for MnSCU; $483.9 million for UM; $116.4 million for the Higher Education Services Office; and $0.8 million for the Mayo Medical Foundation. The amount of state revenue available for student financial aid is about 10 percent of the total higher education appropriation.

Figure 7.5 illustrates trends in state appropriations to the public institutions in current and constant dollars. The appropriations included on this chart are solely for the operation of public postsecondary institutions and do not include state funding for financial aid or other purposes. As this figure reveals, public higher education experienced a cut—both in current and constant dollars—during 1992 and 1993. Moreover, as the constant-dollar figures show, state appropriations for the operation of public higher education—when adjusted for inflation—have remained almost flat for the last 10 years.

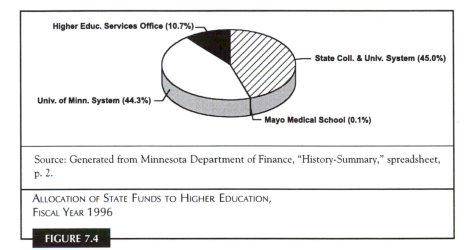

Source: Generated from Minnesota Department of Finance, "History-Summary," spreadsheet, p. 2.

ALLOCATION OF STATE FUNDS TO HIGHER EDUCATION, FISCAL YEAR 1996

FIGURE 7.4

Maintaining postsecondary educational access is a widely shared public policy goal in Minnesota and, as a result, the state has maintained a high level of commitment to its primary financial aid program, the State Grant Program. The State Grant Program makes awards on the basis of financial need to eligible undergraduate residents of the state who attend Minnesota public and private institutions.[26] In fiscal year 1994, Minnesota ranked sixth in total payments, sixth in the number of awards, and fourth in estimated grant dollars per undergraduate student, according to the National Association of State Scholarship and Grant Programs.[27]

The Higher Education Services Office also administers loan programs—as well as a number of categorical grant programs—that apply to particular subgroups of individuals, such as nurses. Figure 7.6 depicts state appropriations to the student assistance programs over the last eight years, in current and constant dollars.

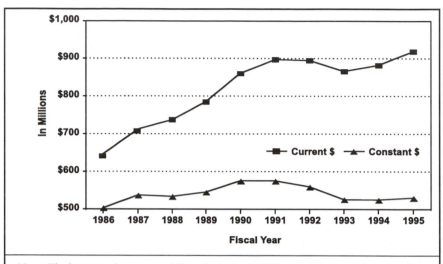

Note: The base year for constant-dollar calculations is 1981. All of the above figures exclude appropriations for Mayo Medical Foundation and the higher education coordinating board.

Source: Generated from Minnesota Department of Finance, "Postsecondary Appropriation Database (Excluding HECB), Real Change in Direct Appropriations," 2 March 1995.

APPROPRIATIONS FOR PUBLIC POSTSECONDARY INSTITUTIONS

FIGURE 7.5

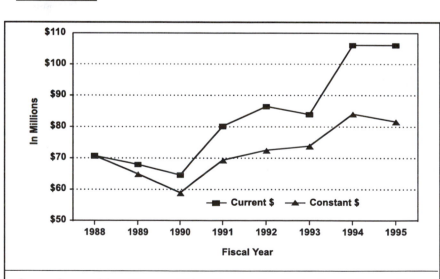

Source: Generated from Minnesota Higher Education Coordinating Board, *Minnesota Higher Education: Recommendations for Change, Technical Report* (St. Paul: 1995), p. 40.

STATE APPROPRIATIONS FOR STUDENT ASSISTANCE

FIGURE 7.6

The total amount of financial aid awarded to undergraduates in Minnesota from all sources—state, federal, and local—totaled about $840 million in fiscal year 1995.[28] The breakdown by type of aid is shown in table 7.4. In 1995, the total dollar amount of loans surpassed grants for the first time—representing a significant shift in the burden of paying for higher education.

TABLE 7.4

FINANCIAL AID AWARDED BY TYPE (IN MILLIONS OF DOLLARS)

	1987		1995	
	Dollars	% of Total Aid	Dollars	% of Total Aid
Grants	226.9	48.8	364.5	43.3
Loans	191.4	41.2	401.2	47.7
Work Study & Jobs at the Institution	46.7	10.0	75.9	9.0
Total	464.9		841.5	

Note: Figures may not add due to rounding.

Source: Minnesota Higher Education Coordinating Board, *Report of Financial Aid Awarded, Fiscal Year 1987* (St. Paul: 1987), p. 3; and Minnesota Higher Education Services Office, *Report of Financial Aid Awarded, Fiscal Year 1995* (St. Paul: 1995), p. 3.

As shown in figure 7.7, the amount of money received through grants and loans to students from all sources grew very rapidly between 1987 and 1995. Loan volume shot up in 1995, increasing from about $300 million in fiscal year 1993 to $400 million in 1995. The growth occurred in federal loans, especially in the Stafford Loan Program and the Parent Loans for Undergraduate Students (PLUS) Program.

In spite of the state's strong commitment to financial aid, the UM system deemed it necessary for the first time in 1995–96 to establish its own student aid program. This program provides undergraduate student financial assistance on the basis of need, just like the State Grant Program. The creation or expansion of programs that recycle tuition income into institution-based financial aid has been a troubling trend to many in the higher education community, because it signals that affordability has become a problem for potential students even with state need-based financial aid programs in place, and it channels institutional revenue away from other areas of needed investment.

At UM, the $1.4 million for the program in fiscal year 1996 was generated from UM's central reserves, and therefore included no tuition. In fiscal year 1997, the $1.44 million for the program will be budgeted from the Operations and Maintenance (O & M) budget, which is made up of state appropriations, tuition, and some investment income. While tuition dollars are not allocated separately from the other sources of income making up the O & M account, it

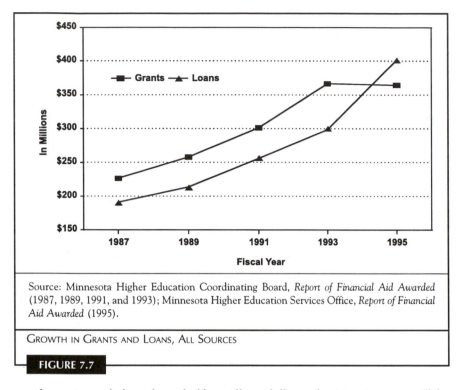

Source: Minnesota Higher Education Coordinating Board, *Report of Financial Aid Awarded* (1987, 1989, 1991, and 1993); Minnesota Higher Education Services Office, *Report of Financial Aid Awarded* (1995).

GROWTH IN GRANTS AND LOANS, ALL SOURCES

FIGURE 7.7

can be estimated that about half a million dollars of tuition income will be recycled into financial aid next year at the university.

TUITION CHANGES

State tuition policy is set in law by intent language that is routinely ignored by the system boards. A Minnesota statute states, "The legislature intends to provide at least 67 percent of the instructional services costs for each postsecondary system."[29] This policy assumes that the system boards will set tuition at 33 percent of instructional costs. But with constitutional autonomy, the UM Board of Regents can establish their own tuition rates. The recently merged MnSCU system has not been held to this standard either.

Figure 7.8 depicts the history of tuition as a percentage of instructional expenditures at each of the four types of public higher education institutions in Minnesota. Tuition as a percentage of instructional expenditures reached a high in fiscal year 1993 of 42.4 percent at the UM system, 39.1 percent at the state universities, 40.6 percent at the community colleges, and 31.6 percent at the technical colleges, before falling slightly in fiscal year 1994.

As in most other states, tuition and fees increased significantly in Minnesota during the first half of the 1990s. The heftiest jump came at UM, where

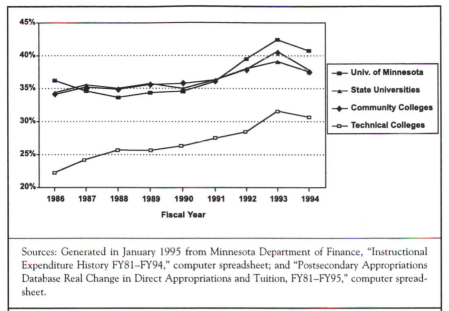

Sources: Generated in January 1995 from Minnesota Department of Finance, "Instructional Expenditure History FY81–FY94," computer spreadsheet; and "Postsecondary Appropriations Database Real Change in Direct Appropriations and Tuition, FY81–FY95," computer spreadsheet.

TUITION AS A PERCENTAGE OF INSTRUCTIONAL EXPENDITURES

FIGURE 7.8

tuition increased 73 percent over the seven-year period (see table 7.5). From 1990–91 to 1996–97, annual tuition and fees increased 39 percent at the state universities, 55 percent at the community colleges, 45 percent at the technical colleges, and 43 percent at the private colleges.

TABLE 7.5

AVERAGE TUITION AND REQUIRED FEES (IN DOLLARS)

	Univ. of Minn.*	State Univs.	Comm. Coll.	Tech. Coll.	Private 4-Year
1990–91	2,630	1,997	1,474	1,496	10,044
1991–92	2,898	2,207	1,598	1,625	10,774
1992–93	3,242	2,276	1,687	1,665	11,467
1993–94	3,381	2,534	1,766	1,756	12,196
1994–95	3,526	2,642	1,834	1,808	12,919
1995–96	4,136	2,618	2,028	1,920	13,574
1996–97	4,549	2,780	2,282	2,174	14,315

Note: The dates represent academic years.

* Resident undergraduate tuition at the College of Liberal Arts.

Source: Data compiled by Minnesota Higher Education Services Office.

Figure 7.9, generated from state department of finance data, charts the history of tuition collected by the state in current and constant dollars. Note that total tuition has climbed over the 10-year period even after adjusting for inflation.

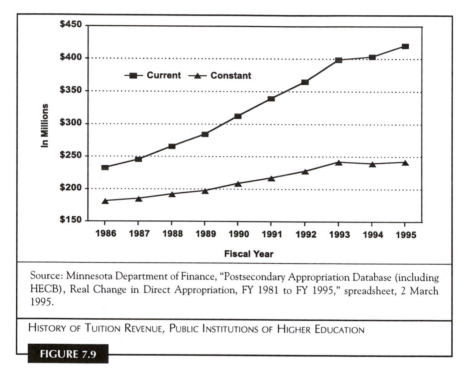

Source: Minnesota Department of Finance, "Postsecondary Appropriation Database (including HECB), Real Change in Direct Appropriation, FY 1981 to FY 1995," spreadsheet, 2 March 1995.

HISTORY OF TUITION REVENUE, PUBLIC INSTITUTIONS OF HIGHER EDUCATION

FIGURE 7.9

State Profiles generates an indicator called the "family share of total funding" that measures the relationship between tuition and overall funding. The family share, which is a ratio of student tuition to total revenues obtained from appropriations and tuition, reflects the extent to which higher education is regarded as an individual or social good. The higher that tuition rises compared to total revenues, the greater the expectation within a state that higher education is of private benefit and therefore a private financial responsibility. If the family share is lower, this reflects a state's opinion that higher education benefits the entire community. In spite of the concerns being raised in the state about the impact of tuition, the family share in Minnesota has tracked very closely to the national average since 1988, suggesting that Minnesota's assumptions about the role of tuition in funding higher education are consistent with assumptions made nationwide.

STUDENT AND FAMILY RESOURCES

In spite of the concern about increases in tuition at public and private institutions in the state, relatively little has been known until recently about the ability of Minnesota's families to pay for higher education. The Minnesota Private College Research Foundation, using a grant from the Lilly Foundation, conducted a survey in 1992 of the financial status of families of students attending baccalaureate-degree-granting campuses in the state.

The study confirmed that participation in the higher educational sector is strongly influenced by family income and that baccalaureate institutions in Minnesota are dominated by students from middle- and upper-income families. According to the study, students at UM came from families reporting the highest median income in 1991 ($48,250), followed by students at the private colleges ($45,500), and then the state universities ($42,250).[30] The disparity in income between students attending the state universities and the UM institutions was over 14 percent. Figure 7.10 illustrates the distribution of 1991 adjusted gross incomes for families of dependent students by system.

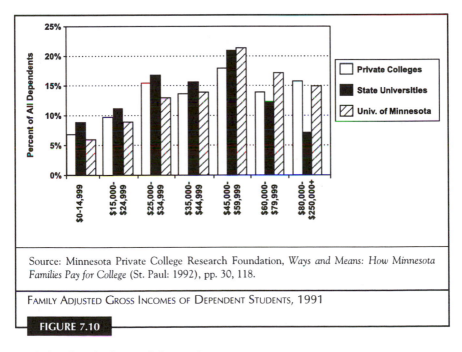

Source: Minnesota Private College Research Foundation, *Ways and Means: How Minnesota Families Pay for College* (St. Paul: 1992), pp. 30, 118.

FAMILY ADJUSTED GROSS INCOMES OF DEPENDENT STUDENTS, 1991

FIGURE 7.10

Other key findings of the study were:

- the higher education financing system is regressive, requiring families with lower incomes to pay a higher percentage of their income for the cost of college;

- students from families with incomes under $35,000 incur much more debt to pay for college than those with incomes above $45,000 (in the aggregate, about twice as much); and
- students from low-income families have the same educational goals as those from wealthier families.

State Profiles provides national comparative data that highlight how much tuition has increased relative to median household income in Minnesota and the nation. "Family payment effort" tracks public net tuition revenues per full-time-equivalent (FTE) student compared to median household income. Figure 7.11 illustrates that tuition has increased at a faster rate than family income, which means that paying for college is taking a bigger bite out of the family budget than ever before. In Minnesota, the peak was reached in 1993, when tuition revenues represented 6.8 percent of median household income.

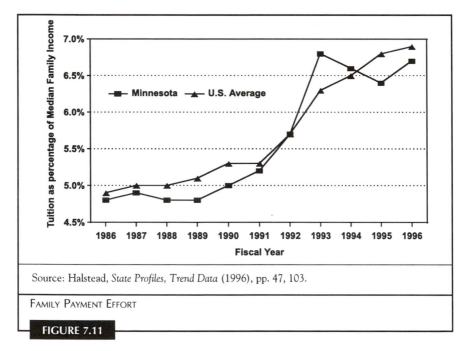

Source: Halstead, *State Profiles, Trend Data* (1996), pp. 47, 103.

FAMILY PAYMENT EFFORT

FIGURE 7.11

Figure 7.12 uses state data to illustrate how tuition and fees as a share of Minnesota per capita personal income compare by public system and type of private institution. Undergraduate resident tuition and fees as a percentage of personal income grew from 1990 to 1995 in all four sectors. The greatest growth was observed at the University of Minnesota, where required tuition and fees (at the College of Liberal Arts) grew from 12.7 percent of per capita personal income in 1990 to 15.5 percent in 1993, and stood at 15.3 percent in 1995.

As shown in figure 7.12, tuition and required fees at the private four-year institutions in the state represent a huge share of Minnesota's per capita personal income. Average undergraduate tuition and required fees at private four-year institutions were $9,230 in 1990, which was over 49 percent of Minnesota's per capita income that year. In 1995, average tuition and fees had risen to $12,919 or 55.9 percent of per capita personal income.

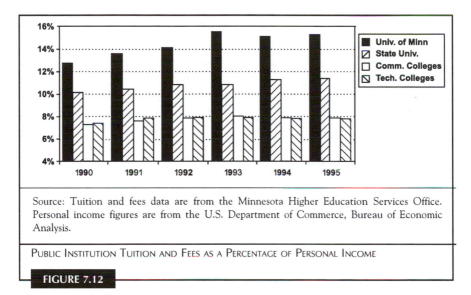

Source: Tuition and fees data are from the Minnesota Higher Education Services Office. Personal income figures are from the U.S. Department of Commerce, Bureau of Economic Analysis.

PUBLIC INSTITUTION TUITION AND FEES AS A PERCENTAGE OF PERSONAL INCOME

FIGURE 7.12

State policy makers are concerned about college affordability, and the legislature appointed a task force on Minnesota financial aid in 1993. One of its recommendations was to adjust the method of calculating state grants to provide additional assistance to the lowest income Minnesotans. The group also urged the legislature to link changes in appropriations for financial aid more closely to projected changes in tuition.

If the state budget continues to shrink, there may be some sentiment in the legislature to adopt an income cap on financial aid. Although private college and vocational school students accounted for about 20 percent of the undergraduates in fall 1993, they received almost half the state appropriations for financial aid. This apparent discrepancy is a function of the formula's recognition of the cost of attending the school of the student's choice. Many families considered to be middle-income families need government assistance to attend institutions with higher tuition rates. In Minnesota, about 12 percent of state grant funds (nearly $11 million) went to families making more than $42,889 in the 1992–93 school year.[31] In spite of generally widespread support for including the more expensive private colleges in the state grant program, some legislators wonder whether a disproportionate share of the student assistance funds are being provided for students in private colleges, even though this aid represents under 5 percent of the state's total investment in higher education.

STATE RESPONSES TO AN ERA OF CONSTRAINED RESOURCES

Minnesota policy makers have grappled with ways to make public higher education more efficient without making great adjustments to the present system of state subsidies. The current approach tries to increase the oversight role with regard to overall system performance, while at the same time permitting greater flexibility in the way the institutions operate. The senate higher education committees have been more aggressive than those in the house of representatives in pursuing the accountability agenda.

Accountability and Performance Incentives

The state legislature devoted significant energy to accountability issues in the 1995 session and specified a number of new provisions in law. For the first time ever, the higher education appropriations bill included $5 million to be released to each of the two higher education systems when the department of finance verifies that they have met performance objectives specified in law. These objectives include: increasing student retention, improving the graduation rate, and increasing the number of women and minority students and faculty.[32]

The governor and legislature also indicated their concern about faculty productivity in 1995 by enacting provisions that

- require all unrepresented system and campus academic administrators to increase their interaction with students through activities like teaching or advising;
- specify the purpose of sabbaticals, require that sabbatical plans be reported annually to the respective boards, and request the UM board of regents to review its sabbatical policies; and
- specify that collectively bargained labor agreements should meet goals such as defining expected work activities and other professional responsibilities of all employees, reassessing layoff procedures, and defining reasonable work-week and work-year provisions for full-time employees.

All these provisions indicate a discomfort within the legislature with working conditions and labor agreements that are viewed as undermining institutional productivity and the instructional mission of the institution.

Deregulation

While exercising greater accountability, the legislature has also indicated a willingness to experiment with removing mandates from higher education institutions and improving operating flexibility at the system and institutional levels.

A provision in a 1995 law requires the board of trustees of MnSCU to designate one of the state universities as a pilot site for improving higher education efficiency and streamlining governmental operations. The stated purpose of the legislation is to "measure the effects of removing a campus from mandates imposed by state agencies, other than basic health and life safety issues, ADA [American Disability Act] regulations, audit requirements, and employment, affirmative action, and collective bargaining issues."[33] The board is to choose a state university that is interested in establishing cooperative arrangements with the private sector and engaging in quality improvement initiatives.

The house of representatives has also recently established a higher education subcommittee on mandates. The subcommittee has solicited suggestions from campus faculty and staff about state mandates that they find onerous and intrusive, and has generated a substantial list of mandates that should be reviewed. An especially egregious example is that campus presidents lack the authority to close colleges due to bad weather—currently a responsibility of the department of employee relations in St. Paul. Legislators on the committees pertaining to higher education are planning to begin the mandate reduction process in the 1996 legislative session. However, many of the regulations were established by other legislative committees, and changes in many of these regulations require approval of these same committees. It remains to be seen how receptive legislators from these other committees will be to this effort.

Telecommunications

Minnesota has also embarked on a program to enhance productivity and efficiency in higher education through the use of telecommunications and instructional technology. The Learning Network of Minnesota, established in 1993 and funded at about $3 million per year, links all campuses electronically through the use of regional and statewide telecommunications networks.

SYSTEM RESPONSES TO AN ERA OF CONSTRAINED RESOURCES

It is difficult to answer comprehensively how individual institutions have responded to the decline in state support, given the number and variety of postsecondary institutions in the state. Research universities have more resources at their disposal than other types of institutions, and thus more flexibility in responding to changes in state appropriations. Given UM's high visibility, there is more information available concerning it than there is for MnSCU.

University of Minnesota System

Figure 7.13 shows the trends in selected revenue sources at UM from 1985 to 1994. The university experienced a 63 percent growth in its educational and general income between 1985 and 1994. Nongovernmental gifts, grants, and contracts increased 146 percent over this period, and tuition revenue increased 80 percent. The university ranks high nationally in its receipt of federal support—eighth in fiscal year 1992.[34] Federal funding increased 79 percent over this same period. In contrast, endowment income; state appropriations; and sales, services, and other income on current funds remained flat or fell since 1991.

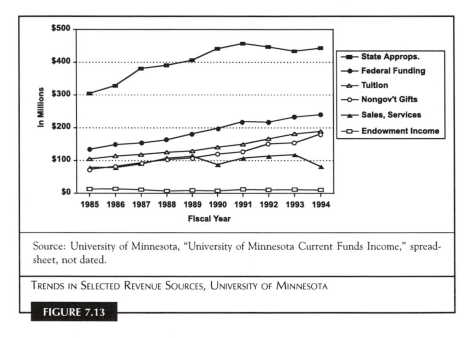

Source: University of Minnesota, "University of Minnesota Current Funds Income," spreadsheet, not dated.

TRENDS IN SELECTED REVENUE SOURCES, UNIVERSITY OF MINNESOTA

FIGURE 7.13

Tuition at UM remains competitive with tuition rates at similar institutions, but it is a source of concern within the state.[35] Institutional research prepared in 1993 attempted to identify the causes of tuition increases above the rate of inflation. They included a decline in state appropriations, a decline in the number of students attending college, and net increases in instructional costs attributable to non-personnel costs and salary costs above the rate of inflation.[36]

Leaders of UM are continually attempting to find ways to make strategic choices about what programs are most essential to the missions of its four institutions. They are doing this to better account for and manage the money the university receives and to reexamine some fundamental assumptions about the nature of the academic enterprise and the employment practices within higher education. Some of the initiatives discussed below affect all four campuses of the system; others (such as the discussion of tenure) do not.

The University of Minnesota embarked on a series of strategic plans over the last decade. The current plan is called University 2000. The planning effort, begun in 1993, involved identifying the system's strategic directions. Since then, the system has tried to make quality investments consistent with those directions. The University of Minnesota is also involved in a partnership with the state for obtaining needed funds for strategic investments. The university administration essentially struck a bargain to internally reallocate a portion of funds and collect a certain amount of tuition from students in exchange for a commitment from the state to help it fund well-defined priorities. This type of cooperation between the governor and legislature paid off for the system in the 1995 session.

The university has engaged in a variety of administrative restructuring efforts to help it save money. One effort has been to implement better accounting and budgeting systems to improve understanding of how money is spent—so that the university can plan more wisely for future spending. In addition, the university has nearly completed a transition to responsibility-centered management. It has utilized early retirement incentives and outsourced a few ancillary services, like the laundry and the library's bindery service. Additionally, the regents initiated a discussion in October 1995 about tenure as it relates to financial compensation and work rules. Board members have assured the university community of their support for academic freedom, but several individual members think that some change in work rules might be necessary.

Minnesota State Colleges and Universities

Since the merger that created the MnSCU system from three previously separate systems has consumed so much energy over the last four years, relatively little planning has been undertaken to adjust for lagging state appropriations. However, the new chancellor Judith Eaton has indicated her willingness to trade performance-based funding for a release from state mandates. She would like to see institutions gain more flexibility and autonomy from the state, enabling them to be more efficient and to harness a more entrepreneurial spirit. The chancellor also believes that the MnSCU system could take much greater advantage of technology to provide distance education. However, this kind of reengineering takes significant capital, and it is not clear how much help the state is willing to provide.

There is some expectation that the system will undertake some campus closings, but the social and economic costs are high, and campus closings result in minimal cost savings in the short term. Given the political difficulty of such efforts and the small financial rewards, the MnSCU system is likely to move slowly to close campuses. However, the system has committed to merging some technical and community colleges, which should result in some savings in personnel costs.

CONCLUSION

When interviews were conducted in October 1995, a sense of resignation characterized attitudes about higher education finance in Minnesota. While news of the budget surplus for the remaining biennium offered relief to higher education officials and legislators in the short term, the federal budget crisis remained unresolved, fueling uncertainty concerning the fiscal demands in the months and years ahead. Legislators' spending choices will continue to be limited by the obligations inherent in state entitlement programs, which could have a serious impact on higher education funding.

The reluctance to significantly alter the current funding model, however, is strong. There is a widely expressed conviction that as long as the legislature is controlled by the DFL party, there is little chance that the current system of state subsidies will be changed in any significant way. In addition, there is no expectation that the existing higher education establishment can reinvent itself in order to achieve any major breakthroughs in the cost structure. Thus, there is fear that without an expressed commitment to strengthen higher education funding in the state, continued flat funding will result in tuition increases. If financial aid does not increase concomitantly, the future could bring some erosion in the access to and quality of public higher education in Minnesota.

NOTES

1. See Minnesota Private College Research Foundation, *Ways and Means: How Minnesota Families Pay for College* (St. Paul: 1992).
2. John Brandl and Vin Weber, "An Agenda for Reform: Competition, Community, Concentration," a report to Governor Arne H. Carlson, November 1995.
3. *Chronicle of Higher Education Almanac* 42, no. 1 (1 September 1995): pp. 6, 66.
4. State of Minnesota, Department of Finance, "November 1995 Forecast," St. Paul, 1995, p. 37.
5. See Kent Halstead, *State Profiles: Financing Public Higher Education, 1978 to 1996 Trend Data* (Washington, D.C.: Research Associates of Washington,

1996) and *State Profiles: Financing Public Higher Education, 1996 Rankings* (Washington, D.C.: Research Associates of Washington, 1996).

6. Halstead, *State Profiles, Trend Data* (1996), p. 22.

7. Ibid.

8. Thomas F. Luce Jr., "Minnesota: Innovation in an Era of Constraint," in *The Fiscal Crisis of the States: Lessons for the Future*, edited by Steven Gold (Washington, D.C.: Georgetown University Press), p. 326–331.

9. Data for 1991 through 1993 are from Luce, "Minnesota: Innovation in an Era of Constraint," p. 332; data for 1994 and 1995 are from the State of Minnesota, Department of Finance.

10. State of Minnesota, Department of Finance, "November 1995 Forecast," p. 6.

11. State of Minnesota, Department of Finance, "1996-97 Adopted Budget," St. Paul, June 1995, p. 7.

12. State of Minnesota, Department of Finance, "Economic Update," St. Paul, April 1995, p. 3.

13. Appropriations, revenue, and other budgetary data are presented in fiscal years, unless otherwise noted.

14. "Summary of the Fiscal Actions of the 1995 Legislature," in *Money Matters* 10, no. 8 (Minnesota House of Representatives, Ways and Means Committee, Staff on Government Finance Issues, 13 July 1995), p. 2.

15. Halstead, *State Profiles: Financing Public Higher Education, 1978 to 1994* (Washington, D.C.: Research Associates of Washington, 1994), p. 8.

16. Halstead, *State Profiles: Trend Data* (1996), p. 46.

17. Geographic access has been the subject of numerous public policy pronouncements but has not been written into state law. As early as 1950, a governor's commission recommended that there be a public or private campus within commuting distance of every Minnesotan, or enough financial aid to allow individuals to relocate. In 1963, when a committee recommended a guideline for placing new campuses, this became known as the 35-mile rule. No new institution could be located within 35 miles of an existing college except in the Twin Cities. In 1969, the Higher Education Coordinating Commission adopted a policy that suggested that a public postsecondary institution could be placed within 35 miles of every community of 5,000 or more inhabitants.

18. Minnesota House of Representatives, Republican Caucus, undated internal memo.

19. Halstead, *State Profiles, Rankings* (1996), p. 19.

20. Halstead, *State Profiles: Trend Data* (1996), table 2, p. 8.

21. Ibid., p. 45.

22. Minnesota Higher Education Coordinating Board, "Enrollment of Students of Color Continue to Increase in Minnesota," St. Paul, 1994, p. 2. (In 1995, the name of this agency changed to the Minnesota Higher Education Services Office.)

23. Minnesota Higher Education Coordinating Board, *Enrollment Analysis and Outlook 1993* (St. Paul: 1993), p. 9.

24. Ibid., p. 11.
25. The Mayo Medical Foundation receives a small appropriation each year ($825,000 in fiscal year 1996) for Minnesota residents enrolled at the medical school and in the Family Practice and Graduate Residency programs.
26. The money is awarded, in a design for "shared responsibility," on the basis of cost of attendance at the institution chosen by the student. This cost of attendance consists of tuition and fees, as well as a living and miscellaneous expense allowance. (The formula does not account for all the costs of attending the most expensive institutions, but uses a maximum award as a way to limit awards to students attending private institutions.) Students are expected to contribute 50 percent of their cost of attendance, while students' families are expected to contribute the remainder. If a family is unable to meet this level of expectation, the difference will be made up by the government in the form of federal Pell Grants and Minnesota state grants. This second 50 percent is called the family-government share.
27. As cited in Minnesota Higher Education Coordinating Board, *Minnesota Higher Education: Recommendations for Change, Report to the Governor and the 1995 Legislature* (St. Paul: 1995), p. 38.
28. Minnesota Higher Education Services Office, *Financial Aid Awarded, Fiscal Year 1995* (St. Paul: 1995), p. 42.
29. Minnesota Statutes 1994, Section 135A.01.
30. Minnesota Private College Research Foundation, *Ways and Means*, "Executive Summary," p. 2.
31. State of Minnesota, Office of the Legislative Auditor, Program Evaluation Division, *Higher Education Tuition and State Grants* (St. Paul: 1994), p. 113.
32. The legislation specifies that the Minnesota State Colleges and Universities will receive $1 million in the second year of the biennium for each of the performance measures achieved. These performance measures were drafted by the legislature, and the definitions are being disputed by the MnSCU system. They include: (1) increase the percentage of the budget directed to instruction and academic resources; (2) increase the number of credits issued through telecommunications between fiscal years 1995 and 1996; (3) increase by at least 2 percent the retention of new entering freshmen on state university campuses who continue into the sophomore year from fiscal years 1995 to 1996 (the appropriation shall be distributed to those campuses that achieve the increase); (4) increase by at least 2 percent the percentage of students in two-year programs who graduate within two years of admission, and the percentage of students in four-year programs who graduate within four years of admission (the appropriation shall be distributed to campuses that achieve the increase); and (5) increase placement rates for occupational programs and transfer rates for academic programs for community and technical colleges.

    The performance measures for the UM system were drafted with the cooperation of campus administrators and there is every expectation that UM will qualify for all the performance-incentive funding. These measures include: (1) increases at the Twin Cities campus, excluding general college, in the percentage of 1996 new entering freshmen ranking in the top 25 percent of their high school class; (2) increases in the rate of retention of new freshmen entering during 1995; (3) increases in the number of new freshmen entering during 1996 who are minority students and increases in the percentage of faculty hired in 1995-96 who are women or minorities; (4) increases in the five-year graduate rate measured between August 1994 and August 1996; and (5) increases in the number of credits issued through telecommunications between fiscal year 1995 and fiscal year 1996.

33. Minnesota Laws 1995, Chapter 212, Section 3, Subdivision 3.
34. National Science Foundation, *Federal Support to Universities, Colleges, and Nonprofit Institutions: Fiscal Year 1992*, NSF 94-329 (Arlington, VA: 1994), p. 157.
35. In fiscal year 1994, undergraduate resident tuition at the University of Minnesota ranked sixth among the Big Ten public universities, according to University of Minnesota, "Tuition Rates: Historic Trends and Market Conditions," internal document, 10 February 1994, p. 2.
36. University of Minnesota, Management Planning and Information Services, "Sources of Tuition Increase in the University of Minnesota System 1971–72 through 1991–92," internal document, revised 10 October 1993.

CHAPTER 8

New York

Politics and the Funding of Higher Education

Kathy Reeves Bracco and Yolanda Sanchez-Penley

*T*his chapter synthesizes interview results with other data sources to illuminate the financing of higher education in New York during the first half of the 1990s. It is based on documents gathered from public offices, higher education institutions, and other relevant sources. Interviews with state officials, educational administrators, faculty, staff, and union officials took place in October 1995.

Economic recession, increased demands for state services, and the political promise of a tax cut contributed to reductions—in constant dollars—in state funding for higher education in the State of New York from 1990–91 to 1995–96. The reductions were partly due to economic difficulties caused by the recession that began with the stock market fall in 1987. By the end of 1993, New York had lost approximately 600,000 jobs; the banking, computer, and construction industries were hit particularly hard.[1]

During the recession, competition for state funds also intensified.[2] The social problems the state faced, particularly in New York City, increased demands for services in health, welfare, and corrections. As a result, New York's colleges and universities faced strong competition for a share of declining state revenues. New York's tax structure made the recession more difficult to weather, since more than half of the state's tax receipts are from personal income. As a result of little or no growth in wages and personal income, sales tax revenues also declined.

From 1990–91 to 1995–96, state general fund spending to higher education remained relatively flat in current dollars, but declined in constant dollars. State spending for higher education as a percentage of the overall state budget also declined during this period. Meanwhile, tuition almost doubled at the state's public institutions. The state has historically had low or no tuition in its public sector.

Unlike other states, New York has structured its state financial aid program—the Tuition Assistance Program (TAP)—as an entitlement. As tuition rates increased, maximum TAP awards rose steadily at the state's two public systems of higher education: the State University of New York (SUNY) and the City University of New York (CUNY). Because of these factors, New York—through incremental policies—shifted its funding from direct support of institutions to direct support of students.

These factors regarding state support also affected the state's independent sector, which is one of the strongest in the nation—enrolling over 40 percent of the students in the state. State elected officials have a long history of supporting the private sector both through direct funding to independent institutions and through financial aid to their students. Yet during the first half of the 1990s, direct state support to independent institutions (Bundy Aid) decreased significantly. During the same period, financial aid to students at independent institutions increased much less than the rate of inflation—and dramatically less than the increase in state aid to students at public institutions.

As in most other states, student loans in New York increased much faster than any other form of student aid. From 1990–91 to 1994–95, loan volume (in dollars) increased 50 percent in New York, while Pell Grants increased 17 percent.

In November 1994, Republican George E. Pataki was elected governor on a platform that promised to cut taxes and shrink government. To reduce taxes the governor had to find ways to reduce spending. In his first budget (for fiscal year 1995–96), the governor made higher education one of the targets for reduced spending, calling for a 31.5 percent cut for SUNY, a 27 percent cut for CUNY, and cuts in TAP, the state's main student financial aid program.

Opposition from the legislature and the higher education community led to a budget compromise that restored some of the proposed cuts, but still reduced state support significantly and raised tuition sharply for another year. In return for reduced cuts in funding, each public system of higher education was to produce a plan, due by 1 December 1995, addressing issues of efficiency and cost effectiveness. These reports were to focus on long-term strategies rather than continued short-term tactics such as maintenance deferrals, hiring freezes, course reductions, and tuition increases.

This budget compromise, which called for the December reports, served as a "wake-up" call for New York state policy makers and educational officials. Some policy makers and educational leaders are asking difficult questions regarding accountability, efficiency, and the role of higher education in economic development. University officials also agree it is time to face up to the realities of increased competition for limited state resources. The University at Buffalo's president, William Greiner, observed in his inaugural address that institutions of higher education are entering a new era, and it is time to "ask harder questions and open the debate [that] will lead the way into the twenty-first century. . . . In the face of sweeping change, we must be prepared to rework everything we do lest it be reworked for us by circumstances which may not be kind."[3]

STATE CONTEXT

New York, with a population of 18.1 million, is the third largest state in the nation. New Yorkers are generally well-educated, particularly in terms of the percentage of the population who have graduate or professional degrees. Over one-fourth of the state's population is minority and 23 percent of its house-holds speak a language other than English at home.[4]

State Economy

New York has recently begun to climb out of the recession of the late 1980s and early 1990s, but the recovery has been slow compared to many other states. After significant declines in employment, the state gained about 40,000 private sector jobs in 1994 (primarily in services)—the strongest job growth in eight years. Employment growth was still sluggish, however, compared with the rest of the country. Although growth in employment remained slow in 1995 and 1996 (at 0.7 and 0.3 percent, respectively), growth in personal income during this period was relatively strong, increasing at over 4.5 percent each year.[5]

New York's economic performance is strongly influenced by national economic trends and policies. In New York, income growth is dependent on industries such as finance, insurance and real estate—sectors very sensitive to national monetary policy. In addition, many of the new jobs in the service sector pay less, offer less security, and provide fewer fringe benefits than the jobs they replaced. These changes affect both the state's rate of income growth and the welfare of the work force.[6]

Despite changes in New York's economic landscape, per capita income was $26,782 during 1995, remaining well above the national average of $22,788. During the same year, however, the state's poverty rate of 17 percent was also above the national average of 14.5 percent.[7]

State Fiscal Structure

Revenue Sources

The largest source of revenue for New York is the personal income tax ($17 billion in 1996), followed by user taxes and business taxes (see figure 8.1).[8] The relative mix of these taxes has remained fairly stable over the past five

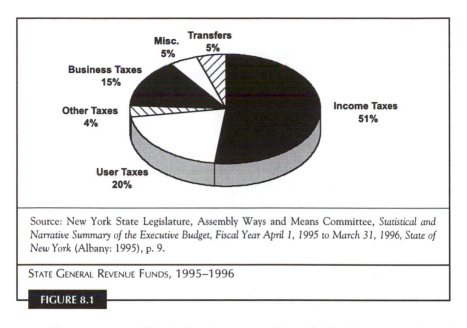

Source: New York State Legislature, Assembly Ways and Means Committee, *Statistical and Narrative Summary of the Executive Budget, Fiscal Year April 1, 1995 to March 31, 1996, State of New York* (Albany: 1995), p. 9.

STATE GENERAL REVENUE FUNDS, 1995–1996

FIGURE 8.1

years. Tax cuts enacted by the legislature in 1994 and 1995, however, reduced income and business taxes and could change the revenue mix in the future.

State revenues remained relatively flat during the first half of the 1990s, rising just over 9 percent from fiscal years 1990–96. The national Consumer Price Index (CPI) for this period was almost 20 percent. Revenues decreased almost 5 percent in 1991, the worst year of the recession in terms of state revenue intake. Revenues were beginning to pick up in 1994 and 1995 in most other states, but not in New York. From 1993 to 1996, state revenues in New York rose only 3 percent, due partly to the tax cuts that took effect in 1995 and 1996.[9]

Appropriations

From fiscal year 1990 to 1996, total state general fund appropriations for all budget categories increased 4 percent in current dollars. This increase is about one-fifth the rate of inflation (as measured by the national CPI). During this period, funding for non-categorical aid decreased 27 percent. Funding for social services and the health and environment category increased 48 and 69 percent, respectively. Funding for education (K–12 as well as higher education) increased 19 percent.[10]

General fund spending for higher education, meanwhile, remained relatively flat in current dollars, and decreased in constant dollars. From 1990–91 to 1995–96, state general fund support for SUNY increased 2 percent.[11] During the same period, state general fund support for CUNY decreased 16 percent.[12] Meanwhile, direct state support of independent institutions (provided through Bundy Aid) decreased 66 percent.[13] The decreases in state funding for the public institutions were somewhat offset by increased state funding for student financial aid, but this was not the case for the private institutions. The inflation rate during this period, as measured by the national CPI, was almost 15 percent.

The declining state support for higher education is more pronounced in terms of the budget share. Although education (K–12 and higher education) has traditionally taken up the largest share of the New York State budget, this is no longer the case. Table 8.1 reveals that K–12 education and higher education, combined, made up about one-third of general fund appropriations in 1990. In 1995, their share of state appropriations dropped to 28.6 percent. Medicaid spending, meanwhile, increased sharply, so that its share of state general fund appropriations eclipsed that of education by 1995. Moreover, table 8.1 shows that largely due to the huge increase in share for Medicaid spending, all other major categories declined in share.

TABLE 8.1

GENERAL FUND BY PROGRAM CATEGORY (IN PERCENT)

	1990	1995	Change 1990–95
K–12 Education	23.3	19.3	(17)
Higher Education	9.3	7.3	(22)
Cash Assistance	8.7	6.3	(28)
Medicaid	18.0	29.4	63
Corrections	4.9	3.8	(24)
Transportation	7.9	6.6	(16)
Other	27.9	27.3	(2)

Note: Because these data are from national sources, 1995 is the most recent year available.

Source: National Association of State Budget Officers (NASBO), *State Budget Report, 1992* (Washington, D.C.: 1993), p. 60; NASBO, *State Budget Report, 1995* (Washington, D.C.: 1995), p. 77.

Recent studies of state spending patterns have shown that New York's downward trend in its share of spending for higher education mirrors national trends. Moreover, on a percentage basis, Medicaid spending showed the sharpest increase in state budget share for both the nation and New York.[14] A major factor in New York's rising Medicaid costs is the increasing number of AIDS patients. Twenty-one percent of all Americans with AIDS are New Yorkers.[15]

Political Environment

Republican George E. Pataki defeated Mario M. Cuomo, the three-term Democratic incumbent, in November 1994. Pataki was elected largely on the strength of his promise to cut taxes and shrink the government. As a "strong governor,"[16] he has line-item veto authority, oversees the negotiation of collective bargaining agreements, and appoints, with senate approval, most of the public university board members in the state. Higher education does not appear to be a high priority for the governor; most of our respondents agreed that his primary concern was employment.

Members of the state assembly serve two-year terms, while senators and the governor serve four-year terms. Although the New York legislature meets year-round, most of the work is done during the first half of the year. Republicans held a majority in the senate over the last five years with a majority of 36 Republicans to 25 Democrats during the 1995–96 session. The Democrats had a 94-to-56 majority in the assembly; this represented a loss to the Republicans of six seats in the 1994 election.

Interviewees expressed concern regarding the "up-state/down-state" geographical split in the legislature. Both the senate, which tends to focus on up-state issues, and the assembly, which tends to focus on down-state (New York City) issues, have higher education committees that address legislation that deals with public, independent, and proprietary institutions in New York. During our visit in 1995, the senate chair, a suburban Republican, was interested primarily in economic development and job creation. The assembly chair, a Manhattan Democrat, was more concerned with tuition and course availability.

Governor Pataki has remained committed to tax cuts even as the state has faced budget shortfalls. He believes that the benefits of higher education are primarily private, and that students should bear more of the costs of obtaining that benefit. In his first budget (fiscal year 1996), Governor Pataki proposed significant budget reductions for higher education institutions, which he argued could recover through tuition increases and improved productivity. One state official explained that the governor and his staff believe that SUNY is over-built and needs to place more constraints on spending. In spite of controversy over the cuts, Governor Pataki achieved most of his legislative agenda; he implemented significant spending and tax cuts and removed 172,000 recipients from the welfare roles.[17]

The focus of Governor Pataki's 1996–97 budget proposal was economic revitalization. Although the state faced a $4 billion budget deficit, he pushed ahead with cuts in personal income and business taxes. He also called for a $1.6 billion reduction in Medicaid with severe cuts in hospitals, nursing homes, and home care. Democrats claimed that this action would devastate the health care industry and result in as many as 150,000 lost jobs. In addition, the governor proposed further cuts in welfare and education,[18] but the legislature restored many of these cuts.

HIGHER EDUCATION: GOVERNANCE AND DEMOGRAPHICS

Higher education in New York is composed of 314 degree-granting, two- and four-year institutions from the public, independent, and proprietary sectors. The public degree-granting institutions comprise two university systems: SUNY and CUNY. Each system has its own board of trustees, established by statute. There are 225 independent two- and four-year institutions and 337 vocational institutions.[19]

State Governance

The University of the State of New York (to be distinguished from the State University of New York) is established in the New York Constitution and encompasses all elementary, secondary, and postsecondary educational institutions, as well as libraries, museums, and other educational organizations. The university has the power to charter, register, and inspect these institutions, license practitioners, certify teachers, and provide state financial assistance.[20]

The board of regents of the University of the State of New York was established by the legislature in 1784. The 16 regents are elected by the legislature, one for each of the 12 judicial districts and four elected at large for five-year terms without pay. The regents appoint the president of the University of the State of New York. The president also serves as the commissioner of education and the chief executive officer of the state department of education.[21]

The regents and the state department of education (the administrative arm of the board of regents) are responsible for general supervision, planning, and coordination for education at all levels. The state department of education's Office of Higher and Professional Education (HPE) concentrates on postsecondary systems. HPE coordinates the development of new campuses and programs and accredits every curriculum in the state. It periodically reviews academic degree programs and proprietary school programs to ensure that they maintain high standards of quality and comply with state and federal requirements. The office has no budget authority for public postsecondary institutions.

The regents are responsible for developing a statewide master plan for higher education. Traditionally, a plan was required every four years, with all sectors of higher education consulted in the process, including the independent sector. The planning process has been streamlined under Governor Pataki, and the planning cycle has been extended to once every eight years.

Most of our respondents agreed that the state board of regents and the master plan have limited influence over higher education and little influence with either the governor or legislature.

In 1974, the New York State Higher Education Service Corporation (NYSHESC) was established to improve postsecondary education opportunities for the people of New York. Its primary responsibility is to centralize the processing of financial assistance—including grants, scholarships, and loans— for all postsecondary institutions in the state. Annually, it now receives one million applications for assistance and administers more than $2 billion in financial aid.[22]

New York Higher Education Sectors

State University of New York

The SUNY system has 64 campuses: 34 four-year colleges and 30 two-year community colleges. The system was established in 1948, making it the last public system established in the United States.[23] The four-year institutions include 4 graduate research universities and 13 comprehensive institutions with selected master's programs. In addition, there are 4 specialized colleges, 4 colleges of technology, and 2 colleges of agriculture and technology. Five statutory colleges are located at independent universities (4 at Cornell University and 1 at Alfred University). These colleges are partially supported by public funds, and are governed through a cooperative arrangement between the SUNY trustees and the governing boards of the independent institutions. The system has 4 health science centers; 2 are free-standing and 2 are associated with the research universities at Stony Brook and Buffalo.[24]

The SUNY system is governed by a board of trustees which consists of 15 members appointed by the governor with the consent of the senate, and 1 student chosen by the student body (ex-officio). The SUNY system's day-to-day operations are overseen by the System Administration Executive Council, which includes the chancellor and vice chancellors.

When Governor Pataki took office, there were seven vacancies on the 16-member SUNY board left unfilled by Governor Cuomo. According to several respondents, the governor has filled these positions with trustees committed to his tax-cutting agenda.

With one exception, each of SUNY's state-operated campuses has an advisory campus council.[25] The council's responsibilities include recommending candidates for the campus presidency, reviewing annual budgets, and managing grounds, buildings, and equipment.

The State University of New York's community colleges have local sponsors (usually one or more counties) that have significant financial responsibilities for the colleges. Community colleges have their own 10-member boards of trustees. The local sponsor appoints 5 members to its board; the governor appoints 4 members, and the student body elects the student representative. Trustees appoint college presidents, recommend approval of the capital and operating budgets, and set policy for academic affairs, student services, and administration.

City University of New York

The state legislature established a municipal college system in 1926. The system was designated as the City University of New York in 1961.[26] Today, the CUNY system has 19 institutions, all located in New York City. Six of the institutions are two-year colleges. One senior college (City College) offers doctorates. Eight offer undergraduate and master's degrees, and three offer baccalaureate degrees. The remaining institution is the systemwide graduate center.

The City University of New York's mission statement describes CUNY as "an articulated system of higher education that is responsible to the needs of its urban setting."[27] State law specifically addresses the need for CUNY to maintain close articulation between senior and community college units. It states that "governance and operation of senior and community colleges should be jointly conducted . . . to maintain the university as an integrated system and facilitate articulation between units."[28] City University of New York is viewed by the legislature as a vehicle for the upward mobility of the disadvantaged in the city.[29]

The board of trustees of CUNY consists of 17 members that govern both senior institutions and the community colleges. The governor appoints 10 members with the consent of the senate; and the mayor of New York City appoints 5, also with the consent of the senate. Two ex-officio members, a representative of the student body, and a representative of the faculty, complete the board's membership. Trustees serve seven-year terms; the student representative serves one year.

Independent and Proprietary Institutions

Independent, nonprofit institutions dominated higher education in New York for almost two centuries.[30] Largely because public systems were established so late in New York, the independent—or private—institutions still have great influence in the state. Independent colleges and universities enroll over 40 percent of the students in New York State. The importance of the independent institutions is evidenced by direct state funding to institutions for degrees awarded to state residents, and by financial assistance for students attending independent institutions.

The independent colleges and universities in New York are operated on a not-for-profit basis. The institutions have their own boards of trustees and most are members of the Commission on Independent Colleges and Universities of the State of New York (CICU).

The 28 proprietary colleges are profit-making, private entities mostly specializing in business and commerce. Proprietary colleges receive no direct state aid.[31]

Current and Projected Enrollments

Head-count enrollment in New York for 1995–96 was 986,468. From fall 1990 to fall 1995, enrollments in state institutions of higher education declined by approximately 1 percent. Changes in enrollment vary by sector, however (see table 8.2). For instance, enrollment increased at CUNY (by 4 percent), decreased at SUNY (by 5 percent), and remained relatively stable at the independent institutions.

TABLE 8.2

ENROLLMENT IN SUNY, CUNY, AND INDEPENDENT INSTITUTIONS

	SUNY	CUNY	Independents	Total
1990–91	403,028	200,688	396,469	1,000,185
1991–92	400,777	200,336	395,816	996,929
1992–93	404,065	202,619	403,995	1,010,679
1993–94	397,637	207,567	401,173	1,006,377
1994–95	393,228	212,812	401,475	1,007,515
1995–96	381,568	208,417	396,483	986,468

Note: This table measures enrollment by head count.
Source: State of New York, Department of Education.

Minority students make up approximately 30 percent of the total student enrollment in higher education in New York.[32] It is estimated that by the year 2000, half of CUNY first-time freshmen will have been born outside the United States. In fall 1994, CUNY reported that 47 percent of their first-year students spoke a native language other than English. The national average is just under 14 percent. This trend, which is expected to continue, will result in increasing numbers of students requiring English language assessment, placement, and instruction.[33]

In fall 1994, 79 percent of all New Yorkers who were freshmen attended college in New York.[34] The State University of New York reported that over 95 percent of its students were residents from the State of New York. Foreign students accounted for 2.0 percent of the enrollment and United States residents from outside New York State accounted for 2.5 percent.[35]

Student enrollment in K–12 public schools is increasing after a period of decline. Enrollment peaked at 3.4 million in the early 1970s, declined to a low of 2.5 million in 1989–90, and is projected to reach 3.0 million students in 2003–04. Over 55 percent of that growth is expected to be in New York City.[36] The state is expecting 166,931 high school graduates in 1996–97 and projects 192,356 by the year 2006–07, an increase of 15 percent.[37] As a result, the state expects moderate enrollment increases in higher education over the next decade.

Kent Halstead reports two indicators of public higher education enrollment. The participation ratio, which divides full-time-equivalent (FTE) students in public institutions by the number of new high school graduates, indirectly measures "the degree to which a state provides attractive and accessible opportunities for higher education students relative to the number of high school graduates."[38] Higher ratios indicate a larger public system in relation to high school graduates, with more opportunity for enrollment. Figure 8.2 shows that New York's participation ratio has been gradually increasing since 1988–89. This ratio even increased somewhat during the 1990s, while enrollments in state public institutions of higher education were decreasing slowly. This is primarily because the number of high school graduates was decreasing at a faster rate during this period.[39]

The second indicator, student enrollment, measures FTE students in public institutions per 1,000 residents. This measure can be interpreted similarly to the participation ratio, but it is applied to the general population of the state rather than just to high school graduates. Figure 8.3 shows that New York's student enrollment ratio, which increased steadily for three years at the end of the 1980s, has remained fairly constant during the 1990s.

During the period shown in figures 8.2 and 8.3, New York's participation and student enrollment ratios remained well below the U.S. average. In 1995–96, for instance, New York ranked 36th out of the 50 states in its participation ratio and 44th in its student enrollment ratio.[40] This can be largely explained by the fact that New York's private institutions play a central role in providing higher education in the state. The participation and student enrollment ratios do not account for the prominent role that private institutions play in many eastern states.

FINANCING HIGHER EDUCATION IN THE STATE OF NEW YORK

State general fund spending for higher education remained relatively flat from 1990–91 to 1995–96, which represents a decrease in constant dollars. The share of state appropriations to higher education also declined during the first half of the 1990s. Many state and university officials expect this downward

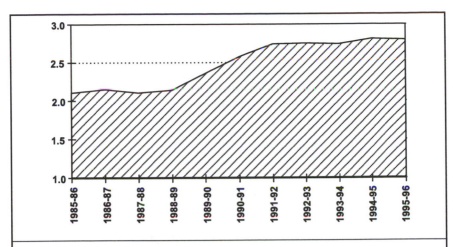

Note: The participation ratio divides the number of FTE public college and university students by the number of new high school graduates.

Source: Kent Halstead, *State Profiles: Financing Public Higher Education 1978 to 1996, Trend Data* (Washington, D.C.: Research Associates of Washington, 1996), p. 65.

NEW YORK PARTICIPATION RATIO

FIGURE 8.2

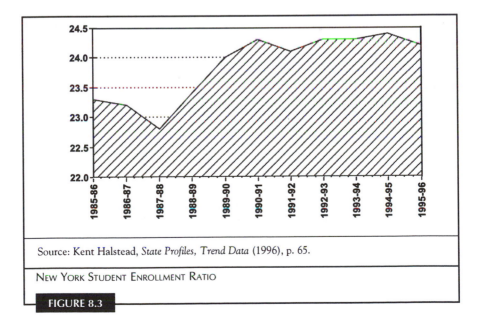

Source: Kent Halstead, *State Profiles, Trend Data* (1996), p. 65.

NEW YORK STUDENT ENROLLMENT RATIO

FIGURE 8.3

trend to continue, particularly as Governor Pataki tries to implement his tax cuts. As one state official said, "New York has joined the national agenda of reducing deficits and downsizing government." According to a recent national study, higher education spending in New York fell from 9.3 percent of total state spending in 1990 to 7.3 percent in 1995.[41]

The percentage of the state budget allocated to *public* higher education has traditionally been well below the U.S. average, as shown in figure 8.4. As this figure reveals, the percentage of the state's budget allocated to public higher education has steadily declined. From 1990–91 to 1995–96, the share of the state budget allocated to higher education fell from just under 4 percent of the state budget to about 3 percent. The 1995–96 share ranked New York 48th in the nation.[42] The large disparity between New York and the national average shown in figure 8.4 is partly attributable to the fact that the state allocates substantial funds for private higher education, which are not reflected in the figure.

Halstead provides other measures of state commitment to funding public higher education. For instance, New York is a high-tax state relative to other states, but the proportion of these taxes going to public higher education placed New York 48th out of 50 states and the District of Columbia in 1994–95.[43] In providing another indicator of state support for public students, Halstead reports that educational appropriations per student are also declining in New York. These declining measures contrast with the "family payment effort," which indicates that New Yorkers are now expending a larger proportion of their median family income to pay for tuition.[44] The increase in the family payment effort, combined with the decreases in the measures of state

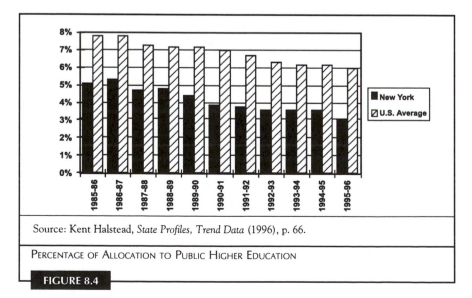

Source: Kent Halstead, *State Profiles, Trend Data* (1996), p. 66.

PERCENTAGE OF ALLOCATION TO PUBLIC HIGHER EDUCATION

FIGURE 8.4

support for public higher education, suggests that a greater portion of the responsibility for paying for higher education is shifting from the state to the individual.

These measures do not take into account independent institutions, which enroll over 40 percent of the college and university students in the state. In addition, the state funds private institutions directly through Bundy Aid, and it supports students at private institutions through TAP. Nevertheless, Halstead's measures show that New York's commitment to *public* higher education has declined on both a percentage and dollar basis.

Sources of Funds

State University of New York

The State University of New York derives about 40 percent of its income from direct state appropriations. The balance is from tuition and fees, federal funds, and other sources. The State University of New York's community colleges are funded by the state, local government sponsors, and tuition and fees. About 33 percent of the operating income at community colleges comes from direct state appropriations. (State aid cannot exceed 40 percent of operating income at community colleges, and tuition revenue may not exceed one-third of the operating income.) Table 8.3 provides a breakdown of SUNY revenue sources from 1990–91 through 1995–96, as well as the CPI for the United States for comparison. The greatest increases in the SUNY budget come from student and other university-generated income, which, when taken together, surpassed the income from state tax dollars in fiscal year 1992–93. The increase in state tax dollars from 1991 to 1996 was only 2 percent, a rate of growth well below the inflation rate of 15 percent for this period, as measured by the national CPI.

The legislature approved a SUNY budget for 1995–96 that included an increase in tuition revenues of $54 million, which translated into a 28 percent tuition hike. In passing this budget, the legislature required SUNY to produce a multiyear plan on productivity issues by 1 December 1995. For the 1996–97 budget, the legislature did not approve any increases in tuition at SUNY.

City University of New York

The City University of New York's senior and community colleges derive most of their funding from state appropriations. The City University of New York funding for 1990–91 through 1995–96 appears in table 8.4. In the six years shown, university funding increased by 11 percent; however, a large portion of this increase was provided by tuition. During the same period, tuition revenues for senior colleges and community colleges increased by 113 percent and 142 percent, respectively.

TABLE 8.3							
STATE UNIVERSITY OF NEW YORK FUNDING SOURCES (IN MILLIONS OF DOLLARS)							
	1991	1992	1993	1994	1995	1996	% Change 1991–96
State Tax Dollars	1,849.6	1,957.6	1,828.2	1,968.5	2,056.2	1,888.3	2.1
Local Sponsorship	251.9	261.2	265.5	274.4	282.2	286.9	13.9
Student Revenue	522.1	658.2	835.8	861.3	906.2	1,089.1	108.6
Other Univ. Income	963.3	1,100.3	1,100.7	1,108.2	1,226.5	1,249.4	29.7
Federal and Other	683.7	679.1	742.0	801.6	832.1	879.9	28.7
One-Time Univ. Income	234.9	0.0	0.0	0.0	0.0	0.0	0.0
TOTAL	4,505.5	4,656.4	4,772.2	5,014.0	5,303.2	5,393.6	19.7
U.S. CPI*							14.8

* The CPI figure is based on calendar rather than fiscal years.

Note: State aid for community colleges increased by 15 percent during the period shown in this table, while state aid for state-operated colleges declined by 1 percent.

Sources: State University of New York, Budget Development Office, 1996. The CPI figure is from the U.S. Department of Labor, Bureau of Labor Statistics, "Consumer Price Index for All Urban Consumers, U.S. City Average," October 1996.

The legislature approved the CUNY budget for 1995–96 that included an increase in tuition revenues of $94.6 million, which translated into a 31 percent tuition hike. Budget approval by the legislature required CUNY to prepare a multiyear plan on work-force development, technology, and other university initiatives by 1 December 1995.[45] For 1996–97, CUNY did not request an increase in tuition.

Independent Institutions

Higher education in New York has historically been dominated by independent institutions. In the late 1960s, however, when CUNY was tuition-free and SUNY charged $400 for tuition, many independent colleges and universities faced dire financial situations and in some cases bankruptcy. Independent institutions argued that if they closed their doors, enrollments at public institutions would increase, the state would have to expand capacity at these institutions, and taxpayers would have to pay the bill. The independents asked the governor to help them weather their financial difficulties, which resulted in the creation of Bundy Aid, a program of direct aid to institutions.

Governor Rockefeller, along with the chancellor of the board of regents of the University of the State of New York, appointed a select committee on the future of private and independent higher education in New York State and charged them to investigate "how the state can help preserve the strength and

---

TABLE 8.4

CITY UNIVERSITY OF NEW YORK FUNDING SOURCES (IN MILLIONS OF DOLLARS)

	1991	1992	1993	1994	1995	1996	% Change 1991–96
State Aid	739.4	682.0	609.0	678.3	732.8	622.7	(16)
City Aid	165.1	119.6	99.1	106.2	110.8	107.5	(35)
Tuition & Other*	246.9	333.0	400.3	424.4	426.6	544.3	120
TOTAL	1,151.3	1,134.6	1,108.4	1,208.9	1,270.2	1,274.5	11
U.S. CPI†							14.8

* Other revenue accounts for less than 1 percent of this category, according to the CUNY budget office.

† The CPI figure is based on calendar rather than fiscal years.

Note: State aid for community colleges increased by 6 percent during the period shown in this table, while state aid for senior colleges decreased by 19 percent.

Sources: The City University of New York, *The Chancellor's Budget Request*, 1991–92 through 1996–97 editions, 1996–97 edition updated February 1996 (New York: 1991–96). The CPI data are from the U.S. Department of Labor, Bureau of Labor Statistics, "Consumer Price Index for All Urban Consumers."

---

vitality of our private and independent institutions of higher education."[46] McGeorge Bundy, president of The Ford Foundation, chaired the committee. Sixteen recommendations were made, the most significant being a program to provide unrestricted aid directly to independent colleges and universities based on the number of degrees awarded. This recommendation was approved by the legislature in 1968, which established Bundy Aid.[47]

In recent years, Bundy Aid has decreased dramatically. Figure 8.5, which illustrates the change in Bundy Aid to independent institutions, depicts the decrease in direct funding for independent institutions. The decline began in 1990–91, and by 1992–93 direct funds to institutions were reduced by half. Figure 8.5, considered alongside the previous discussion of state appropriations to SUNY and CUNY, illustrates that direct state aid to independent as well as public institutions declined in the 1990s.

In 1995–96, independents were given $39 million in direct state aid, but they urged the legislature to provide the maximum statutory limit for direct aid (approximately $122 million).[48]

Budget Process

The State University of New York and CUNY submit preliminary budgets to the state division of the budget during September for the state fiscal year that begins April 1 (the fiscal year for both university systems begins July 1). Formal

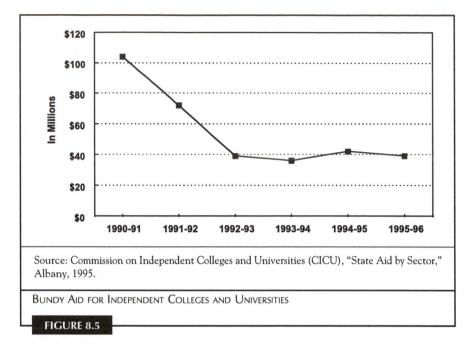

Source: Commission on Independent Colleges and Universities (CICU), "State Aid by Sector," Albany, 1995.

BUNDY AID FOR INDEPENDENT COLLEGES AND UNIVERSITIES

FIGURE 8.5

submissions come later, after the boards of trustees act on the budgets. The division of the budget specifies a list of indexes for inflation adjustment that must be used by the systems, and provides an estimate for institutional revenues (raised through tuition, interest income, etc.). The system governing boards have the authority to set tuition, with approval of the legislature.

The legislature begins with an appropriation for each campus, and then provides appropriations to university-wide and student aid programs. They then subtract the "income offset," or the amount of tuition, fees and other income that they expect the universities to generate. While the budget is scheduled for approval by March 1, the legislature often does not pass a budget until May. After the budget is approved, the governing board of each system adopts an annual financial plan that implements the budget. Should a midyear budget adjustment occur, SUNY and CUNY have the flexibility to develop their own plan for meeting target cuts within 30 days. If they do not meet the 30-day target, the state director of the budget determines where the cuts occur.

The State University of New York and CUNY are given flexibility (relative to other state agencies) to distribute and expend money. The systems do maintain a schedule of payments to individual campuses, however. The systems can move money from one institution to another, but they must provide reasonable justifications if they do so.

The Winter 1995 State Budget Process

Many officials told us that the higher education budget battles for 1995–96 were much more contentious than they had been in the past. This was primarily because the new governor's proposed budget contained a 31.5 percent cut in state support to SUNY ($290 million) and a 27 percent cut to CUNY ($158 million). The reaction was immediate, and even Republicans who generally supported the governor and his platform were not openly supportive of this component. State University of New York officials argued that the governor's proposed budget cuts to SUNY would require closing some smaller rural colleges. Since many Republican legislators are from rural areas that depend on these institutions for economic activity, continued state support for these campuses is generally popular among these Republicans.

Although the final budget cuts were less severe than originally proposed, they were still significant. For instance, SUNY's budget for 1995–96 was cut by $168 million, while CUNY lost $110 million in state support. State funding for the Tuition Assistance Program (which is for students at public and private institutions), however, actually increased 4.7 percent.

The Budget Process for 1996–1997

In fall 1995, as the state university was preparing to submit its budget request for the 1996–97 fiscal year, philosophical differences over the contents of the request created a great deal of tension between the system administration and the SUNY board of trustees. As part of its standard procedures, the state's division of the budget sent a letter providing guidelines for budget preparation. The 1995 letter asked that the budget be based on the previous year's budget plus a 1 percent increase to the base.

The SUNY administration prepared its budget request according to these guidelines, but the result was not acceptable to many of the newly appointed trustees who believed that there should be some cutbacks reflected in the budget. After much discussion, the board of trustees voted down the submitted budget by a 9-to-6 margin. Eventually the trustees moved to submit the budget to the division of the budget "for information only." One former university official noted that this was a unique situation because it was the first time that a governing board refused a request for additional money from the state.

The governor's budget for 1996–97 again proposed reductions for SUNY and CUNY, but the legislature rejected many of them. The governor also included several recommendations from SUNY's December 1995 report, *Rethinking SUNY*, in his budget. The major recommendation, which was adopted by the legislature, creates provisions that allow reserve funds to be carried forward to the next year by the campuses. Previously, these funds would revert to the state. The legislature rejected recommendations for a single budget line for the system and for differential tuition rates across SUNY campuses. Legislators also froze tuition for SUNY and CUNY; in relation to SUNY, they made it clear that the increases above the governor's proposed budget were made so that SUNY would not need a tuition increase (CUNY had not sought an increase).

Tuition

Historically, public tuition rates in New York State have been low relative to the rest of the country. Tuition was not charged at CUNY prior to 1976.

Undergraduate tuition at SUNY's four-year senior institutions averaged $3,400 in 1995–96, a 28 percent increase over the previous year. Tuition at the community colleges averaged $2,167 for 1995–96, a 10 percent increase over the previous year. Figure 8.6 illustrates the trend in SUNY tuition rates over the last six years. Tuition increased by 127 percent at the state-operated campuses and by 58 percent at the community colleges from 1990–91 to 1995–96.

As with SUNY, tuition rates at CUNY have increased rapidly over the last several years. For 1995–96, senior college rates averaged $3,200 for residents, an increase of 31 percent over the previous year. Community college tuition averaged $2,500, an increase of 18.5 percent over 1994–95 levels. Figure 8.7 illustrates the trend in tuition rates for CUNY over the last six fiscal years.

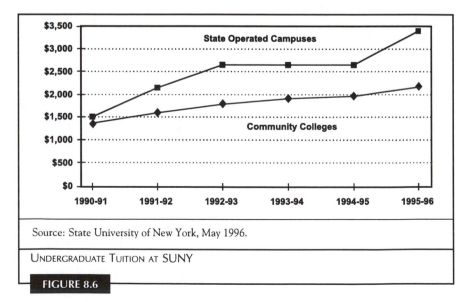

Source: State University of New York, May 1996.

UNDERGRADUATE TUITION AT SUNY

FIGURE 8.6

From 1991 to 1996, tuition increased 156 percent at the senior colleges and 104 percent at the community colleges.

Average tuition rates at New York's independent institutions increased from $10,280 in 1990–91 to $14,182 during 1995–96, an increase of 38 percent. The rate in 1995–96 was well above the national average for independent colleges and universities.

The tuition factor measures the proportion of a public institution's funding (state appropriations plus tuition) that comes from tuition. As a result of tuition increases in the 1990s, students in New York now pay a share of costs greater than the national average. In 1990–91, New York's tuition factor was 22.2 percent, compared to 26.2 percent for the nation. In 1995–96, the tuition factor for New York increased to 32.7 percent, compared to a national average of 31.6 percent.[49]

Governor Pataki's budget proposal for fiscal year 1997, as well as cutting state funding for higher education, called for increases in tuition for fall 1996. According to a recent analysis by the assembly ways and means committee, state support in 1990–91 accounted for 79 percent of the operating costs for higher education, while tuition covered 21 percent of those costs; the governor's proposal would have resulted in state support picking up 54 percent of the operating costs for higher education, with tuition revenues accounting for 46 percent.[50] The legislature chose instead to freeze tuition both at SUNY and CUNY.

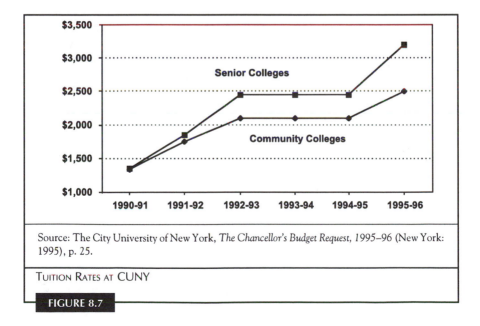

Source: The City University of New York, *The Chancellor's Budget Request, 1995–96* (New York: 1995), p. 25.

TUITION RATES AT CUNY

FIGURE 8.7

Financial Aid

State Funds

New York has long had a policy of supporting students through tuition assistance grants. Over 22 percent of state higher education appropriations is used for student grants—the highest percentage in the country. Approximately $1,148 is awarded in grant aid per FTE undergraduate student, compared to a U.S. average of only $315.

The most prominent state aid program is TAP. The Tuition Assistance Program was initially instituted in 1974 as a need-based program to help students attend institutions of their choice. Originally, its primary purpose was to maintain access to the independent colleges and universities. But during the 1990s for the first time, the amount of TAP funding supporting students at SUNY and CUNY (combined) surpassed the amount supporting students at independent institutions. As table 8.5 shows, TAP expenditures to undergraduates at CUNY and SUNY increased 180 and 97 percent, respectively, while TAP expenditures to undergraduates at independent institutions increased only 7 percent.

The Tuition Assistance Program is an entitlement program; qualifying students who apply for the award receive it. If funds are expended faster than expected, a deficiency appropriation must be enacted. Students are normally eligible for four years of support, but there is a credit accumulation maximum to guard against those who are not making reasonable progress toward a degree. Since 1990, different governors have tried to reduce TAP, leading many to believe limitations on award amounts and stricter criteria for receiving awards are inevitable.

Tuition Assistance Program awards are indexed to net taxable income. When TAP was established, the maximum award paid for approximately half of the average tuition at the independent institutions. In 1995–96, however, the maximum TAP award paid for only 26 percent of the average independent college tuition. Until the mid-1990s, maximum TAP awards covered 100 percent of tuition at CUNY and SUNY. This past year a change was made so that the maximum award paid for 90 percent of tuition at SUNY and CUNY. Table 8.6 shows the changes in the TAP maximum awards, and the percentage of tuition covered by those awards from 1990–91 to 1995–96.

At SUNY and the independent colleges, approximately half the students receive a TAP award. At CUNY, approximately 70 percent receive awards; of these, over half get the maximum award. While steep tuition increases in the public sector mirror those seen throughout the country, the effects of tuition hikes in New York may be somewhat mitigated by the state financial aid programs. Increases in TAP during the first half of the decade helped to maintain student access.

TABLE 8.5

TUITION ASSISTANCE PROGRAM EXPENDITURES (IN MILLIONS OF DOLLARS)

	1991	1992	1993	1994	1995	1996	% Change 1991–96
Undergraduate							
CUNY	56.0	83.3	121.5	131.6	139.4	156.6	180
SUNY	85.9	110.2	149.1	156.4	163.5	169.0	97
Independent	199.8	221.6	231.7	226.9	238.0	213.1	7
Other Degree-Granting							
Institutions	54.9	68.2	69.1	60.4	63.2	60.9	11
All Others	27.3	17.9	17.5	20.1	19.5	12.6	(54)
SUBTOTAL	423.9	501.2	588.9	595.4	623.6	612.2	44
Post-Baccalaureate							
CUNY	0.7	0.7	0.8	0.8	0.7	0.3	(60)
SUNY	4.0	3.8	3.9	3.6	3.5	1.4	(65)
Independent	5.8	5.3	5.5	5.3	5.2	2.0	(66)
SUBTOTAL	10.6	9.7	10.1	9.7	9.4	3.6	(65)
GRAND TOTAL	434.5	510.9	599.0	605.1	633.0	615.9	42

Note: Figures may not add exactly to totals due to rounding.

Source: The University of the State of New York, State Education Department, *Annual Report by the Board of Regents to the Governor and the Legislature on Student Financial Aid Programs* (Albany: 1991– 96 editions).

TABLE 8.6

MAXIMUM UNDERGRADUATE TUITION ASSISTANCE PROGRAM AWARDS

	Maximum TAP Award (in Dollars)			Percentage of Tuition Covered by Maximum TAP Award		
	SUNY	CUNY	Independents	SUNY	CUNY	Independents
1990–91	1,375	1,250	4,125	100	100	40
1991–92	2,175	1,850	4,050	100	100	36
1992–93	2,675	2,450	3,575	100	100	30
1993–94	2,675	2,450	3,575	100	100	29
1994–95	2,675	2,450	4,050	100	100	31
1995–96	3,082	2,902	3,900	90	90	28

Source: Commission on Independent Colleges and Universities.

At the same time, the nature of these awards combined with other budgetary trends in New York during the first half of the 1990s to produce a unique situation. Since TAP awards are entitlements and cover almost the full cost of tuition in the public sector, the amount awarded to students at public institutions rose sharply during the first half of the 1990s. At the same time, state funding of institutions of higher education remained flat. These two trends produced a *de facto* shift in state support away from institutions of public higher education and toward their students.

This trend toward state support of students is not mirrored, however, in the independent sector, for the share of TAP funding that supported students at private institutions declined significantly. At the same time, direct state support to independent institutions (Bundy Aid) decreased. These two trends produced a *de facto* shift in state support from the independent to the public sector and its students.

There are two other financial aid programs that are not entitlements: the Supplemental Tuition Assistance Program (STAP) and Aid for Part-Time Study (APTS). The Supplemental Tuition Assistance Program provides assistance for one additional semester for students who need remediation before their first year of study. APTS is a campus-based program designed to help part-time students with a maximum award of $2,000 per year.

Loans

The annual report of the New York State Higher Education Service Corporation for 1993–94 reported that it expects to increase the volume of direct lending by 40 percent in 1995–96 and 60 percent or more thereafter.

Loan volume (in dollars) increased 50 percent from 1990–91 to 1994–95, while Pell Grants rose only 17 percent during the same time period. Table 8.7 shows selected sources of state and federal student financial assistance. Although most forms of grants and "non-loan" aid increased from 1990–91 to 1994–95, the rapid increase in loan amounts is steadily making loans the dominant source of student financial assistance. The increases in the state grant programs TAP and STAP are notable, as is the rise in grants from independent institutions.

The City University of New York provides those upper division students who are the most needy with relief from the reduction in TAP awards through the state-funded City University Supplemental Tuition Assistance (CUSTA) program. State funding for CUSTA, however, has not kept pace with the increasing number of eligible students. The State University of New York, in the 1992–93 budget, spent $2 million to provide 10,000 students with tuition assistance beyond the state-funded State University Supplemental Tuition Assistance (SUSTA) program.

The "institutional funds" category in table 8.7 warrants further comment. The Commission on Independent Colleges and Universities has noted that the independent sector diverts more than 30 percent of tuition revenues to finance institutional aid. The Commission on Independent College and Universities predicts this number will increase to 40 percent by 1996–97. Furthermore, future tuition increases will be devoted primarily to funding institutional

TABLE 8.7

SELECTED SOURCES OF STUDENT ASSISTANCE (IN MILLIONS OF DOLLARS)

	1990–91	1991–92	1992–93	1993–94	1994–95 (Estimated)	% Change 1991–95
State Funds						
TAP & STAP	435.1	512.0	697.1	703.4	736.2	69
SUSTA & CUSTA*	2.7	2.7	2.6	2.6	2.6	(2)
Aid for Part-Time Study	9.0	11.0	11.1	11.3	13.2	47
Fellowships (SUNY & CUNY)	6.9	6.4	6.3	6.3	6.3	(9)
Federal Funds						
Pell Grants	467.2	563.4	627.4	552.6	546.2	17
College Work Study	5.4	5.9	16.9	18.3	18.2	237
Loans	1,153.6	1,280.6	1,396.9	1,721.0	1,991.9	73
Institutional Funds†	676.0	760.0	905.9	964.3	1,087.3	41

* SUSTA and CUSTA stand for State University Supplemental Tuition Assistance and City University Supplemental Tuition Assistance, respectively.

† Institutional funds are grants from independent institutions.

Source: The University of the State of New York, State Education Department, *Annual Report by the Board of Regents* (1991–95 editions).

aid rather than to paying operating expenses. No data are available in the public sector on using tuition revenues to fund student aid.

Figure 8.8 summarizes New York's financial aid picture by showing the trend in student aid by funding source for all institutions of higher education.

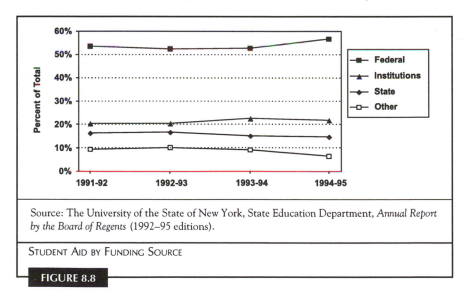

Source: The University of the State of New York, State Education Department, *Annual Report by the Board of Regents* (1992–95 editions).

STUDENT AID BY FUNDING SOURCE

FIGURE 8.8

Of the total funds available for student aid, the largest source is the federal government, followed by aid from institutions themselves.

RESPONSES TO CONSTRAINED RESOURCES

State Responses

Although direct state support to the public and private systems of higher education eroded during the first half of the 1990s, New York has been increasing its state support to students attending public institutions. Moreover, while tuition rates have increased sharply, they are still below the levels in many other states in the region. The governor has proposed, in fact, that New York should charge its college students about the same amount of money for their education as other states in the Northeast.[51] Others have argued, however, along the lines of this editorial in the *New York Times*:

> Access to quality higher education is one of the proudest traditions New Yorkers have. But mere sentimentality is not at work here. An educated work force is surely as crucial to the city's and state's economic health as lower taxes, the goals to which higher education is being sacrificed. . . . Cutting off their access is not only unjust . . . it is economically self-defeating.[52]

Governor Pataki's budget proposals for 1996 and 1997, stimulated spirited reactions from those within higher education. Although the funding levels passed by the legislature were not as low as the governor originally proposed, they did present significant fiscal challenges—and shifts in funding—for higher education. The governor's proposal for 1996 also resulted in higher education officials agreeing to produce studies that would address issues from cost-effectiveness to faculty productivity. According to one policy maker, "We had to box them in," by budget cutting.

Many interviewees expressed concern that declining state support and increasing tuition rates will hurt student access and choice. One respondent countered, however, that higher education was not the only function that received budget cuts, and provided examples of various new priorities for technology that could enhance access: a project to encourage advanced technology and research; a project to develop educational technology; funds for distance learning within the multicampus systems; and funds to allow the faculty to work with multimedia technology. These projects are aimed at providing high-quality, accessible education, while reducing the costs of delivering instruction.

Institutional Responses

SUNY's Responses

One university official said that dealing with less funding is not new. But in the past, SUNY has responded to funding cuts primarily through a "band-aid" approach, taking short-term actions such as increasing class size, using more adjunct faculty, reducing course offerings, consolidating programs, and deferring maintenance. SUNY officials are concerned about the continued use of these short-term tactics and the possible long-term effects on quality.

One major issue confronting SUNY trustees is granting individual campuses more autonomy. Some campus officials believe that having a central administration is inefficient. As one interviewee noted, "It takes years to get a program approved or revised. After a while, you just give up believing that things can change."

The 1996 budget helped SUNY officials seriously consider the purpose and direction of the system. SUNY's agreement to produce the December 1995 report forced the system to address issues of reorganization, efficiency, and productivity.

The board of trustees prefaced SUNY's December report, *Rethinking SUNY*, by stating their commitment to continue to reexamine SUNY in light of the fiscal challenges and the public demand for effective use of tax dollars. The board endorsed several propositions: SUNY exists to provide access to a high-quality education; differentiation of campuses is fundamental; undergraduate education is the highest priority; graduate, professional, and research programs are essential to SUNY's mission and to New York's work-force development and economic health; SUNY is committed to developing academic standards and performance indicators to increase accountability; and the board recognizes its responsibility to plan, prioritize, and allocate resources to the campuses.[53] The report calls for a general reorganization of state university functions, including a redesign of most administrative processes.

Selected activities and actions to be taken include ensuring the ease of transfer from two- to four-year institutions; recognizing the community colleges as centers of quality undergraduate training and work-force training; and reviewing admission policies to maintain quality. In addition, SUNY will review low enrollment programs and recommend whether they should be discontinued. The system has also committed to streamlining the approval process for new programs and to developing options that would shorten time-to-degree. The board will also consider a policy to charge full-cost tuition to students who earn 135 or more credits in order to encourage students to complete their degrees efficiently.

The board has committed to reviewing its budget relationships with various institutions within the system; in turn, it has asked the state for more autonomy in allocating and spending appropriations. Campuses will be asked to increase efforts to attract external funding and use some of the proceeds for financial aid. Several of the trustees' recommendations could have a direct impact on financing the system. For instance, the trustees called for the authority to roll over annual reserves at the campuses, a recommendation that the legislature later approved. The legislature later rejected, however, a recommendation to establish different tuition rates at different campuses.

CUNY's Responses

The City University of New York's restructuring efforts began as early as 1975 when city funding was slashed as a result of New York City's bankruptcies. The declines in state funding during the 1990s exacerbated CUNY's fiscal situation and caused the board of trustees to consider actions to improve productivity.

In the summer of 1995, the CUNY Board of Trustees declared that the system was in a state of "financial exigency," which allowed it to take some cost-saving actions permitted by state law only in times of fiscal crisis. The board voted to terminate 159 tenured faculty and to "abolish, consolidate, or merge" over 30 academic programs at its four-year institutions.[54] Several groups, including the professionals' union and faculty senate, brought a lawsuit against the board for taking these actions. In April 1996, a state court invalidated the trustees' actions, arguing that the state of fiscal emergency identified in February 1995 with the governor's proposed budget had largely disappeared by June 1995, when the board voted on the cost-cutting measures. This ruling was overturned in December 1996 by a state appellate court, which ruled that the trustees had acted "properly and in good faith" in their declaration of a fiscal emergency. This appellate court ruling clears the way for the board to act on its original declaration.[55] Prior to either the lower court or the appellate ruling, however, the board declared a second state of fiscal emergency in March 1996, this time just for the four-year colleges, "paving the way for possible layoffs of more than 1,300 faculty and staff members."[56] The court rulings do not affect this most recent declaration.

Because CUNY began to study issues related to planning, program quality, and student completion prior to the legislature's call for a December 1995 report on efficiency, CUNY administrators believe that their report to the legislature is "a progress report on actions that enable CUNY to operate as effectively as possible within the framework of available resources."[57] Some of the actions CUNY has undertaken are outlined below.

1. The City University of New York is working to restructure and reconceptualize programs in remediation, freshman assessment, basic

skills, and ESL (English as a Second Language). Individual colleges have been given more flexibility in developing admission standards.

2. The board is encouraging strong campus-based planning and distinct campus missions. The board is also developing systemwide initiatives to strengthen fundamental academic activities. Additionally, a policy has been adopted requiring 120 credits for a baccalaureate degree and 60 credits for an associate degree.

3. The City University of New York has implemented guidelines for periodic review of all degree programs, guidelines that outline the basis under which a campus should consider program suspension, closure, or consolidation. The system is already addressing inefficiencies in staffing. The City University of New York has reduced its senior managerial staff by 25 percent and is reviewing additional reductions.

4. Individual campuses are studying ways to improve instructional productivity and coordinate efforts in areas such as purchasing contracts and software licenses.

Responses at Independent Institutions

The Commission on Independent Colleges and Universities has prepared various documents outlining the challenges the independent sector is facing: declining enrollments, declining direct state aid, and high tuition rates relative to public institutions. The Commission on Independent Colleges and Universities is trying to stress the importance of independent institutions to the state, emphasizing that they provide higher education to over 40 percent of four-year students.

The Commission on Independent Universities has encouraged state government to strengthen policies to encourage more New York residents to attend independent colleges and universities. The commission reported that the independent sector has openings for some 30,000 undergraduate students and 12,000 graduate students. The Commission on Independent Colleges and Universities feels this capacity would not only accommodate future demand, but save the state money. The Commission on Independent Colleges and Universities reported that during 1995–96, the state's annual expenditure per student for the independent sector was $935, compared to $10,017 for SUNY and $8,558 for CUNY.[58]

CONCLUSION

During the first half of the 1990s, the combination of a slow economic recovery and a changing political landscape led to some significant shifts in the financing of higher education in New York. Declining or stagnant state funding was offset by increases in tuition in the public sector. These tuition increases resulted in an increase in the percentage of funding from TAP going to students at public rather than independent institutions—and in a shift from direct state support of the public systems to increased state funding of students. Uncertainties about the future level of support for TAP further complicate the picture for a state that enrolls over 40 percent of its students in independent colleges and universities. The fiscal challenges have led to legislatively mandated reports on efficiency and productivity in the public systems. The recommendations of these reports could lead to even greater changes in the financing of higher education in the State of New York.

NOTES

1. Patrick J. Bulgaro, "Economic Pressures and Trends: The Challenges for Higher Education," in *Higher Education in Crisis: New York in National Perspective*, edited by William C. Barba (New York: Garland Publishing, 1995), p. 18.
2. Ibid., p. 19.
3. Ibid., pp. 26–27.
4. *Chronicle of Higher Education Almanac* 43, no. 1 (September 1996), p. 79.
5. New York State Legislature, Assembly Ways and Means Committee, *New York State Economic and Revenue Forecast*, 1995–96 and 1996–97 editions (Albany).
6. New York State Legislature, Assembly Ways and Means Committee, *New York State Economic and Revenue Forecast*, 1994–95 and 1995–96 editions (Albany).
7. *Chronicle of Higher Education Almanac* 43, p. 79.
8. Appropriations, revenue, and other budgetary data are presented in fiscal years, unless otherwise noted. For the state government in New York, fiscal year 1997, for instance, covers the period from 1 April 1996, to 31 March 1997.
9. State of New York, *Comprehensive Annual Financial Report, Fiscal Years 1990 to 1996* (Albany: State Comptroller's Office, 1990–96), exhibit B.
10. Ibid.
11. State University of New York, Budget Development Office, 1996.
12. The City University of New York, *The Chancellor's Budget Request*, 1991–92 through 1996–97 editions, 1996–97 edition updated February 1996 (New York: 1991 through 1996).
13. Commission on Independent Colleges and Universities (CICU), "State Aid by Sector," Albany, 1995.
14. National Association of State Budget Officers (NASBO), *State Budget Report, 1992* (Washington, D.C.: 1993), p. 60; NASBO, *State Budget Report, 1995* (Washington, D.C.: 1995), p. 77.
15. Bulgaro, "Economic Pressures and Trends," p. 23–24.
16. See James Burns, J. W. Peltason, and Thomas Cronin, *State and Local Politics: Government by the People* (Upper Saddle River, NJ: Prentice Hall, 1990), pp. 112, 113.

17. MultiState Associates, Inc., *Multistate Perspective Legislative Outlook, 1996* (Alexandria, VA: 1996), p. 44.
18. Ibid., p. 45.
19. *Chronicle of Higher Education Almanac 43*, p. 79.
20. Aims C. McGuinness Jr., Rhonda Martin Epper, and Sheila Arredondo, *State Postsecondary Education Structures Handbook 1994* (Denver: Education Commission of the States, 1994), p. 201.
21. Ibid.
22. New York State Higher Education Services Corporation, *1993-94 Annual Report* (Albany: not dated), p. 1.
23. William C. Barba, et. al., "Factors That Have Shaped Higher Education in New York State: A Historical and Current Perspective," in *Higher Education in Crisis*, p. 4.
24. Most of the information in this section on SUNY was gathered from SUNY, Office of University Relations, *Overview: State University of New York 1995* (Albany: 1995).
25. The College of Environmental Science and Forestry at Syracuse has a board of trustees composed of 10 members, nine of whom are appointed to seven-year terms by the governor. A student member serves a one-year term and is elected by the student body.
26. The information on the history of CUNY was published on the City University of New York's World Wide Web page, 1996 (http://www.cuny.edu).
27. SUNY, *The Regents 1992 Statewide Plan for Higher Education in New York State* (Albany: 1992), p. 12.
28. State of New York, Education Law 6201, CUNY Art. 125, p. 54.
29. Ibid.
30. Barba, et. al., "Factors That Have Shaped Higher Education," p. 3.
31. Ibid., p. 2.
32. *Chronicle of Higher Education Almanac 43*, p. 79.
33. The City University of New York, *The Chancellor's Budget Request* (New York: September 27, 1995), p. 15.
34. *Chronicle of Higher Education Almanac 43*, p. 79.
35. SUNY, Office of University Relations, *Overview*, p. 32.
36. New York State Legislature, Assembly Ways and Means Committee, *Statistical and Narrative Summary of the Executive Budget, Fiscal Year April 1, 1995 to March 31, 1996, State of New York*, (Albany: 1995), p. 21.
37. *Chronicle of Higher Education Almanac 42*, p. 79.
38. Kent Halstead, "Quantitative Analysis of the Environment, Performance, and Operation Actions of Eight State Public Higher Education Systems," generated for The California Higher Education Policy Center, San Jose, 1995, pp. 25, 70.
39. Kent Halstead, *State Profiles: Financing Public Higher Education, 1978 to 1996 Trend Data* (Washington, D.C.: Research Associates of Washington, 1996), table 2, p. 11.

40. Kent Halstead, *State Profiles: Financing Public Higher Education, 1996 Rankings* (Washington, D.C.: Research Associates of Washington, 1996), pp. 18–19.
41. NASBO, *State Budget Report, 1992*, p. 60; NASBO, *State Budget Report, 1995*, p. 77.
42. Halstead, *State Profiles, Rankings* (1996), p. 22.
43. Ibid.
44. Halstead, *State Profiles: Trend Data* (1996), pp. 66–67.
45. City University of New York, "1995-96 State and City Adopted Budgets for the City University of New York," presentation to the board of trustees of the City University of New York, June 26, 1995.
46. Robert M. Shaw, "Bundy Aid: Policy Implications of Providing Unrestricted State Aid to Private Colleges and Universities," master's thesis, State University of New York, Empire State College, 1994, p. 23.
47. Philip Hanfling, "State Institutional Assistance, in *Public Policy and the Financing of Higher Education in New York*, edited by William McKeough (Hempstead, NY: Hofstra University, 1980), pp. 130–31.
48. Commission on Independent Colleges and Universities (CICU), *Independent Colleges and Universities: The Commitment and Capacity to Serve New York State* (Albany: 1995), p. 25.
49. Halstead, *State Profiles, Trend Data* (1996), pp. 67, 103.
50. New York State Legislature, Assembly Ways and Means Committee, *Statistical and Narrative Summary of the Executive Budget, Fiscal Year April 1, 1996 to March 31, 1997, State of New York* (Albany: December 1995).
51. Malcolm Gladwell, "Proposed Education Cuts Protested in New York," in *The Washington Post* (25 March 1996), p. E31.
52. "Destructive Tuition Hikes," editorial in *The New York Times* (17 March 1995), p. E31.
53. State University of New York Board of Trustees, *Rethinking SUNY*, General Summary (Albany: December 1995).
54. Peter Schmidt, "State Court Overturns Cuts Ordered by City U. of New York," *Chronicle of Higher Education* 42, no. 35 (10 May 1996), p. A41.
55. Peter Schmidt, "Appeals Court Upholds 1995 Cuts at CUNY," *Chronicle of Higher Education* 43, no. 20 (24 January 1997), p. A22.
56. Peter Schmidt, "Trustees Declare Financial Emergency at City U. of New York," *Chronicle of Higher Education* 42, no. 30 (5 April 1996), p. A27.
57. City University of New York, *Progress Report on Academic Program and Other Planning Activities* (New York: December 1995), p. 4.
58. Commission on Independent Colleges and Universities, *Presentation to the Division of the Budget* (Albany: 1995), p. 2.

APPENDIX

Roundtable Participants

T he following individuals, in serving as participants in the Roundtable on the Public and Private Finance of Higher Education, helped to shape the chapters within this book, particularly chapter 3, "Shaping the Future."

Peter Armacost
  President
  Eckerd College

Roger Benjamin
  Director
  Institute on Education and Training
  RAND

David Breneman
  University Professor and Dean
  Curry School of Education
  University of Virginia

Ann Daley
  Regent
  University of Washington

Alfredo G. de los Santos, Jr.
  Vice Chancellor, Educational Development
  Maricopa Community Colleges

James J. Duderstadt
  President Emeritus and University Professor of Science and Engineering
  University of Michigan

Judith S. Eaton
  Chancellor
  Minnesota State Colleges and Universities

Thomas Ehrlich
  Distinguished University Scholar
  California State University

Darryl G. Greer
  Executive Director
  New Jersey State College Governing Boards Association, Inc.

Elaine H. Hairston
  Chancellor
  Ohio Board of Regents

Earl Hale
  Executive Director
  Washington State Board for Community and Technical Colleges

Richard W. Jonsen
  Executive Director
  Western Interstate Commission on Higher Education

Terrence MacTaggart
  Chancellor
  University of Maine

Mario Martinez
  Author, California and Michigan Case Studies
  Arizona State University

C. Kent McGuire
  Program Officer, Education
  The Pew Charitable Trusts

Barry Munitz
  Chancellor
  California State University

Mark Musick
  President
  Southern Regional Education Board

Representative Carolyn Oakley
    Education Chair
    Oregon Joint Ways and Means Committee

Robert T. Tad Perry
    Executive Director
    South Dakota Board of Regents

William Pickens
    Director
    California Citizens Commission on Higher Education

Charles B. Reed
    Chancellor
    State University System of Florida

Richard C. Richardson, Jr.
    Professor
    Division of Educational Leadership and Policy Studies
    Arizona State University

Brian M. Roherty
    Executive Director
    National Association of State Budget Officers

Yolanda Sanchez-Penley
    Author, New York and Florida Case Studies
    Arizona State University

Virginia B. Smith
    President Emerita, Vassar College
    Director, Futures Project
    Higher Education Policy Institute

Assemblyman Edward Sullivan
    Chair, Higher Education Committee
    New York State Assembly

Joan Sundquist
    Author, Minnesota Case Study
    University of Pennsylvania

Rose Tseng
    Chancellor
    West Valley-Mission Community College District

From the California Higher Education Policy Center:
Patrick M. Callan
Joni E. Finney
Gail Moore
Heather Jack
William Doyle

From the Pew Higher Education Roundtable:
Robert Zemsky
Ann J. Duffield
Gregory R. Wegner

INDEX

by Kay Banning